Our Family Mass Resources for the Family Sunday Liturgy **Year B**

Bernadette Sweetman BEd, MREd, is a primary school teacher and catechetical writer. She has lectured on the Graduate Diploma of Education and Masters in Religious Education courses in St Patrick's College, Drumcondra.

OUR FAMILY MASS
RESOURCES
FOR THE FAMILY SUNDAY LITURGY
Year B

Bernadette Sweetman

For my family,
especially my parents, Anne and Seamus,
my husband Dave and daughter Annie.
You all inspire me.
Thank you.

VERITAS
www.veritas.ie

Published 2011 by
Veritas Publications
7–8 Lower Abbey Street
Dublin 1, Ireland
Email publications@veritas.ie
Website www.veritas.ie

ISBN 978 1 84730 329 5
Copyright © Bernadette Sweetman, 2011

All Reflections/Thinking Prayers and Dramatisations of Gospel Readings (unless otherwise noted) © Bernadette Sweetman, 2011

10 9 8 7 6 5 4 3 2 1

The material in this publication is protected by copyright law. Except as may be permitted by law, no part of the material may be reproduced (including by storage in a retrieval system) or transmitted in any form or by any means, adapted, rented or lent without the written permission of the copyright owners. Applications for permissions should be addressed to the publisher.

The readings and Gospel have been taken from the *Columba Lectionary for Masses with Children* (Columba Press, Dublin, 2009)

A catalogue record for this book is available from the British Library

Cover designed by Barbara Croatto, Veritas

Printed in the Republic of Ireland by Turners Printing Company Ltd, Longford

Veritas books are printed on paper made from the wood pulp of managed forests. For every tree felled, at least one tree is planted, thereby renewing natural resources.

Contents

Introduction		**9**
1.	Is this the book for you?	9
2.	Getting the most out of the material in this book	9
3.	An outline of the contents of this book	9
A.	**Getting Started**	**11**
1.	Teamwork!	11
2.	Location and space	11
3.	Practical considerations – being realistic	12
4.	Creating the sense of the Sacred	12
5.	Maximising the liturgical experience	13
6.	Parts of the Mass	15
B.	**Setting the Scene – The Liturgical Year Cycle B**	**18**
1.	Seasons and Feast Days	18
2.	Colours and Themes	18
C.	**Background Information on Readings**	**20**
D.	**Liturgy of the Word**	**30**
I.	Advent	30
II.	Christmas	42
III.	Lent	56
IV.	Easter	78
V.	Ordinary Time	102
	Feasts of the Lord in Ordinary Time	106
	Sundays in Ordinary Time	110
VI.	Some Major Feasts	178
E.	**Appendices**	**187**
Appendix I: Mass Responses and Everyday Prayers (English/Gaeilge); Signing		187
Appendix II: Additional Prayers and Services		195
Appendix III: Dramatisations of Gospel Readings		208
Appendix IV: Penitential Rite		220
F.	**Recommended Resources**	**223**
Postscript		**227**

Our Family Mass: Resources for the Family Sunday Liturgy and *Share the Good News*, the National Directory for Catechesis in Ireland

Reference Guide for the Liturgy of the Word (Year B)

I. Advent — 30
First Sunday of Advent — 34
Second Sunday of Advent — 36
Third Sunday of Advent — 38
Fourth Sunday of Advent — 40

II. Christmas — 42
Feast of the Nativity — 44
The Holy Family of Jesus, Mary and Joseph — 46
Solemnity of Mary — 48
Second Sunday after Christmas — 50
Epiphany of the Lord — 52
The Baptism of the Lord — 54

III. Lent — 56
First Sunday of Lent — 62
Second Sunday of Lent — 66
Third Sunday of Lent — 68
Fourth Sunday of Lent — 70
Fifth Sunday of Lent — 72
Passion Sunday — 74

IV. Easter — 78
Easter Sunday — 82
Second Sunday of Easter — 84
Third Sunday of Easter — 86
Fourth Sunday of Easter — 88
Fifth Sunday of Easter — 92
Sixth Sunday of Easter — 94
The Ascension of the Lord — 96
Seventh Sunday of Easter — 98
Pentecost Sunday — 100

V. Ordinary Time — 102
The Most Holy Trinity (Sunday after Pentecost) — 106
The Body and Blood of Christ — 108
Sundays in Ordinary Time — 110
Our Lord Jesus Christ, Universal King — 176

VI. Some Major Feasts — 178
Feast of Saint Patrick — 178
Feast of the Assumption — 182
Feast of All Saints — 184

Introduction

1. Is this the book for you?

This is the book for you if…

- You are setting up a Family Mass and would like 'ready-to-go' liturgies as well as pragmatic tips and resources to help you get off to a good start.
- You have already established a Family Mass and are looking for fresh ideas, dramatisations of Scripture, 'thinking' prayers, adapted Penitential Rites and homily suggestions for every Sunday liturgy of the year.
- You would like a single volume containing readings, Prayer of the Faithful, ideas for processions and much more, solving the problem of acquiring resources bit by bit.
- You would like a deeper understanding of the liturgical year, background information on the Scripture readings, as well as additional prayers for special occasions.
- You would like to have a wide selection of ideas, dramas and prayers, with the freedom to pick and choose what best suits your local circumstances.

2. Getting the most out of the materials in this book

The materials offered in this book are *suggestions*. You can:

- Use them – as many or as few as you like
- Adapt them – make them suit your community's circumstances
- Be inspired by them – create materials of your own!

The aim of *Our Family Mass* is to provide a ready-made resource for the Liturgy of the Word and to offer advice on the practicalities of operating a Family Mass, thus allowing more opportunity and time for preparation of, involvement in and enjoyment of the liturgical experience.

A Family Mass ministry in the parish will encourage families to participate in parish liturgy and community-building, as well as in reaching out to those in need.
(*Share the Good News: National Directory for Catechesis in Ireland*, no. 134, Irish Episcopal Conference, Veritas, 2010)

3. An outline of the contents of this book

In Section A, *Getting Started*, we provide a useful checklist on optimising your preparations for a Family Mass. From the organisation of a Family Mass team, to the practicalities of space and time, this section will help you be focused and make a positive impact on the establishment (or revival) of your Family Mass.

Section B, *Setting the Scene*, gives information on the liturgical year, Cycle B. At a glance, you can view the different liturgical seasons – when they occur, what celebrations and themes they include, and what colour is associated with each one.

Section C, *Background Information for Readings*, is very useful for thematic liturgical preparations, homily ideas, or just for your own education. We have provided descriptions of each book of the Bible, Gospel or Epistle that features in Year B, including location in the Bible, authorship and date, and the context in which it was written.

Section D, *Liturgy of the Word*, forms the main part of this book. Grouped in liturgical seasons, here you will find a ready-made liturgy for each Sunday of Year B as well as some other major feasts. The contents of each liturgy are presented as follows:

- Colour
- Suggested décor
- Theme
- Entrance and Gospel processions
- Welcome
- Introduction
- Introductions to First Reading and Gospel
- Homily suggestions
- Prayer of the Faithful
- Reflection/Thinking Prayer

There is also an overview of each season which acts as both an introduction to and a summary of the themes, celebrations and activities included.

In Section E, *Appendix I: Mass Responses and Everyday Prayers (English/Gaeilge)*; Signing' is a handy reference guide to the small but significant aspects that can be incorporated into any Mass, family or otherwise.

Appendix II: Additional Prayers and Services includes some ideas that could enhance your family liturgy by referring to other events outside the liturgical year. These include celebrations and feast days not present in Section D, *Liturgy of the Word*, and prayers for special times of the year such as the beginning and end of the school year, Mothering Sunday and Father's Day.

Appendix III: Dramatisations of Gospel Readings provides real opportunities for children to participate in the liturgy whilst conveying the Gospel message for the benefit of the whole congregation. Different styles of drama are included, from mime to role play to tableau. Drama can enliven a liturgy but it should be used intermittently so as to maximise its impact; it would be unrealistic to expect to perform a drama on a weekly basis. Consequently, the option of dramatisation is included in a selection of the liturgies, rather than in each and every one. These are conveniently located together in this appendix.

Appendix IV: Penitential Rite presents thematic adaptations of the *Kyrie Eleison* (Lord, have mercy. Christ, have mercy. Lord, have mercy.). These are grouped according to the seasons of the Liturgical Year and will help to prepare the congregation for a fuller and more meaningful participation in your Family Mass.

The last section, *Recommended Resources*, gives details of books, primary and post-primary resources, CDs, DVDs, retailers, organisations and websites that can be of further assistance in meeting your needs when planning your Family Mass.

Let the little children come to me; for it is to such as these that the Kingdom of God belongs.
Mark 10:14

A. Getting Started

Whether you are at the very beginning of your journey or you have already established a Family Mass in your parish, it may be useful to look over the following questions as a checklist to help you make the most of the experience.

1. Teamwork!

- A Family Mass needs a Family Mass team: who is willing to put in the time and effort (and it can be a lot!) to provide the assistance required?

- In your team, what different talents can your members bring – organisation, overseeing weekly practices, sourcing symbols/artwork, music, etc.? It would be best to give your team members the chance to work at what they are most suited to, have a particular talent for or interest in, and have the necessary time for.

- As children grow older, and younger children arrive, how open is your Family Mass team to accepting new members and ideas?

- How can you maximise cooperation with local schools? Perhaps school work, for example from religion classes, could be incorporated into your Family Mass.

- How can you include people with special needs? Is there someone in your community who could, for example, sign during the Mass, so as to improve the experience of anyone who has particular hearing or other language difficulties?

- Can people with special needs be involved meaningfully in all the different areas of the Family Mass? It is for everyone, and everyone has the right to contribute.

- A good team can flourish with effective leadership. On the other hand, everyone on a team deserves to give input. How can you make sure communication in your Family Mass team is kept open and accepting? Have regular meetings to ensure that your Family Mass is the best it can possibly be.

2. Location and space

- Where will your Family Mass take place? The local church, school hall, etc.?

- What alterations or additional equipment are needed to facilitate a Family Mass? Perhaps extra chairs or microphones?

- If your Family Mass is taking place outside of the local church, for example in the school hall, what furniture will need to be set up – the altar, arrangement of seating to facilitate communion and so on. Who will be in charge of this?

- Within your church environment, where is the best location for readers, participants in processions and so on? Any movement to and from their seats should be kept to a minimum to avoid unnecessary distraction.

- Is there an option to allow younger children gather at the altar for the Gospel reading? If so, do you need special mats or cushions?
- How big is your space? In a Family Mass, where more young children are present, the use of incense can unfortunately be problematic in a small space (think of asthmatic children; or if one child coughs, invariably others follow!)
- Where will you store the items for processions? (Keep in mind that you will hopefully use them again next time.)
- At the Family Mass, where can you place any items for display, such as symbols brought up in a procession, or artwork?
- How can you appropriately decorate the church? See Section B, *Setting the Scene*, for the seasonal colours; you could use them as a basis for your decoration.

3. Practical considerations – being realistic

- If you aim to establish a Family Mass, start off on a small scale. Is it feasible to use everything suggested in this book right from the start? Probably not!
- Can a Family Mass be facilitated every Sunday? If not, how about trying a seasonal approach, for example for Lent/Advent.
- Is it possible to have a Family Mass on feast days that coincide with school days?
- As a rule of thumb, anything that makes a participant (be they young or not so young) feel embarrassed or ill at ease should be avoided. For example, if a reading is too difficult for a child, have a parent read it instead; if someone is too nervous to take part in a procession, ask someone else to do so.

At all times, the focus is on the liturgy, not on any element of performance.

4. Creating the sense of the Sacred

Whether your Family Mass takes place in your local church or school hall, how can you highlight the need for reverence and respect? Here are some useful suggestions:

- Consider an entrance procession. It is not likely to be a regular Sunday Mass experience for most people and it would help mark the beginning of a special occasion.
- Appealing to the senses can be beneficial in creating a different atmosphere.
- Try highlighting a particular act at various Family Masses. For example, the priest could explain why we genuflect before the tabernacle (and then we could all practise it together), or why we stand for the Gospel.
- A Gospel procession including candles, the Lectionary, cross and so on can emphasise that this is God's Word. (Each liturgy provides specific suggestions relevant to themes of that day).

- The Offertory, when the bread and wine are brought as gifts, could be extended to include the actual preparation of the altar. Consider, perhaps during a piece of music, preparing the altar by covering it with a special cloth, placing the collection (if any) and the gifts upon it. It is a visual way of helping the congregation prepare for the Eucharistic Liturgy.

5. Maximising the liturgical experience

The focus should always be on the liturgy – recognition of being in the presence of God, encouraging receptivity to God's Word and ultimately the celebration of the Eucharist. Taking care of the 'little things' will help keep the liturgy centre stage:

- Is the church warm enough and is there enough light?
- Can everyone hear the readers and see processions or dramatisations?
- How can you keep the liturgy fresh and dynamic? For example, it is perfectly acceptable to replace a dramatisation with a song if it is becoming staid or unfeasible.
- How can you bring the locality into your liturgy? For example, if your parish is a fishing community, how might you reflect this in your choice of prayers, symbols or decoration?
- How can you maximise the use of the senses? (see next page)
- Remember: a Family Mass is for the *family*, not just children, so how can you involve parents, grandparents and other family members in a meaningful way?
- Consider giving a task at the end of one liturgy that will be relevant to the next Family Mass. This might be bringing a memento of a baptism in preparation for the liturgy of the Baptism of the Lord, or perhaps asking the congregation to notice particular elements of nature in the week preceding a harvest-time liturgy.

Think about it
Our children will acquire skills such as listening, appreciating the need for silence and praying, as well as developing a sense of belonging and of celebration – from their home life and the wider community. As a family team, how can you assist families as they nurture these things in their children?

Remember
The Family Mass is special for *everyone* involved. Young and old, we can all have a better and more meaningful experience of liturgy when we are comfortable, can see and hear what is going on, when our senses are engaged, and when we feel welcome to participate. It is especially important to involve those with special needs such as impaired mobility, sight or hearing.

It is very important to remember that we acquire meaning through the use of our senses. An effective liturgy recognises this. For young children, appealing to their senses can help make their experience special, and in the long-term, develop a sense of 'sacred space' when they attend a liturgy. But everyone else can benefit too!

	The Senses in a Family Mass
Sound	Ensure audibility and clarity in readings and prayers. Bells; silence; music; encouraging vocal responses and vocal prayer (out loud). All these create an atmosphere of sanctity when used appropriately.
Sight	Ensure clear visibility of the altar, ambo, crucifix and tabernacle. Use of candles or lamps are effective to highlight God's presence. Use of signing for certain prayers (see *Appendix I*) can deepen their meaning and encourage participation. In some cases, the absence of sight can be useful. For example, a reader who cannot be seen could represent God's voice in a dramatisation.
Smell	Flowers and candles can help create 'special' scents for the congregation. Use of incense when appropriate can be tremendously powerful in engaging the congregation.
Touch	Sometimes it may be possible to invite younger children to the altar for the Gospel. At such times, it is beneficial to have special material placed down as cushions/mats for them. This can increase the 'special' associations for their liturgical experience. Alternatively, displays may contain particular materials that can be touched either before or after the liturgy.

From a child's perspective

Young people may find some of the concepts and messages of the readings and Gospels difficult to understand. Try to include some reference to characters from children's programmes or films that could help them understand.

'But why?'

Most of us know lots of children who love asking 'why?'. Wouldn't it be lovely if they wished to question the liturgy? There will be lots of things in the church – objects, places, banners, colours, symbols – that can spark the children's imagination. Many of the readings contain difficult concepts, and perhaps even older members of the congregation might like to ask about the meaning. It is important that when planning your liturgy, reflections and homilies, you take into account the kind of questions that children may like to ask and try to address them in as brief and succinct a manner as possible. Think about it from a child's perspective.

For further information on planning family liturgies, please refer to the *Recommended Resources* section for a useful list of books and websites.

> '… the witness of adult believers can have a great effect upon the children. Adults can in turn benefit spiritually from experiencing the part that the children have within the Christian community. The Christian spirit of the family is greatly fostered when children take part in these Masses together with their parents and other family members …'
> (*Directory for Masses with Children*, 1973, n.11)[1]

6. Parts of the Mass

There follows an outline of the parts of the Mass that may provide opportunities for participation by the family in terms of readings, dramatisations and processions. Remember, these are suggestions. The best Family Mass will be whatever is most suited to the conditions, location and ability of the people involved. At all times, the focus is on the liturgy and the celebration of the Eucharist.

Entrance Procession This can mark the beginning of the celebration. It should include the priest(s), altar-servers, readers and gift-bearers. Symbols can be introduced during the procession and then displayed for the duration of the Mass.

Theme Especially useful during the seasons of Advent and Lent, the theme can provide the overview of the season and the relevance of this particular liturgy to the overall theme. For example, the decoration of the Jesse Tree during Advent or the description of the Lenten Garden could be referred to in the theme.

Penitential Rite The Penitential Rite prepares us to hear the Word of God by helping us to recognise our need for forgiveness and God's grace in our daily lives. It helps to build a sense of community for the congregation. For young people in particular, the atmosphere of togetherness can contribute greatly to their understanding of Christianity as community.

---

[1] *Directory for Masses with Children*, accessed online at http://www.adoremus.org/DMC-73.html [accessed 19 May 2010].

Our Family Mass Resources for the Family Sunday Liturgy **Year B**

Introductions to Scripture Readings Ideally part of every liturgy, the introduction should set the scene for the upcoming Scripture readings. It could begin by making a connection between our everyday experiences and the content of the readings that follow. The introduction is of great benefit in assisting the congregation in 'tuning in' to the liturgy and being more receptive to the Word of God.

'All the elements that will help to explain the readings should be given great consideration so that the children may make the biblical readings their own and may come more and more to appreciate the value of God's Word. Among these elements are the introductory comments which may precede the readings and help the children to listen better and more fruitfully, either by explaining the context or by introducing the text itself.'
(*Directory for Masses with Children*, 1973, n.47)

First Reading This can be read by a member of the congregation. Depending on difficulty level, it could be read by a child or adult minister of the Word.

Gospel Procession To emphasise the sanctity of the Word of God, a procession with candles or the lectionary could be of benefit. At this point, if possible, younger children could gather around the ambo to listen to the Gospel.

Homily The task of the priest or deacon is to bring the Word of God and the Mystery of the Eucharist to the congregation in a meaningful way. It aims to heighten the congregation's awareness of God in their everyday lives, and how this particular celebration of the Eucharistic Liturgy and Liturgy of the Word can bring us closer to God.

> **N.B.** The priest/deacon is the only person who should give the homily (*GIRM* 66). Accordingly, the suggestions in this book are just that – suggestions. They may prove useful in explaining the Word of God by way of contemporary examples or analogies. However, the extent of their inclusion is up to the celebrant.

Prayer of the Faithful (The Universal Prayer) The special relationship of the family of God can be greatly highlighted in this part of the Mass. The priest introduces the Prayer of the Faithful and invites all to pray. The prayers should reflect the needs of the congregation, the parish, the locality, the wider Christian community, and particular global needs, e.g. areas caught in civil war or a natural disaster. The *Roman Missal* sets out the desired sequence:[2]

- For the needs of the Church
- For public authorities and the salvation of the whole world
- For those burdened by any kind of difficulty
- For the local community.

---

2 *Roman Missal* (Veritas, Dublin, 2011), p. XXXIX.

Offertory The only gifts to be brought to the altar at the offertory should be the bread and wine.

Reflection/Thinking Prayer As the introduction is intended to 'tune in' the congregation, the reflection aims to consolidate the main messages of the Scripture readings. The most effective thinking prayers will inspire the congregation to take on board this message and act upon it in their day-to-day lives, thus meaningfully connecting faith and life. There is an opportunity in this section to give the congregation a task for the week in preparation for the next liturgy: for example, on the feast of Christ the King, they could be invited to reflect on how they lived by the Gospel over the past year, before the new liturgical year commences on the following Sunday.

> 'The invitation that precedes the final blessing is important in Masses with children. Before they are dismissed they need some repetition and application of what they have heard, but this should be done in a very few words. In particular, this is the appropriate time to express the connection between the liturgy and life.'
> (*Directory for Masses with Children*, 1973, n.54)

Remember
Many children will encounter stories, poems, prayers and celebrations in the course of their religious education in school or after-school groups. Explore the programmes in use in your locality and avail of their reflections, prayers and ideas. These will be familiar to the younger members of the congregation and are pitched at a level that is easy to understand. Furthermore, what a great way to connect your parish, school and home!

B. Setting the Scene

The Liturgical Year Cycle B[1]

1. Seasons and Feast Days

The liturgical year begins with the season of **Advent** – a time of preparation for the celebration of the birth of Jesus at Christmas. The period of **Christmas** starts on Christmas Eve and continues in joyful celebration until the Baptism of Our Lord.

The time between Christmas and Lent forms part of **Ordinary Time**. Each year, its length varies depending upon the date of Easter. During this period of Ordinary Time, we focus on the mystery of Jesus's life, in particular his early years and the beginning of his public ministry.

Lent, beginning on *Ash Wednesday*, continues to Easter Saturday. It is of forty days' duration (excluding the six Sundays), in remembrance of the time Jesus spent in the wilderness as well as recalling the forty years of wandering in the wilderness by the Israelites before they entered the Promised Land. The final week of Lent, beginning on *Passion Sunday*, is known as *Holy Week*, concluding with the *Easter Triduum* (the three-day celebration of Holy Thursday, Good Friday and Easter Saturday)

Following the sombre and penitential period of Lent, the fifty-day season of **Easter** is jubilant and celebratory. It concludes on *Pentecost Sunday*. The remainder of the liturgical year completes the period of **Ordinary Time**.

In Ireland, the following days are *Holy Days of Obligation*:

> The Immaculate Conception (8 December)
>
> Christmas Day (25 December)
>
> Epiphany (6 January)
>
> St Patrick's Day (17 March)
>
> Assumption of Our Lady (15 August)
>
> All Saints Day (1 November)

If a Family Mass is not practical on any of these particular days, some of the prayers and reflections provided in this book may still be used in the regular liturgy.

2. Colours and Themes

The purpose of a variety in the colour of the sacred vestments is to give effective expression, even outwardly, to the specific character of the mysteries of faith being celebrated and to a sense of the passage of a Christian life through the course of the liturgical year. (*GIRM*, n.345)

---

1 This chapter is based on 'The Physical Environment of the Mass' in Pat Mullins, *The Mass: Understanding What's What* (Veritas, Dublin, 2009), pp. 65–75.

The colours of the liturgical seasons are noted below. Consider incorporating these colours into any artwork, decoration or floral arrangements where it is appropriate.

The theme suggests the mood and atmosphere to be conveyed in the liturgy. This can be achieved with the choice of suitable music, using the prayers provided as well as displaying relevant symbols or artwork.

As with all aspects of liturgy, it is important to confirm in advance with the celebrant(s) that any chosen decoration and music is acceptable.

SEASON/FEAST DAY	COLOUR	THEME
Advent	Violet or Purple	Penitential preparation and expectation of the Incarnation and Christ's return in glory
Gaudete Sunday (*Third Sunday of Advent*)	Rose	Joyful expectation
Christmas	White	Divine Glory
Ordinary Time	Green	Our communion in the mystery of Christ's life through our Baptism and Confirmation
Lent	Violet or Purple	Penitential preparation and expectation as we look forward to renewing our baptismal promises and celebrating the Resurrection
Trinity Sunday **Feasts of Our Lord** (except *Passion Sunday*) **Feasts of Our Lady** **All Saints Day**	White	Divine Glory Communion of the Saints
Passion Sunday **Pentecost Sunday**	Red	Shedding of blood of Jesus Baptism 'with Holy Spirit and Fire'

To Note This book focuses on the Family Mass and therefore the colours and themes for other feast days or special Masses have not been included. Please refer to the *Recommended Resources* section for further information if required.

C. Background Information on Readings[1]

In this section, we provide contextual information for each reading and Gospel from every Sunday liturgy of Year B.

It is hoped that this will broaden your understanding of the liturgy as well as being a useful resource for catechesis.

First, some useful information on the Pentateuch, the Apocrypha, the Synoptic Gospels and the Epistles:

The Pentateuch
All Bibles contain the same first five books in the same order: Genesis, Exodus, Leviticus, Numbers and Deuteronomy. The word 'Pentateuch' comes from the Greek meaning 'five-volumed'. In the Jewish tradition, these are central to the Torah (or 'guidance of God').

The Apocrypha
From the Greek meaning 'hidden' or 'secret', the Apocrypha is a collection of books found in most Christian Bibles, but absent from the Hebrew Bible. They became part of the Canon at a later date. In Roman Catholic Bibles, the Apocrypha are located throughout the Bible, having been attached to the books with which they are thought to be connected. Most of the works were composed between the second century BCE and the second century CE. As many of the works are incomplete, exist only in translation and have unconfirmed authorship and dates, controversy arose about their inclusion in Bibles.

The Synoptic Gospels
Mark, Matthew and Luke are collectively known as the Synoptic Gospels. They all share similar material, although themes and events may be presented in slightly different ways in keeping with the context and time in which each was written. Some theories suggest that the Gospels of Luke and Matthew were influenced by the earlier Gospel of Mark, whilst there is also a possibility of a common external source known as Q.

---

[1] The material in this section is based on John Bowker, *The Complete Bible Handbook* (Dorling Kindersley, London, 2004).

The Epistles

The New Testament contains twenty-one letters, or 'epistles', written by different people as a means of teaching and advising fledgling Christian communities. The majority of the epistles are attributed to Paul whose letters were specifically addressed to communities or individuals (Romans, 1 and 2 Corinthians, Galatians, Ephesians, Philippians, Colossians, 1 and 2 Thessalonians, 1 and 2 Timothy, Titus and Philemon).

Of these, some were written while Paul was in prison and are therefore called 'the Captivity Letters' (Philippians, Colossians, Philemon, Ephesians and 2 Timothy).

1 and 2 Timothy and Titus are sometimes called 'the Pastoral Letters' due to their content on pastoral care, church life and practice.

The remaining letters (James, 1 and 2 Peter, 1, 2 and 3 John and Jude) are known as 'catholic letters', meaning 'universal', as they are not addressed to anyone in particular, but to the Church as a whole.

The remaining letter is that to the Hebrews.

The Book of Genesis

Location: Old Testament; first book of the Pentateuch.

Authorship and Date: Unknown – it is believed to be a collection of narratives and material from different periods of Israel's history.

Genesis tells the story of Creation and how everything has its source in God. There are four main sections: the Garden of Eden and the Flood (Creation and The Fall); Abraham; Jacob; and Joseph. The book is a collection of narratives, poetry and genealogies that combine to present the origins of Israel, and especially Israel's relationship with God.

The Book of Exodus

Location: Old Testament; second book of the Pentateuch.

Authorship and Date: This is still subject to debate. It is generally agreed that the Book of Exodus as we know it today was a collection of material from at least four sources.

The key figure in this book is Moses. Chosen by God as a sign of God's authority, Moses leads the Israelites out of slavery in Egypt, and establishes a covenant with God at Sinai. The Book of Exodus includes many themes and episodes that we encounter in our liturgy and catechesis, including the Ten Commandments, the power of God to free people from oppression and the despair felt by the Israelites in the wilderness mixed with the joyful hope that God will never abandon them.

The Book of Leviticus
Location: Old Testament; third book of the Pentateuch.

Authorship and Date: Unknown. Set in the Wilderness period between the Exodus and the entry of the Israelites into the Promised Land.

Leviticus is often called 'the priestly book' because it contains mostly rules and legislation about the priesthood, feasts, fasts, rituals and the determination of what is 'clean' and 'unclean'. The important Jewish Day of Atonement comes from Leviticus.

The Book of Numbers
Location: Old Testament; fourth book of the Pentateuch.

Authorship and Date: This is still subject to debate. It is generally agreed that the Book of Numbers as we know it today was a collection of material from at least four sources.

The Book of Numbers tells of the 'wilderness experience' of the Israelites after the Exodus and before their entry into the Promised Land. It contains many lists, rules, laws and methods of organising their group, thus giving the name 'Numbers' to the completed work. As well as the practical information given, Numbers tells of the spiritual journey of the Israelites. They grow from being in a state of despair and rebellion amongst themselves and against God, to accepting their destiny as God's people and preparing for a new life in the Promised Land.

The Book of Deuteronomy
Location: Old Testament; fifth book of the Pentateuch.

Authorship and Date: Unknown. Set in the Wilderness Period. This book is probably a collection of the work of several authors.

Deuteronomy marks the end of the Israelites' time in the Wilderness and their imminent entry into the Promised Land. It is presented as a 'last will and testament' of Moses, whereby he reminds the Israelites of the need to renew the Covenant with God. Deuteronomy contains the Ten Commandments. It is a summary of the requirements placed upon the Israelites to uphold the Covenant. Deuteronomy ends with the death of Moses.

The Book of Joshua
Location: Old Testament; one of the Historical Books.

Authorship: Unknown.

Date: Uncertain. It gives an account of the conquest of the Promised Land so it was possibly written within the first few generations of the entry into Canaan.

Joshua succeeded Moses as leader of Israel and this book recounts the successful conquest of the Promised Land in fulfilment of God's promise to Abraham to give Canaan to the obedient people of Israel. It is more a spiritual than a historical account, as it emphasises the fidelity of the Israelites and how their obedience to God relates to the covenantal promise between God and Abraham. Modern readers are cautioned against a literal interpretation of Joshua due to the way in which it neglects the effect of the conquest on the existing inhabitants, and its subsequent influence on views about warfare. The book includes the division of the land among the Twelve Tribes.

The Books of 1–2 Samuel

Location: Old Testament; one of the Historical Books.

Authorship and Date: No author is named but the Oral Tradition of Judaism (the Talmud) attributes this to Samuel, and after his death to Gad and Nathan. It is likely to have been completed during the Exile period.

The Books of Samuel were only separated at the time of the Greek translation, known as the Septuagint. They are in fact one whole book, telling the history of Israel as the civilisation moved from the rule of the Judges to that of the Monarchy, including the reign of David. Consequently, the themes of kingship, obedience and loyalty feature prominently throughout.

The Books of 1–2 Kings

Location: The Old Testament; the Historical Books.

Authorship: Unknown. Jewish tradition associates *Kings* with Jeremiah.

Date: uncertain. Some scholars believe there may have been a version from the late seventh century BCE, whilst the latest events mentioned occurred in around 561 BCE.

The Books of 1–2 Kings traces the history of Israel under the reign of the elderly David through, and beyond, the reign of Solomon. Solomon's reign included the building of the Temple, and later on the division of Israel into the Northern (Israel) and Southern (Judah) kingdoms. Although historical, 1–2 Kings is a theological history because it associates the downfall of Israel with the disloyalty of the Israelites to God. The role of prophets, especially Elijah and Elisha, also features prominently.

The Book of Job

Location: Old Testament; one of the Wisdom Books.

Authorship: Unknown. Likely to have had many authors who adapted and added to an original text.

Date: Probably written c. fifth/fourth century BCE though set in the distant past.

The central theme of this book is a question: 'If God is just and all-powerful, why do the righteous suffer?' Job is the innocent protagonist who suffers. He questions why he is allowed by God to suffer if he has done no wrong. The book challenges the dominant theory of the time that suffering is a result of sin. It also challenges the reader to engage with the topic of human suffering in general as well as the nature and justice of God.

The Books of Proverbs

Location: Old Testament; one of the Wisdom Books.

Authorship and Date: This book is a collection of wisdom from different periods of Israel's history. They are attributed to Solomon but most likely derive from a number of sources.

Many contemporary sayings have their basis in the Book of Proverbs. It is full of advice and guidance on how to live one's life and steer away from foolishness or wrongdoing. As such, the Book of Proverbs is very much viewed from the angle of human experience, more so than other books that focus on the salvation history of Israel.

The Book of Wisdom

Location: Old Testament; Apocrypha.

Authorship: An unidentified Hellenistic author, possibly from Egypt.

Date: Between c. 100 BCE and 100 CE.

The early chapters of Wisdom contrast the lives of the righteous to the 'ungodly'. The book stresses the importance of righteousness and faith as we look to the Final Judgement. Wisdom ultimately calls upon the leaders of the time to remember the true source of their authority and to re-examine how they live. Wisdom is portrayed as a woman, whose virtues and attributes are described in the middle chapters of the book. It also calls upon the reader to remember how God has worked, and continues to work, throughout history.

The Book of Ecclesiasticus (also known as the Book of Sirach)

Location: Old Testament – Apocrypha.

Authorship: In the text, the author identifies himself as 'Jesus, son of Eleazar, son of Sirach of Jerusalem' (50:27).

Date: c. 180 BCE.

Most of this book offers advice and guidelines on how to live a devout life. It identifies proper behaviours in family life, commerce and general society. Wisdom, again personified as a woman, addresses the reader towards the end of the text and also recounts stories of famous kings of Israel, Patriarchs and Prophets.

Isaiah

Location: Old Testament; one of the Books of the Prophets.

Authorship and Date: Chapters 1–39 Oracles of Isaiah, c. eighth century BCE. Chapters 40–55 Followers of Isaiah some two hundred years later in the period of Exile. Chapters 56–66 School of Isaiah, set after the return from Babylon, c. 560–30 BCE.

The book of Isaiah contains sixty-six chapters. Whilst it appears as a single volume, scholars believe there to be three distinct sections from different periods:

Chapters 1–39 are set in the eighth century BCE, a time of political turmoil, during which the Northern Kingdom was conquered by the Assyrian Empire and the Southern Kingdom, Judaea, survived by paying tribute. Key messages in this section include:

- Disapproval of widespread corruption in society
- Disappointment in how politics seems to be taking over people's lives to the neglect of their covenant with God
- Hope in the Messiah – God's Anointed One who will redeem God's people.

Chapters 40–55 have a clear motif of the sovereignty of God, and that salvation is certain despite how bad life was for those in exile at the time. The image of the 'Suffering Servant' appears regularly in these passages. This image later became associated with Jesus Christ. God as Redeemer and Creator also feature significantly in this section.

Chapters 56–66 address those who on their return from exile seek to reconstruct their lives. It speaks of repentance, keeping the laws and ultimately the certainty of salvation and the triumph of God. They also contain passages of particular significance for Judaism: for example, Chapter 58 is the prophetic reading for the morning of Yom Kippur, the Jewish Day of Atonement.

The Book of Jeremiah

Location: Old Testament; one of the Books of the Prophets.

Authorship and Date: Jeremiah; from around 627 BCE to 587/86 BCE.

The Book of Jeremiah is full of anguish and anger. Jeremiah witnessed all the political upheaval that led to the Babylonian Exile. His oracles are predominantly warnings against disloyalty to God and the imminence and certainty of judgement. The personal struggle of Jeremiah in his role as Prophet is also a dominant theme in the book.

The Book of Ezekiel

Location: Old Testament; one of the Books of the Prophets.

Authorship and Date: Ezekiel, an exile taken to Babylonia by Nebuchadnezzar II in 597 BCE; the oracles contained in this record date from 593 BCE to 571 BCE.

Ezekiel was a Prophet who had many powerful visions or oracles, reflecting the power and glory of God. Given that Ezekiel was an exile, his visions largely concerned themselves with the religion of the exiles and the disasters they were to endure. Sin and punishment was a key theme in Ezekiel, with particular reference to Jerusalem as an 'unfaithful wife'. Nevertheless, the book contains the theme of God's reign reaching beyond the confines of Jerusalem and a vision of the restoration of the Temple.

The Book of Daniel
Location: Old Testament; one of the Books of the Prophets.

Authorship: Assumed to be Daniel.

Date: Probably written in the second century BCE, though set in the sixth century BCE.

This book contains lively stories and far-reaching visions. It is a mature work of literature, written in a number of languages and genres, that has influenced modern artists, writers and composers. The first section, mainly narratives, recounts the experiences of four young exiles in Babylon. The overall theme is the maintenance of faith under persecution. The second section presents us with the eschatological visions of Daniel.

The Book of Hosea
Location: Old Testament; one of the Books of the Prophets.

Authorship and Date: Hosea, of the Northern Kingdom of Israel. Between 750 BCE and 720 BCE.

The troubled marriage of Hosea to Gomer, a prostitute (uncertain if this marriage was an historical fact or just an allegory) is a symbol of the infidelity of the Israelites to their Covenant with God. There are lots of references to infidelity and adultery that correspond with the idolatry and paganism that occurred at the time. Hosea calls for repentance and emphasises the enduring love and compassion of God.

The Book of Amos
Location: Old Testament; one of the Books of the Prophets.

Authorship: Amos.

Date: c. 760–50 BCE.

Amos was a businessman and farmer who was called to be a prophet. Social justice was at the heart of his message. Amos challenged the religious officials of his day for empty rituals, elaborate worship and false piety, whilst they neglected and abused the poor and oppressed in society. He chastised the leaders for claiming that their wealth and prosperity was a sign of God's favour, and spoke out against how they passed judgement on others. Instead Amos emphasised the injustice of his day, and stressed that true judgement comes from God alone. Unsurprisingly, Amos was expelled from the Royal sanctuary. The latter chapters relate some visions of God's purpose, moving the overall schema of the book from judgement to hope.

The Book of Jonah
Location: Old Testament; one of the Books of the Prophets.

Authorship: Unknown.

Date: c. sixth century BCE.

Unlike other books of the Prophets, Jonah is not a collection of oracles or visions; it is a vivid story. The plot is that of the relationship between God and humans; obedience and punishment; repentance and forgiveness. The imagery of Jonah is reminiscent of stories from folklore and, likewise, the images and events carry a greater significance. The actions of Jonah highlight the reality of human frailty and fallibility while signifying the importance of repentance and the universal mercy of God. The focus on the sovereignty of God over all nations gives the Book of Jonah a particular place in Christian Tradition in terms of universalism, ecumenism and the call to mission.

The Gospel According to Matthew
Location: New Testament; one of the Synoptic Gospels.

Authorship: Traditionally thought to be Matthew the Apostle (tax collector).

Date: c. 85–90 CE.

This Gospel was most likely written when divisions between Jews and Christians were developing. It presents Jesus as a 'good Jew'. There are many references to the Law, with an emphasis on the need for unity as Jesus completes the Hebrew Scriptures, rather than betraying them. The Gospel has a strong focus on instructing disciples how to be faithful to God, and it contains the largest collection of Jesus' sayings, showing him as our great Teacher.

The Gospel According to Mark
Location: New Testament; one of the Synoptic Gospels.

Authorship: Traditionally identified with John Mark, nephew of Barnabas, who associated with Paul. Some say Mark was an interpreter for Peter. Arguably Mark was the Gospel author closest in time to the historical Jesus.

Date: c. 65–75 CE.

This is the shortest Gospel. It begins with the Baptism of Jesus and ends with his death (although later additions include Resurrection appearances – the authorship of these passages is unclear). The life and ministry of Jesus Christ is central to Mark's Gospel. The first half focuses on Jesus' healing and teaching, highlighting his authority from God. The account of the Transfiguration marks the turning point of the Gospel of Mark. It emphasises the Messianic Secret (how the disciples were ordered not to speak of what they saw or were taught about Jesus as Messiah). The second half presents Jesus as the Suffering Servant. It focuses the reader on our call to discipleship amidst our own frailty and suffering.

The Gospel According to Luke

Location: New Testament; one of the Synoptic Gospels.

Authorship: Traditionally known as Luke, a companion of Paul, and also wrote the Acts of the Apostles.

Date: Unknown, but some scholars argue the author used Matthew as a source and this would date it as c. 80 CE.

Luke contains many accounts of miracles, healings and, overall, Jesus' regard for the poor and marginalised. Jesus is shown as a man of 'compassion' – our ultimate role model for what it means to be truly human. The activity of the Holy Spirit in Jesus' work is a key theme of this Gospel, and the significance of prayer in the life of Jesus, and consequently, for the lives of his followers, is also emphasised.

The Gospel According to John

Location: New Testament.

Authorship: Not mentioned. Traditionally, the 'beloved disciple' has been assumed to be John, son of Zebedee, and therefore the author.

Date: Generally thought of as the latest of the Gospels, c. end of first century CE.

In contrast to the Synoptic Gospels, the Gospel of John does not only recount the events of Jesus' life and death. Instead, known more as a spiritual and theological Gospel, John seeks to explore the meaning of Jesus' life, death and resurrection. This Gospel contains the themes of Jesus Christ as the Word of God and the source of eternal life. There is also greater reference to the 'Paraclete' (Holy Spirit).

The Acts of the Apostles

Location: New Testament; immediately follows the Gospels.

Authorship: Written by the same author as the Gospel of Luke.

Date: c. 80 CE.

This book recounts the beginning of the Christian Church. It seeks to distinguish the movement of Christianity as the followers of Jesus Christ. The descent of the Holy Spirit is integral to the message of this book as it sanctifies the mission of the followers of Jesus in their journeys of evangelisation. It provides accounts of the journeys of the disciples to spread the Good News beyond the confines of Jerusalem, and eventually to Rome. It is in this book that we meet Saul/Paul, the great missionary and author of several of the epistles in the New Testament.

The Letter to the Romans
Location: New Testament; one of the Epistles.

Authorship and Date: Paul. c. 56 CE.

As a missionary, Paul wrote to the Christians in Rome in an attempt to both bolster their faith and extend the reach of Christianity. This letter, which became a basis for theological restatements throughout history, clarifies Gospel teaching and counsels Christians on how to live out their day-to-day lives, both individually and communally, in light of their faith. The major themes of the Letter to the Romans are 'love', 'grace', 'the power of the Spirit' and 'justification by faith'.

The Letter to the Galatians
Location: New Testament; one of the Epistles

Authorship and Date: Paul. Early 50s CE.

This letter deals with controversial matters – in particular, Paul's response to the expectation at the time that Christians should adhere to Jewish Law. He was angered by these obligations being placed upon the newly converted. Firstly, Paul defends his own role as a servant of God and restates the authority given to him to be a missionary for Jesus Christ. He gives the example of Abraham to illustrate the strength and sufficiency of faith. Paul requests that the Galatians be of strong character like Abraham, and live 'by the Spirit'. In this letter, we encounter the terms that gained special significance in the Christian Tradition – 'fruits of the Spirit' (5:22-23) and that 'to be in Christ is to be a new creation (6:15).

The Book of Revelation (also known as the Book of the Apocalypse)
Location: New Testament; final book of the Christian Bible.

Authorship and Date: attributed to John the Apostle, though this is uncertain, c. 95 CE.

The Book of Revelation is written in a particular style of literature called 'Apocalyptic'. As such, it is characterised by vivid imagery, symbolic use of number and place, and the general theme of the end time. The book contains references to almost every other book in the Bible. It features a war between God and Satan marking the end of time, when God will be victorious and Jesus will return.

D. Liturgy of the Word

I. Advent

An Overview

Advent, meaning 'coming', celebrates the coming of Christ.

We recognise three comings of Christ.[1]

Past We remember the birth of Jesus at Bethlehem.

Present We recognise the presence of Jesus in our lives, in the needs of those around us and in the Word and the Sacraments.

Future We look forward to when Jesus comes again at the end of time to bring his faithful people into the Kingdom of his Father.

Main Themes of the Sundays of Advent: Year B

First Sunday of Advent	Humility, watchfulness, awareness.
Second Sunday of Advent	John the Baptist – exemplifying active preparation for the coming of Christ.
Third Sunday of Advent	Joyful expectation; John the Baptist prepares the way for the Lord.
Fourth Sunday of Advent	Jesus, Son of God, is the fulfilment of Scripture.

Visual aids help get the message of Advent across to our families. Two of the most popular are the Advent Wreath and the Jesse Tree.

The Advent Wreath
The greens are bound in a circle which reminds us of hope and eternity.

Each candle on the circle marks the passing of one week and brings us closer to the joyful celebration of the Nativity of Our Lord, denoted by the central candle.

The order and colour of the candles are:

First Sunday	Purple/Violet
Second Sunday	Purple/Violet
Third Sunday	Rose
Fourth Sunday	Purple/Violet
The Nativity of Our Lord	White

---

[1] From www.litmus.dublindiocese.ie/printpagemenus.php?MID=227 [accessed 31 December 2009].

I. Advent

Sun

Apple

Ark/Rainbow

Ladder

Coat

Tablets

Star of David

Letter M

Saw

Chi-Rho

The Jesse Tree[2]

This tree of symbols shows the 'family tree' of Christ. We also belong to God's family and the Jesse Tree provides us with a way of connecting with the figures of the Old Testament who are our ancestors in faith.

The prophet Isaiah spoke about the descendant of King David who would be our Messiah:

> A shoot shall sprout from the stump of Jesse,
> and from his roots a bud shall blossom.
> The Spirit of the Lord shall rest on him;
> a spirit of wisdom and of understanding,
> a spirit of counsel and of strength,
> a spirit of knowledge and of fear of the Lord.
> (Isaiah 11:13)

Each week a small number of symbols can be added to the Jesse Tree, from the bottom upwards, to trace the main events and figures before culminating in the Birth of Jesus.

It is recommended that the number of symbols at each liturgy is kept to a minimum – too many and the message they give will be lost.

Suggested Symbols

Here are some ideas – make sure to choose the ones you think will work best for your liturgy. For more ideas and information on the Jesse Tree symbols, go to www.knocklyonparish.com/faithspirit/educ/jesse.htm.

	SYMBOL	SIGNIFICANCE	SCRIPTURE PASSAGE
1.	Sun, Moon, Star, World	The Creation	Gen 1:1–2:2
2.	Tree, Apple, Angel	The Fall and the Promise	Gen 3:1-15
3.	Ark, Olive Branch, Rainbow	The Covenant with Noah (Flood)	Gen 6:9-22
4.	Ladder	Jacob	Gen 28:10-18
5.	Coat	Joseph	Gen 37:2-11
6.	Tablets	Commandments	Ex 20:1-21, 24:3-8
7.	Star, Harp	David	1 Sam 16:1-13
8.	Letter M	Mary	Lk 1:26-38
9.	Saw	Joseph	Mt 1:18-26
10.	Chi-Rho	Jesus	Lk 2:10-12

[2] This section is based on www.knocklyonparish.com/faithspirit/educ/jesse.htm [accessed 31 December 2009].

Our Family Mass Resources for the Family Sunday Liturgy **Year B**

Suggested readings providing information on Jesse Tree symbols
These simple readings correspond numerically with the symbols given on the previous page.

1. God created humankind in his image. God saw everything that he had made and indeed it was very good.

2. In the Garden of Eden, Adam and Eve disobeyed God and allowed sin to enter the world.

3. God protected Noah, his family and the animals in the Ark from the Great Flood. When Noah sent out a dove, the dove returned with an olive branch, showing that the flood was over, and God had saved them.

4. Jacob dreamed of a ladder reaching to heaven and he was assured God was with him.

5. Jacob loved his son Joseph … he made him a long robe with sleeves.

6. Moses wrote down all the words that the Lord had spoken. The people would follow them as their Commandments.

7. When David was anointed, the spirit of the Lord was with him from that day forward.

8. … And the angel said, 'Hail favoured one! The Lord is with you … Behold you will conceive in your womb and bear a son and you shall name him Jesus' … Mary said 'Behold I am the handmaid of the Lord. May it be done to me according to your word.'

9. 'Joseph, son of David, do not be afraid to take Mary your wife into your home. For it is through the Holy Spirit that this child has been conceived in her.' He did as the angel had commanded and took his wife into his home.

10. Our Lord and Saviour is born.

Think about it
Scripture quotes add sanctity to the otherwise 'normal' tree. If they are difficult to understand, then all the more scope for homilies and the suggestions of finding out more about the symbols during the following week at home.

On the First Sunday of Advent, the **Advent Wreath** could be blessed. Here is a sample blessing from the primary level religious education text *Alive-O 7*:

'God our Father, when we look at our Advent wreath we see its evergreen leaves. They remind us that, through the birth of your Son, Jesus Christ, and through our baptism in Christ, we have a path to the Tree of Life: everlasting life with God who loves us. Each week as we light the different coloured candles we remember that you are the light of the world, especially at this, the darkest time of the year. Bless our Advent Wreath and bless us as we journey through Advent and this dark time of the year. May your light guide us on our way.' Amen.

Similarly, the **Jesse Tree** may be blessed:

'God our Father, this Jesse tree reminds us of all family trees. They take us back a long way, back as far as we can go in the story of our family. This tree reminds us that Joseph and Mary were of the House of David. It reminds us that the roots of our Christian story, our Christian family tree, go back down into the story of the Jewish people and their covenant of love with God in the Old Testament. It reminds us of how long generations of people waited for the coming of Jesus. Now he is coming anew, this Christmas, and we must be awake so that we will not miss him when he comes. It reminds us of the Tree of Life in the Garden of Eden. Bless this Jesse tree, which we will decorate in the weeks ahead, as we prepare to celebrate the birth of your son, Jesus.' Amen.[3]

---

3 Both blessings taken from *Connecting School and Parish: An Alive-O 5–8 Handbook for Classroom Visitations*, compiled by Brendan O'Reilly (Veritas, Dublin, 2007), pp. 65–66.

Our Family Mass Resources for the Family Sunday Liturgy **Year B**

First Sunday of Advent

Colour Purple/violet

Suggested Décor Images from readings, banners reading 'Pay Attention/Watch!'

Theme Humility, watchfulness, awareness

Entrance Procession Candles, selected symbols for Jesse Tree

Gospel Procession Candles, Lectionary

Welcome
Thank you for coming to our Family Mass. Although we came here from different homes, some of us by car, others by foot, we are here together. As we enter this new Church Year and this Season of Advent, let us pause for a moment to remember that together, we are all brothers and sisters in God's family.

Theme *(For Advent Wreath and Jesse Tree) See overview, pp. 30–33.*

Introduction to First Reading
Have you ever had a time when you were upset, afraid, lonely or sick? We want our loved ones, like our parents, to come and help us through it. In our First Reading, we will hear the voice of the desperate Israelites, who lived many years ago. They looked to God for help. We will hear how they begged God to save them from their misery even though they felt that they had brought their unhappiness on themselves.

First Reading
A reading from the prophet Isaiah (63:16-17; 64:1, 3-8)

You, the Lord, are our Father, the one who has always rescued us. Come back for the sake of those who serve you, for the sake of the people who have always been yours.

Why don't you tear the sky apart and come down?

All of us have been sinful; even our best actions are filthy through and through. Because of our sins we are like leaves that wither and are blown away by the wind.

You have hidden yourself from us and have abandoned us because of our sins.

But, you are our Father, Lord. Do not hold our sins against us forever. We are your people. Be merciful to us.

The word of the Lord.

Introduction to Gospel
We've all been told how important it is to pay attention – by our parents, our teachers, our coaches. Jesus told his disciples to pay attention too. In our Gospel, we will hear how Jesus told them to 'watch' and 'be alert'. Let's listen.

Gospel
A reading from the holy Gospel according to Mark (13:33-37)

Be on watch, be alert, for you do not know when the time will come. It will be like a man who goes away from home on a journey and leaves his servants in charge, after giving to each one his own work to do and after telling the doorkeeper to keep watch.

Be on guard, then, because you do not know when the master of the house is coming – it might be in the evening or at midnight or before dawn or at sunrise. If he comes suddenly, he must not find you asleep. What I say to you, then, I say to all: Watch!

The Gospel of the Lord.

Dramatisation of Gospel
See Appendix III, p. 208.

Homily Suggestions
- Explain how this is the first Sunday in the Church's year; that the majority of Gospel readings this year will be from Mark's Gospel. This is the shortest Gospel, but despite its brevity we should expect to listen to powerful passages from Scripture throughout the coming year, passages that will teach us about who we are and who we can be.

- Talk about the symbols of the Jesse Tree/Advent Wreath.

- Refer to how the Israelites in the First Reading were waiting for God. Similarly we are waiting during Advent to celebrate how Jesus came among us.

- Mention the line from the First Reading: 'Why don't you tear the sky apart and come down?' What a powerful image! The Israelites desperately wanted some sign that God had not abandoned them. Ask the congregation to think of a time that they might feel that they need some reassurance of God's presence.

- Refer to the Gospel. Ask the congregation to imagine the man leaving his servants in charge of his house. What does he expect them to do? Why should the doorkeeper keep a 'look-out' for the master's return? What might happen if the doorkeeper fell asleep and didn't see the master returning? On the other hand, what could happen if the doorkeeper saw the master and told the servants he was on his way?

- Connect the two readings and refer to the banners 'Pay Attention/Watch!'. On the one hand, we might be looking for God. But on the other hand, we must always pay attention because God is at work where we might least expect. Ask the congregation to look around. Remind them that through Baptism, we are all brothers and sisters in God's family. God lives in each one of us and the challenge is to accept that God even dwells in those with whom we don't get along! Give some examples of how God is at work through us all the time and we might not be paying attention – e.g. in an act of kindness, a gesture of welcome.

- Remind the congregation how God is present in creation – nature, wildlife – and therefore we have a duty to act with an environmental awareness of the presence of God.

- During the coming week, suggest paying more attention to each other and to the world around you – not to just be concerned with your 'stuff' or whatever is going on in your life. Think about other people, remembering that God is in them too.

- As a parting question, ask the congregation whether they think that NOT paying attention to God within ourselves, others and the world around us is a good or bad thing to do? Give a few moments to allow them to think about whether they pay attention to God in their lives.

Prayer of the Faithful

We pray for our families. Help us to be kind to each other, remembering that each one of us is a child of God.

We pray for our Church. May her message of God's love be heard, listened to and taken to people's hearts.

We pray for our leaders. Help them to pay attention to the guidance of the Holy Spirit as they work for a better world.

We pray for those who are lonely, sick or in any need. May they be comforted.

We pray for our parish family. As we begin our new Church year, help us to be more aware of the presence of God in each other and all around us.

Reflection/Thinking Prayer

Imagine you have a checklist of all the things you are paying most attention to this Advent.

Maybe these questions are on your list:

- When do your holidays start?
- What presents do you want?
- What films are on TV?
- How much money will all this cost?

Think back on today's readings. Here are some different questions you could ask yourself during the coming week:

Do I give time to my friends and family, and not be wrapped up in my own 'stuff'?

Do I look after my pets and the environment in which I live?

Do I remember to treat others the way I would like to be treated?

Do I pay attention when I pray?

In this, the First Week of Advent, am I really ready to welcome Jesus?

⊕

Our Family Mass Resources for the Family Sunday Liturgy **Year B**

Second Sunday of Advent

Colour Purple/violet

Suggested Décor Images from readings, 'to do' lists

Theme John the Baptist – exemplifying active preparation for the coming of Christ

Entrance Procession Candles; sackcloth; stopwatch

Gospel Procession Candles, Lectionary

Welcome
Welcome to our Family Mass. We are one week closer to Christmas. Are you getting excited? Are you getting busy preparing to celebrate the Birth of Jesus? At our Mass today, just like at every other Mass, we prepare ourselves to welcome Jesus in the Eucharist, the Bread and Wine. Let's take a moment of silence to remember that special reason that brings us together here today.

Theme (For Advent Wreath and Jesse Tree) See overview, pp. 30–33.

Introduction to First Reading
Busy. Busy. Busy. Our First Reading today is full of tasks to do, places to go and things to say. We hear an excited voice in our reading, letting the people know the wonderful news that God is coming and we need to get ready.

First Reading
A reading from the prophet Isaiah (40:1-5, 9-11)

'Comfort my people,' says our God. A voice cries out, 'Prepare in the wilderness a road for the Lord! Clear the way in the desert for our God! Fill every valley; level every mountain. Then the glory of the Lord will be revealed, and all mankind will see it. Jerusalem, go up on a high mountain and proclaim the good news! Speak out and do not be afraid. Tell the towns of Judah that their God is coming!'

The word of the Lord.

Introduction to Gospel
In our Gospel today we meet John the Baptist. He acted on the words we heard in the First Reading. He set to telling people about how someone special was coming. John baptised people in the River Jordan and told them that the person coming was so much greater than he. Listen carefully. What does John say about this special person?

Gospel
A reading from the holy Gospel according to Mark (1:1-8)

So John appeared in the desert, baptising and preaching. 'Turn away from your sins and be baptised,' he told the people, 'and God will forgive your sins.' Many people from the province of Judaea and the city of Jerusalem went out to hear John. They confessed their sins and he baptised them in the River Jordan. John wore clothes made of camel's hair, with a leather belt round his waist, and his food was locusts and wild honey. He announced to the people, 'The man who will come after me is much greater than I am. I am not good enough even to bend down and untie his sandals. I baptise you with water, but he will baptise you with the Holy Spirit.'

The Gospel of the Lord.

Dramatisation of Gospel
See Appendix III, p. 208.

Homily Suggestions
- Refer to the focal object of the sackcloth. Ask the congregation to think about how uncomfortable and itchy this material would be, and what it must have been like to eat locusts (perhaps explain them as a type of grasshopper) and wild honey. Explain that John was a great prophet of God, and yet he didn't treat himself to special things. Instead, John wanted everyone to focus on his message, the coming of the Saviour.

- Recall the excitement in the First Reading. Compare this to the excitement felt by the congregation in the days coming up to Christmas. Ask them to think of what they are excited about.

- Refer to the focal object – a stopwatch. Just like in the First Reading, we can become excited and busy in the run-up to Christmas. It is a good idea, however, to stop every now and then to remember why we celebrate Christmas in the first place.
- Connect the two readings by reminding the congregation how John wanted people to concentrate on the one coming after him, who we believe to be Jesus. Suggest that we should think of ways to show our excitement about the coming of God.
- Talk about the symbols of the Jesse Tree/Advent Wreath.

Prayer of the Faithful

We pray for our families. Help us to make time to spend together and just enjoy being in each other's company.

We pray for our Church. Bless all the clergy, religious and lay people who put so much work into helping us to prepare during this season of Advent.

We pray for our leaders. Help them to put first the needs of the poor and marginalised in our society.

We pray for those who do not feel ready to welcome God into their hearts. May our prayer strengthen them and help them to turn to God with love.

We pray for our parish community. Help us to work together to make our neighbourhood a welcome home for God.

Reflection/Thinking Prayer
(Spoken quickly)

Christmas lights and decorations

Shopping lists galore.

Parties, presents, invitations.

More, more, more!

(Spoken slowly)

But, take a breath. Stop and think.

Remember why we're here.

We gather together to celebrate.

The Birth of Jesus is very near.

⊕

Our Family Mass Resources for the Family Sunday Liturgy **Year B**

Third Sunday of Advent

Colour Rose

Suggested Décor Images from readings

Theme Joyful expectation; John the Baptist prepares the way for the Lord

Entrance Procession Candles, selected symbols for Jesse Tree

Gospel Procession Candles, Lectionary

Welcome
Welcome to our Family Mass. Today we celebrate the Third Sunday of Advent. It is also called Gaudete Sunday, meaning 'joyful expectation'. In other words, we are happily looking forward to what lies ahead. Let's take a moment of silence to remember all that we have to look forward to, and hope for. With our inside voice, we say 'thank you' to God.

Theme
(For Advent Wreath and Jesse Tree) See overview, pp. 30–33.

Introduction to First Reading
This reading comes from the Prophet Isaiah. It tells us about being chosen by God to do wonderful things. As we listen, try to remember what wonderful actions are listed.

First Reading
A reading from the prophet Isaiah (61:1-2)

The Sovereign Lord has filled me with his spirit. He has chosen me and sent me to bring good news to the poor, to heal the broken-hearted, to announce release to captives and freedom to those in prison. He has sent me to proclaim that the time has come when the Lord will save his people and defeat their enemies. He has sent me to comfort all who mourn.

The word of the Lord.

Introduction to Gospel
For centuries before Jesus, the Jewish people hoped for a Messiah – someone specially chosen or 'anointed' by God – to be their Saviour. Some expected a mighty king like David. Others expected a prophet like Elijah. When the authorities in charge of Jerusalem heard rumours about John who was baptising people in the River Jordan, they questioned him like a suspect, trying to find out if he was the one for whom the Jewish people were waiting. Let's listen.

Gospel
This reading requires three participants.
A reading from the holy Gospel according to John (1:19-28)

Narrator The Jewish authorities in Jerusalem sent some priests and Levites to John.

Delegate Who are you?

Narrator John did not refuse to answer, but spoke out openly and clearly.

John I am not the Messiah.

Delegate Who are you, then? Are you Elijah?

John No, I am not.

Delegate Are you the Prophet?

John No.

Delegate Then tell us who you are. We have to take an answer back to those who sent us. What do you say about yourself?

Narrator John answered by quoting the prophet Isaiah:

John I am the voice of someone shouting in the desert: make a straight path for the Lord to travel!

Delegate If you are not the Messiah nor Elijah nor the prophet, why do you baptise?

John I baptise with water, but among you stands the one you do not know. He is coming after me, but I am not good enough even to untie his sandals.

Narrator All this happened in Bethany on the east side of the River Jordan, where John was baptising.

The Gospel of the Lord.

Homily Suggestions

- Suggest finding out more about today's symbols on the Jesse Tree.
- Refer to the different colour candles on the Advent Wreath for today.
- Refer to the wonderful actions in the First Reading. Emphasise how Jesus showed his divinity through actions, not just words. Consequently, we must show that we care with more than words.
- Refer to how we hear passages from Isaiah during Advent. Connect these to John the Baptist as the figure in the desert calling 'Prepare a way for the Lord'. Emphasise that we are part of that preparation too. Even outside the season of Advent, we should always strive to prepare a way for the Lord – to be as welcoming as we can be.
- In addition, bring attention to the desert image ('a voice in the desert'). The desert can conjure images of emptiness and loneliness. But the readings today teach us about hope. Compare 'a voice in the desert' to 'a light in the darkness'. Despite whatever 'desert' we might find ourselves in, there is always the hope of God's love.
- Bring attention to the anxieties and sadness that can be experienced at this time of year, e.g. those in mourning awaiting their first Christmas without a loved one, those who find it hard to pay the Christmas bills. Ask the congregation to think about how they might be active in reaching out to those in need, just as John actively prepared the way for the Lord.
- This liturgy might include a speaker from an Outreach programme or charity.

Prayer of the Faithful

We pray for our mammies and daddies who help us to get ready for so many things, and who are always there when we need help.

We pray for our Church. May she bring hope to those in despair.

We pray for our leaders. Help them to care for those in need in our society.

We pray for those who find this time of year difficult. May they be comforted.

We pray for our parish family. Help us to be active in reaching out to those who need help in our community.

Reflection/Thinking Prayer

A voice in the desert

Calls 'Prepare a way for the Lord'.

A light in the darkness

Shows the way.

Here we are in the darkness of winter

Looking out for that bright star

Shining hope, peace and love upon us all.

☩

Our Family Mass Resources for the Family Sunday Liturgy **Year B**

Fourth Sunday of Advent

Colour Purple

Suggested Décor Images from readings

Theme Jesus, Son of God, is the fulfilment of Scripture; 'Children of God'

Entrance Procession Candles, selected symbols for Jesse Tree

Gospel Procession Candles, Lectionary

Welcome
Welcome to our Family Mass. It's good to be together in God's presence. Let's take a moment to quieten ourselves and get ready to welcome God's love into our hearts.

Theme *(For Advent Wreath and Jesse Tree) See overview, pp. 30–33.*

Introduction to First Reading
David was a fine king many years before the birth of Jesus. Before he was king, David was just an ordinary shepherd boy – nothing special really. But God chose him to be leader of Israel. Our First Reading gives us an account of how God spoke to a person called Nathan about David.

First Reading
A reading from the second book of Samuel (7:1-5, 8-12, 14, 16)

But that night the Lord said to Nathan, 'Tell my servant David that I, the Lord Almighty, say to him, "I took you from looking after sheep in the fields and made you the ruler of my people Israel. I have been with you wherever you have gone, and I have defeated all your enemies as you advanced. I will make you as famous as the greatest leaders in the world. I have chosen a place for my people Israel and have settled them there, where they will live without being oppressed any more. Ever since they entered this land, they have been attacked by violent people, but this will not happen again. I promise to keep you safe from all your enemies and to give you descendants. When you die and are buried with your ancestors, I will make one of your sons king and will keep his kingdom strong. He will be the one to build a temple for me, and I will make sure that his dynasty continues forever. I will be his father, and he will be my son."'

The word of the Lord.

Introduction to Gospel
Our First Reading ended with the line 'I will be his father, and he will be my son'. In our Gospel, we hear how the Angel Gabriel appeared to Mary and explained how God wished for her to be mother to his Son, Jesus. Let's listen to this beautiful passage where we hear Mary saying yes to God, putting all her trust in God's plan for her, even when she didn't fully understand it.

Gospel
This reading requires three participants.
A reading from the holy Gospel according to Luke (1:26-38)

Narrator In the sixth month of Elizabeth's pregnancy God sent the angel Gabriel to a town in Galilee named Nazareth. He had a message for a girl promised in marriage to a man named Joseph, who was a descendant of King David. The girl's name was Mary. The angel came to her and said:

Angel Peace be with you! The Lord is with you and has greatly blessed you!

Narrator Mary was deeply troubled by the angel's message, and she wondered what his words meant.

Angel Don't be afraid, Mary; God has been gracious to you. You will become pregnant and give birth to a son, and you will name him Jesus. He will be great and will be called the Son of the Most High God. The Lord God will make him a king, as his ancestor David was, and he will be the king of the descendants of Jacob forever; his kingdom will never end!

Mary I am a virgin. How, then, can this be?

Narrator The angel answered:

Angel The Holy Spirit will come on you, and God's power will rest upon you. For this reason the holy child will be called the Son of God. Remember your relative Elizabeth. It is said that she cannot have children, but she herself is now six months pregnant, even though she is very old. For there is nothing that God cannot do.

Mary I am the Lord's servant, may it happen to me as you have said.

Narrator And the angel left her.

The Gospel of the Lord.

I. Advent

Homily Suggestions
- Briefly explain about First Reading:
  - Nathan – assumed to be one of the authors of 2 Samuel
  - 2 Samuel is one of the historical books
  - King/royal terminology – 'dynasty', 'kingdom', 'greatest leader', 'ancestors', 'descendants'
  - David was a shepherd boy until he was chosen by God to be the King.
- Highlight the connections between the two readings:
  - David: Joseph was of the House of David
  - Final line of First Reading: 'I will be his father, and he will be my son' and the Gospel reference to Jesus as 'Son of God'
  - Both passages end with an agreement/promise/acceptance of God's will.
- Emphasise how Jesus was the fulfilment of Scripture – in a way, connecting it all together.
- Contrast the two images that emerge of leaders – the First Reading shows a mighty king, royal and strong; the Gospel shows us an infant.
- Bring attention to how Baptism unites us to Christ, making us children of God – in a sense, when we hear the final line of the First Reading, we can apply that to ourselves, i.e. God is our Father and we are his children (sons and daughters). Extend this to invite a brief reflection on how we treat ourselves, and each other, as children of God.
- Highlight the bravery of:
  - the shepherd boy David, who rose to the challenges set against him; explain how he became a great leader
  - the virgin Mary, who agreed to God's request despite being 'deeply troubled'.
- Ask the congregation to think about how they may be challenged or troubled, and how they can show similar bravery in living out Gospel values and rising to the task of being a 'child of God'.
- Emphasise how the greatness of the little infant Jesus influences how we should think about all children. Each child is a little treasure. Refer to Jesus's teachings on children and the Kingdom of God (e.g. Mark 10:13-16).
- Address the children of the congregation, affirming that they are very special to God.
- Ask how we would prepare for a family birthday. As Jesus' birthday approaches, invite reflections on how, as children of God, we can all prepare for the birthday of our Father.
- Refer to the Advent Wreath/selected symbols of the Jesse Tree.

Prayer of the Faithful
We pray for all mothers and fathers. We are grateful for all the love and care they show us. Be with them especially at this time of family and celebration.

We pray for our Church. Bless all the clergy, religious and laypeople as they make their final preparations for Christmas.

We pray for our leaders. Help them to follow the examples of David and Jesus, by governing wisely and fairly, with a special care for the children in our society.

We pray for those who are saddened at this time of year by the loss of a parent or child. May your love give them comfort.

We pray for our parish family. Help us to live and work together in peace and respect as children of God.

Reflection/Thinking Prayer
Christmas is just around the corner

It's barely a week away.

Have you got everything ready

To celebrate Jesus's birthday?

What do you think Jesus would like?

Something home-made or something bought?

Or maybe you could do an act or deed

That reflects what Jesus taught.

After all, Jesus led by example

He showed us how to love one another

This week, let's try to live as children of God

Remembering that Jesus is our brother.

II. Christmas

An Overview

Christmas is marked by the joyful celebration of the birth of Christ.

God so loved the world, he sent his only son to live in it – to take upon himself the sins of all people and be their Saviour and Redeemer through the Paschal Mystery.

In contrast to the muted violet/rose colours of Advent, the Church should be bright and reflect the joy of the season.

White is the liturgical colour for Christmas and can be highlighted in the following simple ways:

- Bringing attention to the white of the central candle of the Advent Wreath
- White is the bright light of the star that led the visitors to the Baby Jesus
- White represents the purity and divine glory of Jesus Christ.

The focus of the Church's celebration of Christmas is on the birth of Jesus Christ.

It follows that the central display for Christmas should be a crib. Depending on your local circumstances and space available, the crib should be placed in such a way that it is clearly visible. A backdrop of the night sky and star, or foreground additions such as straw or rocks could be locally sourced or made in an art activity in school. The construction of the crib could be an activity for a group before the Mass – it all depends on your own circumstances. The figure of the Baby Jesus and the figures of the Three Kings should be retained for their placement during the relevant liturgies.

(Many different sizes and styles of crib are available. See *Recommended Resources* for some suppliers.)

Give it a go!
Ideally, the crib should be a sacred space in the Church, as well as a welcoming one. Prayers could be printed and displayed, as well as images from the Christmas story and subsequent Gospel readings. Consider placing some information near the crib that parishioners can bring home. These might include:

- Information on the first crib (St Francis of Assisi)
- Colouring pages of images from the Gospel passages of the Christmas season
- Crosswords/word searches relating to the Christmas story.

During the week, parishioners can be encouraged to visit the crib, look at the artwork and offer their prayers at this sacred space.

Dramatisation of the Gospel during Christmas
It is likely that many children will be taking part in nativity plays in their schools during the Advent season, and so dramatisation of the Gospel seems slightly redundant at this time. For this reason, while a nativity play is included, dramatisations are largely absent from the samples provided, with suggestions for songs instead.

And remember ...
Dramatisations of the Gospel are there if you *want* to use them. They are not obligatory and would become an ineffective chore if overused. We must also accept that there are many other events and celebrations taking place at Christmas, outside of the liturgies. Children are understandably preoccupied with parties, school holidays, gifts, special dinners and visitors. Instead of downplaying these special events in preference for the Christmas story, try to capture their excitement and channel it in the context of the wonder and joy of the birth of Jesus Christ. Our aim is to bring our Christmas liturgies to life within the real experiences of the family. Have a look at the following ideas:

- Invite younger parishioners to make a Christmas card for Jesus and leave it at the crib

- Set up a facility where people can bring their unwanted gifts to the Church (or a similar venture for *before* Christmas time where small gifts would be collected) for distribution to local charities or groups

- Encourage the children to tell their friend Jesus all about their experiences at Christmas time.

Our Family Mass Resources for the Family Sunday Liturgy **Year B**

Feast of the Nativity

Colour White

Suggested Décor Images from readings banners reading 'Immanuel', 'Rejoice', Crib/Manger/Nativity Scene

Theme Divine Glory, Birth of our Saviour

Entrance Procession Candles, banners, Baby Jesus figure for manger

Gospel Procession Candles, Lectionary

Welcome
Welcome to our Family Mass. Happy Christmas! We are all excited and looking forward to the day. Let's just take a moment to quieten ourselves and remember that today we celebrate Jesus' birthday.

Introduction/Theme *(including lighting central candle of Advent wreath and placing last symbol on Jesse Tree)*

During Advent, we have waited and prepared. Week after week, we lit the candles of our Advent Wreath. Today we light our central white candle. It is the birthday candle of Jesus. Happy Birthday Jesus!

Introduction to First Reading
The prophet Isaiah spoke about a child. This child, a boy, would be our ruler and king. He would bring joy, peace and light to the world. Let's listen to our First Reading to hear how Isaiah described it.

First Reading
A reading from the prophet Isaiah (9:1-7)

The people who walked in darkness have seen a great light.

They lived in a land of shadows, but now light is shining on them.
A child is born to us!
A son is given to us!
He will be called our ruler.
He will be called, 'Wonderful Counsellor,' 'Mighty God,' 'Eternal Father,' 'Prince of Peace.'

The word of the Lord.

Introduction to Gospel
The child spoken of in our First Reading was born to Mary and Joseph in Bethlehem. We now listen to the story of his birth from Luke's Gospel, and we hear how news of his birth began to spread.

Gospel
A reading from the holy Gospel according to Luke (2:1-14)

Joseph went from the town of Nazareth in Galilee to the town of Bethlehem in Judaea, the birthplace of King David. Joseph went there because he was a descendant of David. He went to register with Mary, who was promised in marriage to him. She was pregnant, and while they were in Bethlehem, the time came for her to have her baby. She gave birth to her first son, wrapped him in strips of cloth and laid him in a manger – there was no room for them to stay in the inn.

There were some shepherds in that part of the country who were spending the night in the fields, taking care of the flocks. An angel of the Lord appeared to them, and the glory of the Lord shone over them. They were terribly afraid, but the angel said to them, 'Don't be afraid! And this is what will prove it to you: you will find a baby wrapped in strips of cloth and lying in a manger.'

Suddenly a great army of heaven's angels appeared with the angel, singing praises to God:

'Glory to God in the highest heaven, and peace on earth to those with whom he is pleased!'

The Gospel of the Lord.

Dramatisation of Gospel
See Appendix III, pp. 209–215.

44 —

Homily Suggestions

- Compare conditions of the First Christmas to our experience of Christmas: warmth, shelter, toys, food – it helps to put things into perspective. Encourage the congregation to think of all those around the world whose Christmas might be cold, lonely or unhappy.

- Encourage the congregation to have fun today. Be happy and enjoy – because it is amazing that God sent us his only Son, that Jesus came to us in the form of a little child; all because of God's love for us. This is such great news that we should sing, dance, have fun and enjoy our celebrations, so long as we keep in mind 'the reason for the season'.

- Comment on the Nativity scene/Crib – point out the figures and explain them, thus reinforcing the Gospel passage.

- Remind the congregation that Christmas is not just one day – God sent us Jesus for all time. All the joy we feel today, we should try to have in our lives every day. If we find ourselves to be more giving around this time of year – having the 'Christmas spirit' – wouldn't the rest of the year be happier if we were to keep that 'Christmas spirit' all year round?

- Ask the congregation to think about the saying 'Christmas is for children' – some people might agree, especially if they are speaking about presents etc. Think about it – we hear in our Gospel of Jesus as a baby. We see the wonder in children's eyes all around. Remind the older members of the congregation that they were children once too, and really they are still children, only older. We are all children of God, and we should try to live our lives with that beautiful childlike quality – wonder, seeing things as if for the first time, using our imagination and having fun.

Prayer of the Faithful

We pray for our mammies, daddies and all our family. May we enjoy a happy and healthy Christmas together.

We pray for our Church family – from the tiniest babies to those who have already joined God in heaven. May we remember them in our celebrations today.

We pray for our leaders. May they be guided by your light to work for peace in our world.

We pray for those on their own this Christmas – the sick, and those who are away from home for any reason. Help them to feel your loving presence today.

We pray for our parish. Help us to keep alive the Spirit of Christmas in our community throughout the year.

Reflection/Thinking Prayer

As our Mass comes to an end, let's think about our situation and that of Jesus and his mammy and daddy. We probably have a delicious dinner planned later on. Maybe Mary and Joseph didn't even know where they were going to get something to eat – there wasn't any room at the inn, remember? We are likely to be playing with new toys and games later on today. What might Jesus have had? Joseph was a carpenter; perhaps he made a rattle somehow. The shepherds would be arriving to visit – that would be nice, even though they might not have much by way of presents. But they might pray, sing and wonder at the amazing birth of this special baby.

At some point today, let's remember to be thankful for all the things we have and for all the effort that other people like our mammies and daddies are putting into making our day special. Maybe we could imagine an extra seat at our dinner table, for Jesus; an extra present under the tree, for Jesus; and an extra smile, hug or handshake – something that helps us to say 'Happy Birthday Jesus!'

✜

Our Family Mass Resources for the Family Sunday Liturgy **Year B**

The Holy Family of Jesus, Mary and Joseph

Colour White

Suggested Décor Images from readings, photos of families

Theme Divine Glory – the value of family, lifelong trust in God

Entrance Procession Candles, family photos, picture of the Holy Family

Gospel Procession Candles, Lectionary

Welcome
Welcome to our Family Mass. We are together here to celebrate as Jesus asked us. Let's take a moment to prepare to listen to the Word of God.

Theme
Today we bring to the altar two special pictures: one of the Holy Family – Jesus, Mary and Joseph; another of a modern-day family. Our families can be small or big; we might all live together or we might not. All families are joined together by the bond of love. Today, we will remember the strong and faithful family of Jesus and we will pray that our families can grow to be just as strong and full of faith.

Introduction to First Reading
Do you have anything special at home that used to belong to someone older in your family, like your grandparents or great-grandparents? A family treasure? People often pass their special things onto their children. In our First Reading, God promises to give a great reward to Abram but Abram questions the use of a reward when he has no children to pass it on to. But Abram was also a man of strong faith. Let's listen to what happened.

First Reading
A reading from the book of Genesis (15:1-6; 21:1-3)

Abram had a vision and heard the Lord say to him, 'Do not be afraid, Abram. I will shield you from danger and give you a great reward.' But Abram answered, 'Sovereign Lord, what good will your reward be to me, since I have no children? You have given me no children and one of my slaves will inherit my property.' The Lord took him outside and said, 'Look at the sky and try to count the stars, you will have as many descendants as that.' Abram put his trust in the Lord, and because of this the Lord was pleased with him and accepted him.

The Lord blessed Sarah, as he had promised, and she became pregnant and bore a son to Abraham when he was old. The boy was born at the time God said he would be born. Abraham named him Isaac. Abraham was a hundred years old when Isaac was born.

The word of the Lord.

Introduction to Gospel
Mary and Joseph were Jewish. When a child is born in a Jewish family, it is customary to bring the infant to the Temple. This takes place in our Gospel today. An ordinary event for any Jewish family, but because the baby was Jesus, the event became extraordinary.

Gospel
A reading from the holy Gospel according to Luke (2:22, 39-40)

At that time there was a man named Simeon living in Jerusalem. He was a good, God-fearing man and was waiting for Israel to be saved. The Holy Spirit was with him and had assured him that he would not die before he had seen the Lord's promised Messiah. Led by the Spirit Simeon went into the Temple. When the parents brought the child Jesus into the Temple to do for him what the law required, Simeon took the child in his arms and gave thanks to God:

'Now, Lord, you have kept your promise, and you may let your servant go in peace. With my own eyes I have seen your salvation, a light to reveal your will to the gentiles and bring glory to your people Israel.'

There was a very old prophetess, a widow named Anna. She was now eighty-four years old. She never left the Temple; day and night she worshipped God, fasting and praying. She gave thanks to God and spoke about the child to all who were waiting for God to set Jerusalem free.

The word of the Lord.

Song 'God called Abraham' (from *Alive-O*).[1]

---

[1] Geraldine Doggett, from *Alive-O 8 Teacher's* Book (Veritas, Dublin, 2004), p. 291.

Homily Suggestions

- Refer to First Reading: Abram did not ask God for a child – yet God granted him this gift of family. Abram's faith was central.

- In both readings, the elderly feature prominently. Emphasise how lifelong trust in God is a key theme and something to which we aspire. Mention how we learn our faith from our elders, and how they are due great respect from us. Give concrete examples of how we can respect our parents/grandparents, for example visits, spending time together, listening to their stories, helping out, being mannerly and so on.

- Mention the focal objects (family pictures and picture of the Holy Family). Ask the congregation to think about what family means to them – special occasions; arguments; our relatives; home being a safe haven. Ask them to compare this image to that of Abram's family and the Holy Family.

- Invite the congregation to imagine ways they could improve their family life, for example setting aside times for all being together; eating meals together; planning events for just the family; keeping in touch more, and so on. Perhaps refer to the film *The Sound of Music*, where the family were too ordered and regimented – they just needed fun time together.

- Encourage the families in the congregation to set aside time to pray together – even just a grace before meals, a thank-you prayer or a blessing for an event.

Prayer of the Faithful

We pray for our mammies and daddies. Help them to be strong and faithful like Abram, Joseph and Mary, especially when being a parent is difficult.

We pray for our Church family. Help us to grow in love and peace.

We pray for our leaders. May they have the support of their families in their work, and may they keep the value of family life at the heart of their policies.

We pray for those who are lonely and for families dealing with grief or separation. We ask you to comfort them in their pain.

We pray for our community. May the families in our parish be happy and healthy.

Reflection/Thinking Prayer

'Trust me, I won't let you fall,'

said Grandad, as he held onto my saddle.

I tried to cycle with no stabilisers.

But instead all I did was wobble.

Morning soon turned into afternoon

And then the light began to fade.

I was ready to quit and never try again

When Grandad whispered 'Don't be afraid'.

I didn't want to let Grandad down,

He'd stayed out with me here all day.

As I turned to say thanks, I got a surprise –

He was far behind, waving and shouting 'hooray!'

☩

Our Family Mass Resources for the Family Sunday Liturgy **Year B**

Solemnity of Mary

Colour White

Suggested Décor Images from readings, images of Mary

Theme Divine Glory – the Divine Motherhood of Mary

Entrance Procession Candles, statue/picture of Mary, picture of Mary and Jesus

Gospel Procession Candles, Lectionary

Welcome
Welcome to our Family Mass. Thank you for coming today. It's good to be together in God's presence.

Theme
Today we celebrate Mary as Mother of God. Mary agreed to God's request to be mother to Jesus – she gave birth to him, looked after him and supported him all through his life. We thank Mary for her faith, and we look to her as a model of motherhood.

Introduction to First Reading
A blessing is when you wish someone well. After Moses freed the Israelites from slavery, they travelled in the wilderness to the Promised Land. Moses wanted them to always keep their faith in God during their difficult journey, and for God to bless them. So he taught the people to say a special blessing. Let's hear about it now in our First Reading.

First Reading
A reading from the book of Numbers (6:22-27)

The Lord commanded Moses to tell Aaron and his sons to use the following words in blessing the people of Israel:

May the Lord bless you and take care of you;

May the Lord be kind and gracious to you;

May the Lord look upon you with favour and give you peace.

And the Lord said, 'If they pronounce my name as a blessing upon the people of Israel, I will bless them.'

The word of the Lord.

Introduction to Gospel
In our Gospel today we will hear more of the Christmas story – the visit of the shepherds and how Mary responded to their visit. Imagine how she must have felt, the proud mammy having people come to see her newborn son. Maybe she was grateful that he was okay, maybe she was wondering about what might happen as her baby grew older. Listen now to the Word of God.

Gospel
A reading from the holy Gospel according to Luke (2:16-21)

The shepherds hurried off and found Mary and Joseph and saw the baby lying in the manger. When the shepherds saw him, they told them what the angel had said about the child. All who heard it were amazed at what the shepherds said. Mary remembered all these things and thought deeply about them. The shepherds went back, singing praises to God for all they had heard and seen; it had been just as the angel had told them.

A week later, when the time came for the baby to be circumcised, he was named Jesus, the name which the angel had given him before he had been conceived.

The Gospel of the Lord.

Song 'Magnificat' (from *Alive-O*).[2]

Homily Suggestions
- Blessings – think about when you say a blessing: when someone sneezes; when you make the sign of the cross (explain reference to God in your thoughts, hearts and hands); when someone leaves; wishing someone luck. Aren't blessings wonderful!

- Encourage people to bless each other.

- Describe Mary – her youth, her faith in God getting her through very difficult situations, an unusual pregnancy, a birth in a stable – all the time unsure of what the future might bring. What kind of person do you think Mary was? What attributes does she have that we could aspire to?

---

2 Frances O'Connell, from *Alive-O 8 Teacher's Book* (Veritas, Dublin, 2005), pp. 304–305.

- Refer to how Mary 'remembered all these things and thought deeply about them'. Mary was intelligent – she wondered about things. She may have been quiet, but she was very thoughtful and reflective.
- Look at the statue/pictures of Mary, and of Mary with Jesus. What do they portray – Tenderness, gentleness, love, protection? Think also about the care, strength, faith and uncertainty that Mary must have felt during her lifetime.
- Think about our mothers – the responsibility they have for us, the unconditional love, the bond between mother and baby, the expectations we have that they will always be there for us.
- Bless all mothers, that they may be strengthened in their roles by the example of Mary.

Prayer of the Faithful
We pray for mammies everywhere. Bless them and keep them safe.

We pray for our Mother Church. May she nurture, comfort and protect her children.

We pray for our leaders. May they, like Mary, have faith in you when faced with difficult times.

We pray for our mothers who have already joined you in heaven. May they rest in peace.

We pray for our community. Help us to treasure our mothers and remember to make them feel special.

Reflection/Thinking Prayer
Together, let's pray:

Hail Mary, full of grace

The Lord is with you

Blessed are you among women

Blessed is the fruit of your womb, Jesus.

Holy Mary, Mother of God,

Pray for us sinners

Now and at the hour of our death

Amen.

✠

Our Family Mass Resources for the Family Sunday Liturgy **Year B**

Second Sunday After Christmas

Colour White

Suggested Décor Images of Jesus, banner reading 'Word of God'

Theme Jesus – the Word of God

Entrance Procession Image/figure of Jesus, candle, banner 'Word of God'

Gospel Procession Candles, Lectionary

Welcome
Welcome to our Family Mass. Together, we listen to special readings – the Word of God – and together our hearts will be filled with God's love.

Theme
Today we learn how Jesus is also called the 'Word of God'. In a similar way to how our thoughts can become real and effective when put into action, we will listen to how Jesus was the Word of God, given flesh and blood.

Introduction to First Reading
There are words in our First Reading that are, at first, hard to understand. For example, 'the most high' is another way of saying 'God'. Imagine the 'word' in this reading like a seed, finding a place to take root, in order to grow and bring fruit and beauty to its surroundings.

First Reading
A reading from the book of Ecclesiasticus (24:1-2, 8-12)

I am the word spoken by the most high. I looked everywhere for a place to settle, some part of the world to make my home. Then my Creator, who created the universe, told me where I was to live. 'Make your home in Israel,' he said. 'The descendants of Jacob will be your people.' I served him in the sacred Tent and then made my home on Mount Zion. He settled me in the Beloved City and gave me authority over Jerusalem. I put down roots among an honoured people whom the Lord had chosen as his own.

The word of the Lord.

Introduction to Gospel
In our faith, we call Jesus the 'Word' with a capital 'W' – the only word amidst silence, the only light amidst darkness, the spark of life amidst nothingness. Let's listen to how the Gospel of John describes Jesus as the Word of God.

Gospel
A reading from the holy Gospel according to John (1:1-18)

Before the world was created, the Word already existed; he was with God, and he was the same as God. The Word was the source of life, and this life brought light to mankind. The light shines in the darkness, and the darkness has never put it out. The Word was in the world, yet the world did not recognise him. The Word became a human being and, full of grace and truth, lived among us. We saw his glory, the glory which he received as the Father's only Son.

The Gospel of the Lord.

Song 'Words' (from *Alive-O*).[3]

Homily Suggestions

- Emphasise that what we associate with the term 'words', for example reading, writing, speaking, is not exactly the same as the meaning of 'Word of God'. Also, emphasise that the 'Word of God' is not just for those who are able to speak, read or write.

- Refer to First Reading – the Word sought a place to settle and grow, choosing God's people as its 'fertile soil'. Compare this to how we listen to the 'Word of God' at our liturgies. Invite the congregation to reflect on how they listen (or not) and whether they are 'fertile soil' in which the Word can 'take root'.

- Ask the congregation to examine how the Word of God can be given flesh in the actions and words that we use in our daily lives. How do their lives reflect this?

- Refer to the focal objects (the image/figure of Jesus, light and banner). Emphasise Jesus as our model for being human. Suggest that in our thoughts and actions we should ask ourselves, 'What would Jesus say/do?'

---

3 Geraldine Doggett, from *Alive-O 8 Teacher's Book* (Veritas, Dublin, 2004), p. 335.

Prayer of the Faithful

We pray for our families. Help us to be kind with our words and caring with our actions.

We pray for our Church. Help all those who work to bring the Word of God to new places and people.

We pray for our leaders. May they follow the example of Jesus, bringing light and peace to the world.

We pray for those who find it hard to follow Jesus. May listening to the Word of God bring them greater understanding, and the desire to strengthen their relationship with God.

We pray for our parish community. Bless our Ministers of the Word, our Scripture study and prayer groups.

Reflection/Thinking Prayer

In listening and talking
May Jesus be our friend.

In reading and writing
May Jesus be our teacher.

In our thoughts and actions
May Jesus always be present.

Help us to speak and act
With truth and faith.

We ask this through Christ our Lord.
Amen.

⊕

Our Family Mass Resources for the Family Sunday Liturgy **Year B**

Epiphany of the Lord

Colour White

Suggested Décor Images from readings, stars

Theme Divine Glory

Entrance Procession Candles, star, Three King figures for crib/objects representing gifts of the Magi

Gospel Procession Candles, Lectionary

Welcome
Welcome to our Family Mass. Together, we will hear the Word of God; let's try to listen as best as we can.

Theme
Today, we place the three kings into our crib. The light of a star led them to the baby Jesus. With them they brought three gifts:

Gold – to wish the baby Jesus wealth and good fortune.

Frankincense – to wish him a loyal and faithful people.

Myrrh – to wish him peace and a long and happy reign among his people.

We also realise today that God has given us a wonderful gift – his Son Jesus, the light of our world.

Introduction to First Reading
We prepare to listen to a reading from the prophet Isaiah. In it, we will hear about a great light – the glory of God that shines upon us. We will hear about how people gather, bringing gifts in celebration. Listen carefully; can you hear any words that make you think of our celebration today – the visit of the Three Kings?

First reading
A reading from the prophet Isaiah (60:1-6)

Arise, Jerusalem, and shine like the sun;
The glory of the Lord is shining on you!
Other nations will be covered by darkness,
But on you the light of the Lord will shine;
The brightness of his presence will be with you.
Nations will be drawn to your light.
And kings to the dawning of your new day.
Look around you and see what is happening:
Your people are gathering to come home!
Your sons will come from far away;
Your daughters will be carried like children.
You will see this and be filled with joy;
You will tremble with excitement.
The wealth of the nations will be brought to you;
From across the sea their riches will come.
Great caravans of camels will come, from Midian and Ephah.
They will come from Sheba, bringing gold and incense.
People will tell the good news of what the Lord has done!

The word of the Lord.

Introduction to Gospel
In our Gospel today, we hear about the Three Wise Men. They were guided by a star to worship the baby Jesus. They brought special gifts. Listen carefully and see if you can find out:

· What gifts they brought?
· What happened when they met King Herod on their way?
· Why they returned home using a different route?

Gospel
A reading from the holy Gospel according to Matthew (2:1-12)

Jesus was born in the town of Bethlehem in Judaea, during the time when Herod was king. Soon afterwards, some men who studied the stars came from the east to Jerusalem and asked, 'Where is the baby born to be king of the Jews? We saw his star when it came up in the east, and we have come to worship him.'

And so they left, and on their way they saw the same star they had seen in the east. When they saw it, how happy they were, what joy was theirs! It went ahead of them until it stopped over the place where the child was. They went into the house, and when they saw the child with his mother Mary, they knelt down and worshipped him. They brought out their gifts of gold, frankincense and myrrh, and presented them to him.

Then they returned to their country by another road, since God had warned them in a dream not to go back to Herod.

The Gospel of the Lord.

Song 'Light of Christ' (from *Alive-O*).[4]

Homily Suggestions

- Highlight the connections between the First Reading and Gospel passage.
- Provide some background for the Three Kings/Wise Men: names (Balthazar, Melchior, Caspar); their education (astronomers and Scripture scholars).
- Refer to the difference between the exuberant gifts of the Three Kings to the conditions of Jesus' birth in a stable with the animals.
- Ask the congregation to imagine the visit:
  - Might Mary or Joseph be expecting visitors?
  - How might Mary or Joseph react to such gifts?
  - Might the Three Kings be surprised to find their 'King of the Jews' in a manger?
- Refer to the dream that warned the Three Kings about their return route. Recount earlier angels' messages from the last few weeks' liturgies, all seeking to reassure and protect.
- Look at the images of stars. Their light can only be seen in darkness. Like in the First Reading, when the 'people walked in darkness', the glory of God shone brightly. Remind the congregation that when we seem lost, or caught in a feeling of darkness and despair, the light of Jesus will always guide us along the right path.
- Explain the word 'Epiphany':
  - Like a 'lightbulb over your head' in a story when someone figures out an answer
  - Compare to a wonderful feeling of 'I understand/I get it!' that follows when you finally work out a puzzle, riddle or problem.
- Explain why today is called the feast of the Epiphany.

Prayer of the Faithful

We pray for our families. Help us to be good friends to each other on our journeys through life.

We pray for our Church. May she be a shining light, showing your love for all.

We pray for our leaders. Help them to use their talents as they work towards a greater and brighter future for all.

We pray for anyone suffering in the darkness of depression and despair. May your beacon of light lead them out of their pain.

We pray for our parish. May your light of love shine on all our homes.

Reflection/Thinking Prayer
A Shining Light

There is a lighthouse off our coastline
Standing on an island, tall and proud.
It shines its light to keep sailors safe
From the rocks that can run them aground.

Your light, my Lord, is like that lighthouse
Shining brightly across the sea
Like the beautiful star, on that special night
That the Three Wise Men did see.

Help us to follow your light, Lord Jesus
And just like the sailors, we will be safe
And like the Three Kings who journeyed far,
We will be guided by the light of our faith.

✠

---

4 Bernard Sexton and Frances O'Connell, from *Alive-O 8 Teacher's Book* (Veritas, Dublin, 2004), pp. 302–303.

Our Family Mass Resources for the Family Sunday Liturgy **Year B**

The Baptism of the Lord

Colour White

Suggested Décor Images from readings, baptismal symbols

Theme Divine Glory, celebration of the anointing of Jesus with the Holy Spirit and the beginning of his public ministry. As Christians, we share in this Mystery

Entrance Procession Baptismal candles, chrism, water, baptismal register

Gospel Procession Candles, Lectionary

Welcome
Welcome to our Family Mass. Let's take a moment to remember that we are in a special place. Together, we will hear the Word of God, let's try to listen as best as we can.

Theme
Today we celebrate the Baptism of Jesus. Most of us were babies when we were baptised. We might not remember it, but it was a very important day in our lives. God called us to live as his children.

Today we bring to the altar some special things:
- A baptismal candle – Jesus is our light, and God calls us to be a light for others
- The chrism and water with which we are baptised – we all belong in God's family
- The baptismal register – where all our names are recorded to mark this great event.

Introduction to First Reading
Imagine you were given a job. You would be told what your responsibilities were and what you were expected to do as part of that job. Our First Reading is like the job description for Jesus. Let's listen and see if we can learn more about how Jesus is our Saviour.

First Reading
A reading from the prophet Isaiah (42:1-4, 6-7)

I, the Lord, have called you and given you power to see that justice is done on earth.

Through you I will make a covenant with all peoples; through you I will bring light to the nations.

You will open the eyes of the blind and set free those who sit in dark prisons.

The word of the Lord.

Introduction to Gospel
Jesus was an adult when he was baptised and from that day he began to travel and teach people how to live as children of God. Today, we listen to Mark's account of the amazing events that happened immediately after Jesus asked John the Baptist to baptise him in the River Jordan.

Gospel
A reading from the holy Gospel according to Mark (1:7-11)

Not long afterwards Jesus came from Nazareth in the province of Galilee, and was baptised by John in the Jordan. As soon as Jesus came up out of the water, he saw heaven opening and the Spirit coming down on him like a dove. And a voice came from heaven, 'You are my own dear Son. I am pleased with you.'

The Gospel of the Lord.

Dramatisation of the Gospel
See Appendix III, p. 215.

Homily Suggestions

- Recount the main points of the Scripture passages – justice, covenant, light, Saviour, anointing of Jesus with the Holy Spirit at his baptism, recognition of Jesus's divinity, start of Jesus's ministry.
- Briefly explain elements of baptismal rite, for example oil, water, gown and candle.
- Clarify the connection between the anointing of Jesus with the Holy Spirit and how we receive the Holy Spirit in our baptism.
- Looking at how Jesus spent the remainder of his earthly life, what does that mean for how we should live our lives?
- Mention how the Sacraments of Initiation bring us into God's family and consequently the responsibilities of Jesus (for example, those in First Reading) become our own responsibilities. Invite the congregation to reflect on how they are faring in carrying out their Christian responsibilities?
- Remind the congregation of their baptismal promises. Invite them to renew them together.

Prayer of the Faithful

We pray for our families, especially our mammies and daddies. We thank them for bringing the care and love they show to us.

We pray for our Church, especially for those who are preparing for baptism. May they find a happy home in God's family.

We pray for our leaders. Help them to follow the way of Jesus in being of service to others.

We pray for those who have forgotten their baptismal promises. May your light guide them back to living their Christian responsibility.

We pray for our parish. Bless all those who have been baptised in the last year, and all those who prepare candidates for baptism.

Reflection/Thinking Prayer[5]

Think back on our Gospel reading today. We invite you to look upwards and close your eyes.

Imagine the sky. It is cloudy. The clouds disappear and you can see heaven. It is more beautiful than anything you have ever seen – you can almost feel the happiness, the peace, the warm feeling of love. Imagine hearing the words spoken to Jesus, 'You are my own dear Son. I am pleased with you.' (*Pause for a few moments.*)

Please open your eyes.

God calls us all to be his children. This week, let's make a special effort to be more like his dear Son, Jesus – more gentle, friendly and kind; to say hello, to smile, to help out at home.

⊕

---

[5] Adapted from Ed Hone & Roisín Coll, *All Together: Creative Prayer with Children* (Veritas, Dublin, 2009), p. 102

III. Lent
An Overview

The season of Lent is a period of preparation for Easter – the pinnacle of the Church's year at which time we celebrate the Paschal Mystery. Consequently, Lent involves an examination and active refinement of who we are as Christians. It is a time when we look carefully at ourselves and ask are we the best Christians we can be, and, if not, how can we improve?

The areas of penance, self-reflection, conversion and the catechumenate can be difficult topics to present to children. Consequently, during the season of Lent, the Family Mass will need to optimise the use of visual aids and symbols and, ideally, to connect with the work done in the school context. All of this will assist in enabling the younger members of your congregation to give meaning to this important liturgical season.

See the *Recommended Resources* section for a list of materials from the religious education programmes currently in use in schools.

How can we present Lent to children?

Lent can be effectively presented to children as:

- A journey
- A time to re-connect, re-build, re-form
- A time to differentiate between what we really need and what we take for granted
- A time of beginning and ending (and beginning again, of course!)
- Turning *away* from sin, turning *towards* God (conversion and repentance)
- 'Keep-fit' for the soul and spirit.

Take your time

The liturgies and additional activities suggested for the Lenten season are quite extensive. But relax! Just treat them as they are meant to be – suggestions and ideas! Pick and choose what you would like to try, or what you think might work for your particular Family Mass. Remember to keep in mind the overall length of the liturgy. For example, if you choose to try out a Lenten Garden, maybe use the reading for it instead of a theme and/or reflection. It's up to you.

Just like the Wreath and Jesse Tree in Advent, it is a good idea to have an activity for the season of Lent. What follows are some ideas.

A Lenten Garden
A large flowerpot or window box would be suitable for this purpose. The premise is the transformation of a wild, overgrown, litter-strewn and unfruitful space into a beautiful, productive and flourishing garden. This is a visual representation of the efforts we make during Lent to turn around our own lives – getting rid of bad habits and putting in their place better attitudes, thoughts and behaviours.

Week by week, a reader can describe the changes in the Lenten garden and make comparisons to how we can similarly improve our lives. Sample readings are provided below but these can be adapted and supplemented to suit your local circumstances. Such an activity can be a great focal point for the liturgies and can be expanded to include participation from local farmers (vegetables), gardeners (flowers), hardware stores (ornaments) and schools (decorations/painting the pot or box).

What do you think?
It might be an idea to separate the reading for the Lenten Garden into two parts. The first, focusing on the garden itself could form part of the introduction to the Mass. The second, suggesting improvements to be made in our lives, could be used at the end of the Mass as a parting task for the week.

Week 1 *The Garden is a mess of litter, weeds, stones and poor soil. The pot or box is in poor condition also.*

'Look at the state of that! This is no lovely garden. It's full of litter and weeds. What little soil there is, is bone dry – nothing could grow there. There are rocks where there should be flowers. Even the box could do with a fresh coat of paint.

'If you could make the garden look well, what jobs do you think need to be done first? Let's start with the litter. This week, we will tidy up the garden and get rid of that awful litter.

'This week, we will get rid of the litter in our lives. What do we not need? What is taking up space in our lives? Do we spend too much time on the computer and not enough time talking with our family? Do we rush our school work so can get to go out to play? Do we eat too much junk food and not enough healthy food? Are our rooms untidy, with clothes and toys scattered everywhere? This week, pick something to improve in your life.'

Week 2 *The Garden is free from litter, but is still in poor condition as described in Week 1.*

'Take a look at the garden now. The litter is all gone. There's more space. We can do some work. What's next? How about the weeds? Some people say that weeds are flowers that just grow in the wrong place! Colourful flowers would be better than weeds. The weeds will steal the sunlight and water from the flowers though. This week we better get rid of the weeds.

'The weeds in our garden have grown there for some time. It's a bit like our bad habits: sometimes we do things for a long time just because we are used to doing them, but they might not be good things. Maybe we sit around too much and are a bit lazy. Should we think about maybe getting out and

Our Family Mass Resources for the Family Sunday Liturgy **Year B**

about for some exercise? What about saying please and thank you? Or saying prayers at night? Maybe we have a habit of forgetting them or rushing through them. This week, let's try to pick some habits we have and not only break them, but make new and better habits.'

Week 3 *The Garden is free from litter and weeds. The soil remains poor and stony. The general condition of the box is also poor.*

'We're getting there, aren't we? At least our garden is clean. There is no litter. The weeds have all been dug up. But nothing will grow in poor soil. It's time to freshen up the soil, put in some compost and take out any stones. We must have good soil to grow our flowers. That's what we will do this week – we will freshen up the soil.

'The soil in our garden will be the home for our flowers. Flowers need a good home with enough room to grow, a safe place in which to extend their roots, and plenty of nourishment to keep them healthy. We can compare ourselves to that soil. Are we a welcome home for Jesus? Do we give time to Jesus? Do we listen and allow God to be part of our lives? Are we kind to each other like Jesus wants us to be? Perhaps this week we might make a special effort to be kind, and to make time to pray to our friend Jesus.'

Week 4 *The Garden is in much better condition. The soil is good though the box is still not ready.*

'Our garden is ready for planting. We need some seeds and bulbs. We need to be careful when we sow them. We must give them room to put down their roots. Which seeds and bulbs will we choose? Perhaps we could ask someone who knows more than we do about gardening. Yes, this week we will ask some advice from a gardener about planting in our garden.

'We have made a great effort so far this season to give up things that we don't need, things that aren't good for us. Wouldn't it be good if we could take *up* things that *are* good for us, and good for those around us. Good habits instead of the bad ones – like colourful flowers instead of the weeds in the garden. Sometimes it's hard to know what is the right thing to do. When we need help deciding, we can ask our mammies, our daddies, our teachers, our priests. We can pray to God and ask God for help too. This week, let's try to listen more to the advice we get from others, and listen more to how God wants us to act.'

Week 5 *The Garden is in good condition. The flowers are growing but they need water. The box still needs painting.*

'What a difference a few weeks makes. Do you remember how awful our garden looked before? Now there is no litter, no weeds, no stones. We have good soil and our plants are beginning to grow. Still, they don't look as healthy as they can be. We need water and plenty of light. This week, we will water our plants and make sure our garden gets some light.

'Light and water help our flowers to bloom and grow strong. Jesus is our light of the world. When we let Jesus shine his light on us – when we really listen to the Word of God and when we love as Jesus asked us to – we can grow and

58 —

bloom as wonderful children of God. And just as the water feeds the flowers and keeps them going, the water of our baptism keeps us going too. We can always turn to Jesus when we need that little bit of encouragement.'

Week 6 *The garden is flourishing. All that remains to do is freshen up the box itself and add some ornaments.*

'Wow! Now that's a garden! What beautiful flowers – how lovely to see our hard work pay off! But something still isn't quite right. Ah, the box needs a fresh coat of paint. Maybe a couple of little ornaments would give it that extra sparkle. Then it will be all ready in time for Easter.

'Our Lenten journey is almost at an end. We have worked hard at being better people. Now we should be ready to show our new selves to the world. How might we show that we are good people, the kind of people God knows we can be? Well, how about smiling more, greeting passers-by in the street, remembering to do what we say we will do. It's all very well to *think* we have done a good job of giving up bad habits and taking up good ones – we have to *show* it. Let's do that this week.'

On Easter Sunday, the Lenten Garden should be in the best condition possible – colourful, clean, healthy and decorated.

A Lenten Rockery

A collection of stones could be displayed on the first Sunday of Lent, representing the wilderness and desert that we encounter in the Scripture readings. The members of the congregation are invited to take a stone and keep it with them during the weeks of Lent – they could use it as a prayer stone, or place it somewhere in their house to remind them of the meaning of Lent. The stones can be brought to each subsequent liturgy to maintain the connection from week to week.

During Holy Week, the stones can be returned to help build a tomb for display at Easter. The stones can symbolise how God, in the flesh and blood person of Jesus, took our 'hearts of stone', our sins, and saved us.

A Faith Friend

Are you familiar with the tradition of Kris Kindle in the weeks before Christmas? Well, a faith friend is similar. You can pick a name at random (perhaps from a basket, or better still, the names could be on paper leaves on a tree!) and remember that person in your prayers throughout Lent. At Easter, you could meet with the person or perhaps, in the case of younger children, encourage them to make an Easter card for their faith friend.

Focal Objects for the Sundays of Lent

First Sunday
Sand Symbolic of the desert. Lent is a time for us to examine the 'full' and the 'empty' areas of our lives. Where do we need to inject more life? More effort? More charity? More time for God? What do we take for granted?

Second Sunday
Light The 'light at the end of the tunnel'. We follow Jesus as our Light of the World. We trust in the light of God that no matter what, we will be saved from the darkness. (*Also a symbol used in baptism.*)

Third Sunday
Water The necessity of water to our lives. Jesus is the spring of the eternal water of life. Our lives can become 'dry', 'withered' and 'barren', but through our baptism we can 'drink this eternal water of life'. (*Also a symbol used in baptism.*)

Fourth Sunday
Oil The anointing of David. Jesus is 'the Anointed One'/the Messiah. The power of touch, of healing and of re-connecting in our relationships. (*Also a symbol used in baptism.*)

Fifth Sunday
Budding Branch New life emerging from apparent barrenness. Death can test our faith. But in death, Jesus brings us to new life.

Passion Sunday
Palm The arrival of Jesus into Jerusalem.

Ash Wednesday and Holy Week
It is likely that younger members of the congregation will encounter Ash Wednesday and perhaps some of Holy Week as part of their school-based religious education. Since these days do not fall on Sundays, and are not Holy Days of Obligation, we have not included a full liturgy on each. However, many families attend some prayer services or visit the church during these days, so we have provided some prayers and reflections that could be incorporated into the main parish liturgy, as well as highlighting some wonderful services from current religious education programmes. You can find all this in *Appendix II*, p. 195.

Songs for Lent
The primary school programme *Alive-O* contains a number of songs that are relevant to Lent. Not only would many children be familiar with them, but listening to them after the Gospel, either on CD or with a choir, would be a welcome alternative to dramatisation. Both methods can enrich the liturgical experience for the entire congregation, but there are already a number of Scripture readings in dialogue format during this season. As Lent is a solemn season of preparation for Easter, a simple song that reinforces the theme of the Mass is adequate. In addition, from a pragmatic point of view, practise for the Passion Sunday readings and any other services during Lent will already take up a lot of time.

In each liturgy, some songs are suggested. For information on where to find these songs, please refer to the *Recommended Resources* section.

Remember: it's good to appeal to as many senses as possible!

A final word: Lent and Length!
As you go through the liturgies of this season, you will notice that many of the Gospel readings in particular are quite long. There is a strong visual element in these Lenten liturgies through a broad use of symbols with accompanying explanatory readings. Keeping in mind the age range of the congregation, it's probably best that other elements of the Mass be kept short so that attention will be retained. For example, the reflections are brief and we have omitted the dramatisations in favour of a song. Amongst your team, discuss how you might need to adapt your Family Mass to prevent it from being overwhelming for your congregation.

Our Family Mass Resources for the Family Sunday Liturgy **Year B**

First Sunday of Lent

Colour Purple

Suggested Décor Images from readings, rainbows

Theme Our Lenten journey

Entrance Procession Bowl of water, bowl of sand, cross

Gospel Procession Candle, Lectionary

Welcome
Welcome to our Family Mass. It's time now to quieten ourselves, to prepare to listen to the Word of God and to celebrate the Eucharist together.

Theme
Reference to Lenten Garden/Rockery/Faith Friend (*where applicable – see overview, pp. 57–59*).

Today, we bring some special items to the altar:

A bowl of water In our First Reading, we will hear about Noah and the Great Flood. We know that water is life-giving. It nourishes us and the world around us. But too much water – a flood – can swamp and overwhelm. At the beginning of our Lenten journey, we might ask ourselves what do we have too much of? What takes our attention away from what really matters, away from God and each other?

A bowl of sand We will hear about the desert in our Gospel today. In contrast to a flood, a desert has little or no water. A desert seems like an empty and lifeless place. Today, let's think about what areas of our life we could put more energy into and bring to life. Can you think of any talents that you could use more? What could you do in this season of Lent that would bring the life-giving Spirit of God into your life and into the lives of those around you?

A Cross Our Lenten journey will end at Easter, when we will remember and celebrate the Paschal Mystery – the life, death and resurrection of Jesus. The cross reminds us that whatever we choose to give up or do during this season of Lent, our focus must always remain on the true destination of our journey – a greater love for God and deeper belief in the Good News.

Introduction to First Reading
Do you remember Noah and the Great Flood? Noah loved God, and out of love God told Noah to build a boat called an Ark. Into the Ark, Noah was to bring his family and some animals. God told Noah that everything would be washed away by a Great Flood, but that when a rainbow appeared it would be a sign for Noah that it was all over and it would be safe to leave the Ark. This is where we join our First Reading.

First Reading
A reading from the book of Genesis (9:8-15)

God said to Noah and his sons, 'I am now making my covenant with you and with your descendants, and with all living beings, all birds and animals, everything that came out of the boat with you. With these words I make my covenant with you: I promise that never again will all living beings be destroyed by a flood; never again will a flood destroy the earth.'

The word of the Lord.

Introduction to Gospel
Jesus was baptised by John in the River Jordan. Our Gospel reading gives us an account of what happened next. As you listen, think about these questions:

- Where did Jesus go?
- What did Jesus do afterwards?

Gospel
A reading from the holy Gospel according to Mark (1:12-15)

The Spirit made Jesus go into the desert, where he stayed forty days, being tempted by Satan. Wild animals were there also, but angels came and helped him.

After John had been put in prison, Jesus went to Galilee and preached the Good News from God. 'The right time has come, and the kingdom of God is near! Turn away from your sins and believe the Good News!'

The Gospel of the Lord.

Song 'Light of Christ' (from *Alive-O*).[1]

---

1 Bernard Sexton and Frances O'Connell, taken from *Alive-O 8 Teacher's Book* (Veritas, Dublin, 2004), pp. 302–303.

Homily Suggestions

- Refer to the Lenten Garden/Rockery/Faith Friend (if applicable).

- Explain to younger children that Lent can be a time during which we prepare to be our best selves for Easter – liken it to 'keep fit' for our feelings, thoughts, behaviours, spirits and souls.

- With reference to the Gospel, explain the word 'temptation'. For younger members of the congregation, refer to ideas of 'selfishness', as well as the idea of 'giving up/giving in/taking the easy way'.

- Recap on Gospel and answer the questions from the introduction to the Gospel (i.e. that Jesus entered the desert, and afterwards preached to believe in the Good News).

- Expand on the 'usual' activities during Lent – giving up/avoiding temptation/doing something extra. Lent can be a time for practising putting others first. For example, in *Toy Story 2*, Buzz and his friends risk everything to rescue Woody. They put his needs first. Offer some suggestions for the congregation to try during Lent.

- Refer to the rainbow image from the introduction to the First Reading.

  • Rainbows only appear when there is both rain and sunshine, i.e. good times following bad times. Ultimately rainbows are a sign of hope, and our hope will always rest in God (who gave the rainbow to Noah)

  • Imagine Lent as a journey along the rainbow. At the end of this rainbow journey is Easter (refer to the focal object of the Cross).

- Examine the image of the Flood (refer to the focal object of water). We know that we need water for nourishment and cleaning. We also have fun with water, like when we go swimming or sailing. But a flood is when there is too much water. Ask the congregation to think about what they might have too much of in their lives, and how it might be taking their attention away from God and from others. For example, do we spend too much time on our phones or games consoles and not give enough attention to our families? Do we let someone else do so much for us that we have become lazy and don't bother using our own talents for the good of others? Do we forget that we are lucky to have enough to eat, good clothes or warm homes, without giving our time or efforts to help those who do not have enough? Give some time for reflection.

- Examine the image of the desert (refer to the focal object of sand). Ask the congregation to think about the apparent emptiness of the desert. Compare this to our quiet times. Emphasise that it can be good to have quiet time, silence and peace – we can attune ourselves to God during periods of quiet. Also refer to the loneliness that we might be unaware of in our neighbours, especially the elderly. Remind the congregation that we must be ready to reach out to others and think of ways to keep them from being lonely or left out.

Prayer of the Faithful
We pray for our mammies, daddies and all who look after us. We thank them for providing for our needs with love and care.

We pray for our Church. Bless all the faithful as we journey through Lent.

We pray for our leaders. Help them to work towards peace, justice and equality for all, especially those most in need.

We pray for those for whom Lent does not seem important. Help them to realise that there is a place for everyone on this Lenten journey. Guide them back to the Good News.

We pray for our parish family. During this season of Lent, help us to always be grateful for what we have, and to provide for those who have not.

Reflection/Thinking Prayer
God gave hope to Noah with the sign of a rainbow.

Let's think about our Lenten journey like a colourful rainbow:

Red. Lent is our chance to stop, look and listen.

Orange. Like a flashing amber traffic light, Lent is the time to double-check our habits and thoughts before we proceed on our journey.

Yellow. The colour of the daffodils we see growing at this time of year. As spring takes hold in nature, let's ask ourselves what areas of our lives need love and care to help us grow into better people.

Green is for Go! What good habits and practices can we start this Lent?

Blue is the colour of the sea and the sky. We remember that we are responsible for the world around us. During this season of Lent, how can we try to be more environmentally friendly and look after the plants and animals that are also creations of God?

Purple. This is the most important colour for Lent. It is the colour of preparation and royalty. We are getting ready for Easter when we celebrate the Paschal Mystery of our King, Jesus Christ.

Our Family Mass Resources for the Family Sunday Liturgy **Year B**

Second Sunday of Lent

Colour Purple

Suggested Décor Images from readings, mountaintops

Theme Our Lenten Journey – a transformation

Entrance Procession Candle/light, image of mountaintop

Gospel Procession Candles, Lectionary

Welcome
Welcome to our Family Mass. Let's take a moment to prepare to listen to the Word of God and celebrate the Eucharist together.

Theme
Reference to Lenten Garden/Rockery/Faith Friend (*where applicable – see overview, pp. 57–59*).

Today is the second Sunday of Lent. We continue on our journey towards Easter, trying to be better people. Sometimes our journeys can be difficult. It seems hard to know what God wants for us. Today we remember that Jesus is always there for us. We bring a light to the altar to remind us of Jesus's presence in our everyday lives. It also reminds us of the light of God within each one of us. It is up to us to let that inner light shine brightly for all to see.

We also present the image of a mountaintop. This place features in both Scripture readings today. A mountaintop is a private place, somewhere to be away from the hustle and bustle of our busy lives. During Lent, we should take some time to be on our own, some quiet time when we can listen more carefully to the guidance of God in our lives.

Introduction to First Reading
Abraham wanted a son for a very long time. After many years, he finally had a child called Isaac, whom he loved dearly. In our reading today, we listen to a terrifying time in Abraham's life.

First Reading
This reading requires four participants.
A reading from the book of Genesis (22:1-2, 9-13, 15-18)

Narrator Some time later God tested Abraham; he called to him.

Voice of God Abraham, Abraham!

Abraham Yes, here I am!

Voice of God Take your son, your only son, Isaac, whom you love so much, and go to the land of Moriah. There on a mountain that I will show, offer him as a sacrifice to me.

Narrator When they came to the place which God had told him about, Abraham built an altar and arranged the wood on it. He tied up his son and placed him on the altar, on top of the wood. Then he picked up the knife to kill him.

But the angel of the Lord called to him from heaven.

Angel Abraham! Abraham!

Abraham Yes, here I am!

Voice of God Don't hurt the boy or do anything to him. Now I know that you honour and obey God, because you have not kept back your only son from me.

Narrator Abraham looked around and saw a ram caught in a bush by its horns. He went and got it and offered it as a burnt offering instead of his son.

The word of the Lord.

Introduction to Gospel
Just as we did in the First Reading, we go to a mountaintop for our Gospel today. Jesus brought his friends there to be away from the crowds. Let's listen to the amazing events that occurred.

Gospel
A reading from the holy Gospel according to Mark (9:2-10)

Jesus took with him Peter, James and John, and led them up a high mountain, where they were alone. As they looked on, a change came over Jesus, and his clothes became shining white – whiter than anyone in the world could wash them. Then the three disciples saw Elijah and Moses talking with Jesus. Peter spoke up and said to Jesus, 'Teacher, how good it is that we are here! We will make three tents, one for you, one for Moses, and one for Elijah.' He and the others were so frightened that he did not know what to say.

Then a cloud appeared and covered them with its shadow, and a voice came from the cloud, 'This is my own dear Son – listen to him!' They took a quick look round but did not see anyone else; only Jesus was with them.

The Gospel of the Lord.

Song 'Light of Christ' (from *Alive-O 8*).

Homily Suggestions
- In reference to the First Reading, acknowledge how horrifying it seems – a father told to kill his son! Emphasise that it is difficult to relate to the image of God asking Abraham to kill Isaac. Explain how today's reading is about reminders:

  • Abraham had waited for Isaac for so long. This event reminds Abraham of how Isaac was a gift from God and that God is the source of everything. Abraham was tested, but by recognising that everything rests in God's hands, he passed his 'test'

  • Ask the congregation to think of what and who they treasure – how would it feel to have to give up this person? Does this help us to remember to be grateful for all the love in our lives?

- In reference to the Gospel, explain that Moses and Elijah were prophets and that the disciples would have been very familiar with them from their faith. Recap on the Transfiguration – Jesus transformed into his glorious form (refer to the focal object of light). This reminds us of the light or glory of God.

- Examine how Scripture says that after the Transfiguration, there was 'only Jesus'. It's as if the light remains within Jesus instead of the glorious visible light. Similarly, by virtue of our Baptism, we have the same 'inside light'.

  • Invite the congregation to reflect on how we have this 'inside light'. Do we allow our 'light' to shine? Do we recognise the 'light' within other people?

- Refer to the focal object of the image of the mountaintop. Lent is a time for us to take some time away from the hustle and bustle of everyday life, to allow ourselves simply to be in the presence of God and become more aware of how we are capable of being better people.

Prayer of the Faithful
We pray for our families. Help us to be thankful for the gift of each other, and to recognise the goodness in every one of us.

We pray for our Church. Guide her in her mission of bringing the glory of God to all the world.

We pray for our leaders. Help them to work towards a world where everyone's dignity as a unique and special individual is recognised.

We pray for those who are alone, or who feel unloved in any way. Help them to know that they are all gifts from God.

We pray for our parish family. During this Lent, be with us as we make a special effort to re-connect with God and recognise the value of each other.

Reflection/Thinking Prayer
Light of truth, Light Divine
Love of love, Light of mine
Help me to make my Light shine
Shine for all to see.

Light of hope, Light of learning
Light in my heart, for God yearning
Help me to be grateful and caring
As Jesus asks me to be.

✠

Our Family Mass Resources for the Family Sunday Liturgy **Year B**

✝ Third Sunday of Lent

Colour Purple

Suggested Décor Images from readings

Theme Our Lenten Journey – the opportunity to check our progress in faith

Entrance Procession Candles, image of fire

Gospel Procession Candles, Lectionary

Welcome
Welcome to our Family Mass. Thank you for making the effort to come here today. It is good to be together in God's presence.

Theme
Reference to Lenten Garden/Rockery/Faith Friend (*where applicable – see overview, pp. 57–59*).

We bring an image of fire to the altar. We will hear in our reading today about Moses who first encountered God in a burning bush. We will listen to how the disciples remembered a passage from Scripture about love feeling like a fire inside you.

Our Mass today is a checkpoint along our Lenten journey – a chance for us to ask ourselves are we really doing our best?

Introduction to First Reading
For many years, the Israelites were forced to stay in Egypt as slaves. Moses led them to freedom. Afterwards, God spoke to Moses, giving him guidelines for the Israelites as to how they should live their lives. We have come to know these as the Ten Commandments. Let's listen.

First Reading
A reading from the book of Exodus (20:1-17)

God spoke and these were his words:

'I am the Lord your God who brought you out of Egypt, where you were slaves. Worship no God but me. Do not make for yourselves images of anything in heaven or on earth or in the water under the earth. Do not bow down to any idol or worship it, because I am the Lord your God and I tolerate no rivals. Do not use my name for evil purposes, for I, the Lord your God, will punish anyone who misuses my name. Observe the Sabbath and keep it holy. You have six days in which to do your work, but the seventh day is a day of rest dedicated to me. On that day no one is to work, neither you, your children, your slaves, your animals, nor the foreigners who live in your country. Respect your father and your mother, so that you may live a long time in the land that I am giving you. Do not commit murder. Do not commit adultery. Do not steal. Do not accuse anyone falsely. Do not desire another man's house; do not desire his wife, his slaves, his cattle, his donkeys, or anything else that he owns.

The word of the Lord.

Introduction to Gospel
At the time of Jesus, the Temple was much like what our Church building is today – the place where people gather to celebrate their faith. It is a very special place. In our Gospel today, we listen to how Jesus arrived at the Temple in Jerusalem and found it full of stalls where people were buying and selling all sorts of things. He got very angry. Why do you think Jesus was angry? Let's listen.

Gospel
A reading from the holy Gospel according to John (2:13-25)

It was almost time for the Passover Festival, so Jesus went to Jerusalem. There in the Temple he found men selling cattle, sheep and pigeons, and also the money-changers sitting at their tables. So he made a whip from cords and drove all animals out of the Temple, both the sheep and the cattle; he overturned the tables of the money-changers and scattered their coins; and he ordered the men who sold the pigeons, 'Take them out of here! Stop making my Father's house a market-place!' His disciples remembered that the Scripture says, 'My devotion to your house, O God, burns in me like a fire.'

The Gospel of the Lord.

Song 'The Ten Commandments' (from *Alive-O*).[2]

---

2 Fr Peter O'Reilly, from *Alive-O 7 Teacher's Book* (Veritas, Dublin, 2003) p. 327.

Homily Suggestions

· Present the Ten Commandments in modern format *(see below)*.

· In reference to the Gospel, emphasise that the image of an angry Jesus can appear at odds with the more prevalent images of Jesus. Suggest that it demonstrates Jesus' humanity and should enable us to feel even closer to him. Explain that Jesus' anger came out of his disappointment at the disrespect being shown at the Temple.

· Invite the congregation to reflect:

  • How do you treat your Church? Are you respectful of the presence of God? Do you allow other people to pray in silence? Do you pay attention?

  • How is your Lenten journey progressing? Are you keeping up your promises?

Prayer of the Faithful

We pray for our mammies and daddies. Help us to always show them love and respect.

We pray for our Church. May she be a shining example to all of how to live as faithful children of God.

We pray for our leaders. Help them to lead by example, by being respectful, charitable and fair.

We pray for those who have lost their way and forgotten how to live a life of faith. May their faith be renewed and strengthened.

We pray for our parish family. May our love for God guide us in building a stronger community.

Reflection/Thinking Prayer

In our reading today, we heard the Ten Commandments – guidelines for living a good life. How are you getting along? Let's ask ourselves some checkpoint questions:

• Do you think about what God would want when you make all your decisions?

• Do you speak kindly and pray with your heart?

• Do you give some special time just for God?

• Do you love and respect your parents?

• Do you look after your pets and the world around you?

• Do you keep your promises and tell the truth?

• Are you grateful for what you have?

How are you doing so far this Lent?

Are you keeping up the promises you made?

Are you getting rid of bad habits?

The Ten Commandments in modern format

1. Love the Lord your God alone, with all your heart.
2. Respect the Lord's name.
3. Keep the Lord's Day holy.
4. Honour your parents.
5. All life is in God's hands; do not destroy life.
6. Be faithful in marriage.
7. Do not steal.
8. Do not speak falsely of others.
9. Do not desire a person who already belongs with another.
10. Do not be greedy for things that already belong to others.

✠

Our Family Mass Resources for the Family Sunday Liturgy **Year B**

Fourth Sunday of Lent Laetare Sunday (*meaning 'Be Joyful'*)

Colour Rose can be used today instead of purple

Suggested Décor Images from readings, Lenten Garden/Rockery (if applicable), pictures of doctors/nurses

Theme Anointing with oil; the healing power of touch

Entrance Procession Candles, container of oil

Gospel Procession Candles, Lectionary

Welcome
Welcome to our Family Mass. Together, in this special place, we will hear the Word of God; let's try to listen as best as we can.

Theme
Reference to Lenten Garden/Rockery/Faith friend (*where applicable – see overview, pp. 57–59*).

Last week, we brought water to the altar. Today, we bring some oil. At our baptism we are also blessed, or anointed, with special oil. Those of you who will make your confirmation this year will be blessed again on that day. Both water and oil are things we can touch, and when we do, we learn what they feel like. Our senses are important to today's celebration.

Introduction to First Reading
Meet David. A normal boy. He wasn't the eldest in his family; in fact he was the youngest. He probably wasn't the tallest or the strongest. David spent his days on the mountains looking after his father's sheep. But God saw that David *was* special, *very* special indeed. Let's listen to find out more.

First Reading
A reading from the first book of Samuel (16:1, 6-7, 10-13)

The Lord said to Samuel, 'Get some olive oil and go to Bethlehem, to a man named Jesse, because I have chosen one of his sons to be king.' Samuel did what the Lord told him to do and went to Bethlehem. He told Jesse and his sons to purify themselves, and he invited them to the sacrifice.

When they arrived, Samuel saw Jesse's son Eliab and said to himself, 'This man standing here in the Lord's presence is surely the one he has chosen.'

But the Lord said to him, 'Pay no attention to how tall and handsome he is. I have rejected him, because I do not judge as a man judges. Man looks at the outward appearance, but I look at the heart.'

Then Jesse called his son Abinadab and brought him to Samuel. But Samuel said, 'No, the Lord hasn't chosen him either.' Jesse then brought Shammah. 'No, the Lord hasn't chosen him either,' Samuel said. In this way Jesse brought seven of his sons to Samuel. And Samuel said to him, 'No, the Lord hasn't chosen any of these.' Then he asked him, 'Have you any more sons?'

Jesse answered, 'There is still the youngest, but he is out taking care of the sheep.'

'Tell him to come here,' Samuel said. 'We won't offer the sacrifice until he comes.' So Jesse sent for him. He was a handsome, healthy young man, and his eyes sparkled. The Lord said to Samuel, 'This is the one – anoint him!' Samuel took the olive oil and anointed David in front of his brothers. Immediately the spirit of the Lord took control of David and was with him from that day on. Then Samuel returned to Ramah.

The word of the Lord.

Introduction to Gospel
Please close your eyes. You cannot see your family. You cannot see beautiful colours. You could not see where it is safe to walk or see the toys you love to play with. Now open your eyes. Aren't we very lucky if we can see? In our Gospel, we hear how Jesus helped a blind man to see. But there is more to seeing than just looking at what is around us. Listen now to the Word of God.

Gospel
A reading from the Gospel according to John (9:1-41)

As Jesus was walking along, he saw a man who had been born blind. Jesus spat on the ground and made some mud with the spittle; he rubbed the mud on the man's eyes and said, 'Go and wash your face in the pool of Siloam.' So the man went, washed his face and came back seeing.

His neighbour, then, and the people who had seen him begging before this, asked, 'Isn't this the man who used to sit and beg?'

Some said, 'He is the one,' but others said, 'No he isn't; he just looked like him.' So the man himself said, 'I am the man.'

Then they took to the Pharisees the man who had been blind. The day that Jesus made the mud and cured him of his blindness was a Sabbath. The Pharisees, then, asked the man again how he had received his sight. He told them, 'He put some mud on my eyes; I washed my face, and now I can see.'

Some of the Pharisees said, 'The man who did this cannot be from God, for he does not obey the Sabbath Law.'

Others, however, said, 'How could a man who is a sinner perform such miracles as these?' And there was a division among them.

So the Pharisees asked the man once more, 'You say he cured you of your blindness – well, what do you say about him?'

'He is a prophet,' the man answered.

The Gospel of the Lord.

Song 'Light of Christ' (from *Alive-O 8*).

Homily Suggestions
- In reference to the First Reading – David, who later became a king (recall story of Goliath/Joseph of the House of David), began as a seemingly normal boy.
- Reference to Oil of Baptism (bringing attention to the focal object of the container of oil) – origin of anointing with oil. To be 'marked for God's work'; oil as a precious item, not for everyday use etc.
- Anointing with oil involves the sense of touch. Jesus cured the blind man with his touch. Refer to the healing power of touch – hugs that make you feel better, rubbing a sore knee after a fall, etc. Ask the congregation to think of doctors and nurses who help heal our pains, and counsellors who help with pain we cannot see.
- Both readings refer to 'seeing'. David might not have looked different to anyone else, but God 'saw' something special in him. The blind man was cured so he could see. Emphasise that we don't always need our eyes to *really* see. When we open our hearts, we can *feel* the world around us, the love of our mammies and daddies, the love God has for us.
- Really seeing with our hearts = believing.
- Bringing together today's liturgy with last week – water and oil of our baptism marks us for God's work, enables us to 'see' the truth of God's love for us.
- Bring the congregation's attention to how the readings are preparing us for Easter, i.e. the controversy caused by curing the blind man sets the tone for the eventual arrest of Jesus.

Prayer of the Faithful
We pray for our families, especially the youngest children, those with special needs and those who are sick. May they always know how much they are treasured.

We pray for our Church. May she spread your Good News so that people all over will know that they are special and that you love them.

We pray for our leaders. Guide them to look after those in need in our society especially those who are sick and those who have special needs.

We pray for doctors, nurses, counsellors, carers and all those who look after people who are sick or have special needs. Bless them in their work and may they always know that their efforts are appreciated.

We pray for those in our community who are preparing for the Sacrament of Confirmation. Be with them on their journey.

Reflection/Thinking Prayer
When I was happy, you patted me on my back.
When I was frightened, you held me tight.
When I was sad, you hugged me.
When I was cold, you wrapped me in a warm blanket.
When I fell and hurt my knee, you rubbed it and made it better.
When I was nervous, you held my hand.
When I was sick, you healed me.
When I was born, you welcomed me in your loving arms.
Thank you.

Our Family Mass Resources for the Family Sunday Liturgy **Year B**

Fifth Sunday of Lent

Colour Purple

Suggested Décor Images from readings, images/items representing spring/new life

Theme Our Lenten Journey – new life in Christ

Entrance Procession Candles, budding plant/branches

Gospel Procession Candles, Lectionary

Welcome
Welcome to our Family Mass. Let's take a moment to remember that we are in a special place. Together, we welcome God into our hearts.

Theme
Reference to Lenten Garden/Rockery/Faith Friend (*where applicable – see overview, pp. 57–59*).

Today, we bring to the altar a branch or plant. Not long ago, it was bare – its leaves and flowers long gone. But look – buds have formed on it. Soon all around us, the trees and plants will blossom. Leaves will grow. Nature comes to life once again.

As we near the end of our Lenten journey, we will soon celebrate how Jesus was raised from the dead and gave hope and New Life to us all.

Introduction to First Reading
A covenant is a special promise, one that changes how you lead your life. In the Hebrew Scriptures, we learned about Abraham, Noah and Moses. These were great leaders and prophets of God. They taught about God and about how to live a life in which you promised to always put God first. In our reading today, we hear how God spoke to another prophet called Jeremiah and commented on how the Israelites had broken their covenant with God in the past. Let's listen to hear what God told Jeremiah about a new covenant. What or who does it make you think of?

First Reading
A reading from the prophet Jeremiah (31:31-34)

The Lord says, 'The time is coming when I will make a new covenant with the people of Israel and with the people of Judah. It will not be like the old covenant that I made with their ancestors when I took them by hand and led them out of Egypt. Although I was like a husband to them, they did not keep that covenant. The new covenant that I will make with the people of Israel will be this: I will put my law within them and write it on their hearts. I will be their God, and they will be my people. None of them will have to teach his fellow countryman to know the Lord, because all will know me, from the least to the greatest.'

The word of the Lord.

Introduction to Gospel
We are approaching Easter when we remember and celebrate the passion, death and resurrection of Jesus. Today's Gospel gives us an insight into a private moment that Jesus had before all these events took place. He is troubled, concerned and worried. When you listen, see if you can find out why Jesus was anxious and how can you connect this passage with our First Reading.

Gospel
A reading from the holy Gospel according to John (12:24, 27-28, 31, 33)

Jesus said, 'I am telling you the truth, a grain of wheat remains no more than a single grain unless it is dropped into the ground and dies. If it does die, then it produced many grains. Now my heart is troubled, and what shall I say? Shall I say, Father, do not let this hour come upon me? But that is why I came, so that I might go through this hour of suffering. Father, bring glory to your name!'

Then a voice spoke from heaven, 'I have brought glory to it, and I will do so again.'

The Gospel of the Lord.

Song 'Beginnings and Endings' (from *Alive-O 5*).

Homily Suggestions
- Reiterate the explanation of 'covenant' – for younger children, the importance of keeping promises is familiar and relevant. Invite the congregation to examine whether they live their life as 'one promised to God'.

- Examine the image of the 'troubled' Jesus. Much like the 'angry' Jesus from a couple of weeks ago, we can relate to the humanity of Jesus, especially in difficult times. Focus on the hope of new life: Jesus looks forward rather than dwelling on his anxiety – so must we.

- Bring attention to the focal object of the budding branch – how spring brings new life, colour; animals awaken from hibernation; birth of young animals on farms. Encourage the congregation to take more notice of this in the coming weeks, to spend time in nature.

- Refer to beginnings and endings. This is a familiar theme to children, e.g. recycling/cycles of life in nature/new friendships, etc. Recommend the story, *The Fall of Freddie the Leaf* by Leo Buscaglia. (See *Recommended Resources* for more information.)

- Mention some phrases like, a new player might 'breathe new life' into a team who was not doing well, or by 'turning over a new leaf' you get rid of bad habits and try to do things better – i.e. 'the old habits are dead'. This can help children make connections between today's readings and their activities for Lent.

- Today's readings prepare us for the Easter story. Make reference to the fact that in a couple of weeks we will hear the important story of Jesus' death and how he rose, giving us new life in the process.

- For those who have experienced death in their family, acknowledge how death tests our faith – it can be hard to keep believing when bad things happen. But we mustn't lose hope. Our emphasis is always on hope. Not to focus on what's gone, but to look forward to what is to come, always remembering that God is there for us.

- Refer to the Lenten Garden/Rockery (if applicable).

Prayer of the Faithful
We pray for the members of our families who have died. May they rest in peace and look forward to eternal life with you.

We pray for our Church – for those here on earth, for those preparing for heaven and for those already in your loving presence.

We pray for our leaders. May they always hold on to the hope that they can make a difference in our world, to bring about justice and peace for all.

We pray for anyone who feels troubled. May your light guide them out of the darkness of their worry.

We pray for our parish community. Help us to look after our wildlife and nature in this exciting time of new life, so that we may reflect the hope of the new life you have given to us.

Reflection/Thinking Prayer
We have listened to the Word of God together, and heard that God never gave up on us, despite how others broke their covenant with God. In Jesus, we always have hope. We have a fresh start. We have new life.

We thank you God that:
Where there is hunger, you bring nourishment.
Where there is sickness, you bring healing.
Where there is anger, you bring kindness.
Where there is fear, you bring courage.
Where there is loneliness, you bring comfort.
Where there is cold, you bring warmth.
Where there is tiredness, you bring energy.
Where there is sadness, you bring joy.
Where there is doubt, you bring hope.
Amen.

⊕

Our Family Mass Resources for the Family Sunday Liturgy **Year B**

Passion Sunday

Colour Purple

Suggested Décor Images from Gospel, palms, cross

Theme The Passion of Jesus

Entrance Procession Candles, palms, cross

Gospel Procession Candles, Lectionary

To Note The length of today's Gospel means that there is no First Reading. In this liturgy, we have recommended segmenting the Gospel to enable the congregation to absorb its meaning more fully.

Welcome
Welcome to our Family Mass. Thank you for coming. It is good to be together in God's presence. Today's Mass is a little different because we are entering into Holy Week before we celebrate Easter. Let's take a moment to quieten and to prepare ourselves.

Theme
Reference to Lenten Garden/Rockery/Faith Friend (*where applicable – see overview, pp. 57–59*).

As we near the end of our Lenten journey, we bring to the altar some palms and a cross. These mark the beginning and the end of Jesus' time in Jerusalem. As he arrived, the people were delighted to see him. They waved these palms in excitement, like we wave flags at parades. In memory of Jesus as our Lord, we now bless these palms.

Blessing of the Palms

After the special meal called the Passover that Jesus and his friends shared, Jesus was arrested. He had done nothing wrong. But some people were afraid of him – afraid that the people of whom they were in charge would listen to Jesus and not to them anymore. So they put him to death on a cross. Because of this, the cross is a symbol of all that we believe. We display it today to remember all that Jesus did for us.

To Note Today's Gospel amalgamates passages of Gospel with dramatisations. Consider supplementing these with tableau, or having the 'readers' suitably attired to add a visual aspect to the reading.

Introduction to Gospel
We present today's Gospel in four parts. The first brings us to the time of Jesus' trial. We will imagine what it felt like for one of the soldiers there. In the second section, we will meet Simon of Cyrene who helped Jesus carry his cross. Next, we will hear about the Governor – the person in charge – whose name was Pontius Pilate. Lastly, we will listen to the Centurion. He was a guard, or army officer, at the Crucifixion of Jesus.

Gospel
This reading requires five participants.

Interviewer You were one of the soldiers who guarded Jesus of Nazareth in the Praetorium. He was made to wear the mock robes of a king. Why was that?

Soldier It has always been the custom for us soldiers to make sport of the criminals who are condemned to die. It's almost part of their sentence. We heard the story that this man from Nazareth claimed to be the king of the Jews. So we made him king for the laugh to make fun of him and pretended to honoured him with mock bows and mock gestures and put a mock robe over his shoulders. It passed the time for us, and for him too, I suppose, as he waited to die.

Interviewer You don't seem to have enjoyed your fun?

Soldier The fun went sour for me. You see, he was different. I mocked him, but there was something about him that made me want to respect him. I felt that he wanted the best for me … that he cared about me. It was a strange feeling. Afterwards when we marched him to Calvary I was there beside him. I was close to him. It made me feel good. I had mocked him and taunted him with the title 'king.' He was a king, in his own way, a real king.

Reader The soldiers took Jesus inside to the courtyard of the governor's place and called together the rest of the company. They put a purple robe on Jesus, made a crown out of thorny branches, and put it on his head. Then they began to salute him: 'Long live the King of the Jews!' They beat him over the head with a stick, spat on him, fell on their knees and bowed down to him. When they had finished mocking him, they took off the purple robe and put his own clothes back on him.

74 —

Song 'Imagine You Were There' (from *Alive-O 8*).

Interviewer Simon from Cyrene, you helped Jesus of Nazareth to carry his cross.

Simon I don't know why they picked on me but they did. At first I was furious at being made to carry the cross with a criminal, but a bit along the way we became friends.

Interviewer That was a strange thing.

Simon The strangest thing that ever happened to me! He made me feel good. He made me feel important. He made me feel that I mattered. There was a charm about him. He reached out in friendship to me. I was honoured to carry the cross with him. I can't explain it but it happened.

Reader Then they led him out to crucify him. On the way they met a man named Simon, who was coming into the city from the country, and the soldiers forced him to carry Jesus's cross. They took Jesus to a place called Golgatha, which means 'The place of the skull.'

Song 'Circle of Friends' (from *Alive-O 8*).

Reader At every Passover Festival, Pilate was in the habit of setting free any one prisoner with the rebels who had committed murder in the riot. When the crowd gathered and began to ask Pilate for the usual favour, he asked them, 'Do you want me to set free for you the king of the Jews?' He knew very well that the chief priests handed Jesus over because they were jealous.

But the chief priests stirred up the crowd to ask instead for Pilate to set Barabbas free for them. Pilate spoke again to the crowd, 'What then, do you want me to do with the one you call the king of the Jews?' They shouted back, 'Crucify him!' 'But what crime has he committed?' Pilate asked. They shouted all the louder, 'Crucify him!'

Pilate wanted to please the crowd, so he set Barabbas free for them. Then he had Jesus whipped and handed him over to be crucified.

Interviewer Governor Pilate, sir, Jesus of Nazareth died today on the cross. Did he have to die?

Pilate He should not have died. I tried everything to save him. I tried to persuade his accusers that there was no case against that man. I offered to release a prisoner, hoping they would choose the Nazarene. They chose that heartless murderer Barabbas instead. I did what I had to do.

Interviewer You condemned him to die.

Pilate The Governor cannot flinch from his duty. I had to save the city from riots and public disorder. His death was wrong, but the city and the people have been spared turmoil and disruption. His death was for the good of all the community.

Interviewer Was he guilty?

Pilate He broke no law. But he claimed he was the Son of God. That wasn't against the law. But that's what caused the trouble; that's what caused his death.

Interviewer Sent to the cross for claiming to be God's Son. A dreamer perhaps, but not a criminal.

Song 'Stabat Mater' (from *Alive-O 5*).

Interviewer Centurion, sir, what did you make of Jesus of Nazareth?

Centurion It was my duty to see that the sentence of the court was carried out. My men and I took the prisoner, Jesus of Nazareth, under guard to Calvary. We carried out the sentence of the court and crucified the prisoner according to Roman law. We then stood in loose formation at the foot of the cross to guard and observe the prisoner.

Interviewer What did you observe?

Centurion He died after three hours and I made my report to the authorities, giving the time of his death and the usual details.

Interviewer Was that the end of it?

Centurion That should have been the end of it, but I kept thinking about him. He was no ordinary criminal, no ordinary man. He was a man of God. The way he acted, the way he talked, the way he suffered, the way he made you feel, it was out of the ordinary. I felt blessed in some way by being near him. God was with him. When he died there was a strange silence. The world seemed to hush all around as if to honour him. I can't figure it out. I feel his story is not over yet. His death will be the beginning of something. I'm sure of that.

Reader The army officer who was standing there in front of the cross saw how Jesus had died. 'This man was really the Son of God!' he said.

Allow for a few minutes of silence, during which we kneel.

Homily Suggestions

- Bring attention to the palms and cross as markers of Jesus' time in Jerusalem.

- Briefly recall the events in the Gospel, asking the congregation to imagine they were there. How would they feel?

- Mention the Stations of the Cross as images of this journey. Invite the children to come to the church with their families during the week – perhaps to specific liturgies. Make reference to the upcoming services especially on Holy Thursday, Good Friday and Easter Saturday.

Encourage the congregation to put aside time this week to reflect on the events of Holy Week. Suggest displaying a cross or some of the blessed palm as a focal object for prayer time at home.

Prayer of the Faithful

We pray for our mammies and daddies. They do so much for us, often giving up what they would like to do so they we have what we need, or simply so that we have fun. Help us to say thank you and may they always know they are loved very much.

We pray for our Church. May the prayers and services of this Holy Week help our Church to grow closer to Jesus.

We pray for our leaders. May they be humble in their work, always putting the needs of their people first.

We pray for anyone who suffers pain, cruelty or imprisonment. May they be strengthened by Jesus' courage.

We pray for our community. Bless us this week as we join together in prayer to remember how Jesus suffered in order to save us.

Reflection/Thinking Prayer

God loves us and cares for us all the time.
All through his life, Jesus loved those who shared their life with him.
He also loved God and knew that God loved him.
Jesus died on the cross rather than stop loving God or his friends.
This week, let's try to remember the journey that Jesus had in Jerusalem:
His trial, carrying the cross, his death.
We will remember his love for us all.
Jesus, we bless you and adore you.
Amen.

✠

IV. Easter

An Overview

Easter is a single celebration lasting fifty days. It begins with the Easter Vigil and ends on Pentecost Sunday ('Pentecost' means 'fiftieth day'). During this time, we celebrate the joyous Resurrection of Jesus, his victory over death and our salvation and redemption. Our readings bring us along on the journey of faith with the disciples as they encounter the Risen Jesus. Following the Ascension of the Lord, we celebrate the outpouring of the Holy Spirit on Pentecost Sunday – the birthday of the Church.

Easter is the most important part of the liturgical year. It commemorates the core of Christianity – the Resurrection, and the presence of the Risen Christ in the Church.

Being realistic

These mysteries are difficult to present, especially to younger people. For example, it is easier for most people to relate to the birth of Jesus at Christmas than to grapple with the Resurrection! In addition, in contrast to the preparatory seasons of Advent and Lent, where there was a 'goal' ahead, Easter is a prolonged celebration. It is naturally more challenging to maintain interest and meaning when the season begins with the central event. Not only that, but we must take into account the longer evenings and the possibility of holidays as reasons why the Easter liturgies may be more challenging to engage the congregation's imagination over the entire season.

Central features of the Easter Season

Paschal Candle

Lit during the Easter Vigil, this candle is inscribed with the date and the Greek letters Alpha (Α) and Omega (Ω). Christ who was 'in the beginning' and will be 'at the end' is the Light of the World.

Singing of the Alleluia

Absent during Lent, the melody of the Alleluia reflects the joyous tone of the entire season.

The Presence of the Risen Christ

'In the here and now' could well be a motto for the liturgies of Easter. We celebrate how Jesus conquered death, saving us all, and we praise God for the *ongoing* presence of the Risen Christ in our Church, our sacraments and our day-to-day lives.

Outreach and Community

The Resurrection is not just a singular event. It ripples through into our lives and into the heart of our communities. Pentecost Sunday celebrates the coming of the Holy Spirit and the inauguration of the Church and her mission. Therefore, the impact of the Easter events on our lives is central to a meaningful celebration of the season. How we act as a community, how we live out the teachings of Christ and how we embody the core values of Christianity – these should all be emphasised in our liturgies.

Planning your Easter Liturgies
Whatever you plan to include in your liturgies for Easter, consider incorporating the following:

- An atmosphere of joy, happiness, excitement and possibility!
- Bright, cheerful and positive décor
- Presenting Pentecost as the arrival of the Holy Spirit and the birthday of the Church (thus creating a 'goal' similar to the preparatory seasons of Advent and Lent).

Pentecost and Sign Language
All too often, we think about the 'gift of speaking in many tongues' to the neglect of those in our congregation who are deaf. God's message is for everyone, including those who cannot speak or hear in the same way as others.

The celebration of Pentecost provides a great opportunity to highlight the inclusion of deaf people in our society. How about using some sign language? Many children will be familiar with the gestures used with the 'Our Father' in the *Alive-O* programme and this is suggested in the liturgy provided.

If you are interested in finding out more about using sign language in your liturgy, check out the National Chaplaincy for Deaf People's DVD on *Liturgical Signs and Prayers* (2005). For more details, see the *Recommended Resources* section.

Easter Challenges
A central feature of the season of Easter is Christian Outreach. Believing in Jesus, the importance of community and spreading the Good News are all main aspects of the Easter liturgies. To make this more concrete, we have included a series of Easter 'challenges' throughout the season. Each one resonates with the theme of the individual liturgy and seeks to involve the congregation in 'putting into practice' the aspects of our faith that can be called 'Christian outreach'.

An Easter Storyboard Display

The liturgies of Year B include great imagery and particular phrases that can help all parishioners, young and old, engage with the question Jesus posed – 'Who do you say I am?' – as well as inviting them to reflect on what impact the Paschal Mystery has on them. Some of the images and themes from this Easter cycle are listed below.

- The 'realness' and 'touchability' of the Risen Christ when he appeared to the disciples
- The Good Shepherd
- The Vine
- The repetition of the phrase 'Peace be with you'
- The Keystone
- The Greatest Commandment: Love One Another
- The Commissioning of the Disciples
- Jesus prays for his disciples
- The Gifts and Fruits of the Holy Spirit.

Explore them in your Family Mass team and consider how you could organise a display that would encourage the congregation to engage with the presence of the Risen Christ in their daily lives, especially beyond the 'confines' of the Mass.

Our Family Mass Resources for the Family Sunday Liturgy **Year B**

Easter Sunday

Colour White

Suggested Décor *Lenten Garden – resplendent, *Rockery – tomb. Images from readings, empty tomb, cross, banners reading Alleluia/Christ is Risen

Theme The Joy of the Resurrection

Entrance Procession Candles, flowers, banners: Alleluia/Christ is Risen

Gospel Procession Candles, Lectionary

Welcome
Welcome to our Family Mass. Today is a glorious day for us. Let's prepare to celebrate together in the Presence of God.

Theme
Alleluia! Hurray! Jesus is risen. Today, we celebrate life! All our preparations in our Lenten journey have been worth it, and much more! Because of the Resurrection, the Risen Jesus is with us on *all* our journeys through life, right there beside us, holding our hand.

Introduction to First Reading
Imagine what it must have been like for the disciples – they saw their friend, Jesus, die on a cross. They must have been very scared. He was their leader, what now? But then Jesus rose from the dead, the same Jesus but now in all his glory. The disciples set out on their new mission, to baptise people in his name so that they too could welcome the Risen Jesus into their lives. Listen to how Peter spoke about his friend Jesus.

First Reading
A reading from the Acts of the Apostles (10:34, 37-43)

Peter began to speak: 'I now realise that it is true that God treats everyone on the same basis. You know of the great event that took place throughout the land of Israel, beginning in Galilee after John preached his message of baptism. You know about Jesus of Nazareth and how God poured out on him the Holy Spirit and power. He went everywhere, doing good and healing all who were under the power of the Devil, for God was with him. We are witnesses of everything that he did in the land of Israel and in Jerusalem. Then they put him to death by nailing him to a cross. But God raised him from death three days later and caused him to appear, not to everyone, but only to the witnesses that God had already chosen, that is, to us who ate and drank with him after he rose from death. And he commanded us to preach the Gospel to the people and to testify that he is the one whom God has appointed judge of the living and the dead. All the prophets spoke about him, saying that everyone who believes in him will have his sins forgiven through the power of his name.

The word of the Lord.

Introduction to Gospel
The disciples had lost their friend. Jesus had died on the cross and his body was in a tomb. Jesus' friend Mary Magdalene went to visit the tomb, only to discover something amazing. Listen to what happened.

Gospel
A reading from the holy Gospel according to John (20:1-9)

Early on Sunday morning, while it was still dark, Mary Magdalene went to the tomb and saw that the stone had been taken away from the entrance. She went running to Simon Peter and the other disciple, whom Jesus loved, and told them, 'They have taken the Lord from the tomb, and we don't know where they have put him!'

Then Peter and the other disciple went to the tomb. The two of them were running, but the other disciple ran faster than Peter and reached the tomb first. He bent over and saw the linen wrappings but he did not go in. Behind him came Simon Peter, and he went straight into the tomb. He saw the linen wrappings lying there and the cloth which had been around Jesus' head. It was not lying with the linen wrappings but was rolled up by itself. Then the other disciple, who had reached the tomb first, also went in; he saw and believed.

The Gospel of the Lord.

Given the number of services during Holy Week, any practices for dramatisation of the Gospel during this liturgy will probably be difficult to organise. A song is suggested as an alternative. Also, it might be beneficial to bring attention to some of the Easter symbols and decorations of the Church. In this sample, they are incorporated into the 'Homily Suggestions' that follow.

Song 'This is the Day' (from *Alive-O*).[1]

Homily Suggestions
- Ask the congregation to think of their happiest memories or of events that bring great joy, for example birthdays, family occasions and so on. Focus on this feeling of happiness and relate it to the joy of Easter and the word 'Alleluia' (also explaining the return of the 'Alleluia' into the Mass).
- Make reference to the following, where applicable (depending on décor):
  - Lenten Garden/Rockery
  - Paschal Candle
  - Empty Tomb
  - Bright, colourful decoration of the Church
  - Significance of white for the Easter season.
- Invite the congregation to imagine themselves at the time after the Crucifixion. Facts are facts: Jesus died. Now, he is risen. Encourage the congregation to believe along with the disciples. Highlight how this is a mystery and that it is okay not to fully understand it. Instead ask the congregation to focus on the joy; the triumph of good over evil; the ongoing of presence of the Risen Jesus in our lives.

Prayer of the Faithful
We pray for our families. May we all have a happy Easter.

We pray for our Church. May all our brothers and sisters in faith around the world celebrate the joy of this Easter morning.

We pray for our leaders. May they work for peace and a worldwide belief in the triumph of good over evil.

We pray for all who have lost their faith. May hearing the Good News of this Easter Sunday help them to find their way back to you.

We pray for our community. Together, may we keep the happiness of this day alive in our hearts, and may it guide our actions as we work together in your name.

Reflection/Thinking Prayer[2]
The Risen Jesus was with the disciples. They were filled with joy when they realised that he was alive. The Risen Jesus is alive today and with us. Let us be full of joy as we say together:

Response *(repeat after leader)* The Risen Jesus is alive and with us

He is with us each and every day (R)

He is with us when we play (R)

He is with us when we work (R)

He is with us among those whom we love (R)

He is with us at school as we learn (R)

He is with us as we gather together at Mass (R)

May we, like the disciples, recognise that the Lord Jesus is with us always. Amen

*If the Lenten Garden and/or Rockery idea was used, they are brought to completion today. The introduction could include a reference such as:

Today, we see our Lenten Garden in all its glory, full of life and colour.

Today, we see how our Lenten rocks have gathered to surround the open tomb of Jesus. He took our sins upon himself, the sins represented by these rocks, and now they surround the tomb he left when he saved us from our sins and defeated death.

⊕

---

1 Mary Amond-O'Brien, from *Alive-O 8 Teacher's Book* (Veritas, Dublin, 2004), p. 325.

2 Adapted from part of service in The Resurrection: Term 2, Lesson 10, taken from *Connecting School and Parish: An Alive-O 1–4 Handbook for Classroom Visitations* (Veritas, Dublin, 2001), pp. 132–133.

Our Family Mass Resources for the Family Sunday Liturgy **Year B**

Second Sunday of Easter

Colour White

Suggested Décor Images from readings

Theme Giving Witness to the Risen Lord Together

Entrance Procession Candles, banners reading 'Give Witness', 'Together', bowl of water and small bottle of food colouring

Gospel Procession Candles, Lectionary

Welcome
Welcome to our Family Mass. We are a family. We are all God's children. Let's take a moment to quieten ourselves, to remember we are in God's house, and to prepare to celebrate Mass together.

Theme
We bring two banners for display today. The first reads 'Give Witness', the second says 'Together'. These reflect the actions of the disciples as we will hear in our readings today. These will be explained later in the Mass.

Perhaps it is best if we were to also demonstrate their meaning. We have a bowl of water. Imagine this is each one of us. Here is some food colouring. Imagine this is God. When we pour some of the food colouring into the water, the water changes — it has become united with the food colouring. They cannot be separated. When we give witness to God together, we are also changed. We are united to God and God can shine out through us.

Introduction to First Reading
What a difference Jesus made! He invited his disciples to follow him. They left behind their everyday lives to help Jesus spread the Good News. After the Resurrection, the disciples continued their work with even greater determination. Their work of spreading the Good News can also be called 'giving witness to God'. They lived by their teachings. Everyone was treated fairly. Everyone mattered.

First Reading
A reading from the Acts of the Apostles (4:32-35)

The group of believers was one in mind and heart. No one said that any of his belongings was his own, but they all shared with one another everything they had. With great power the apostles gave witness to the resurrection of the Lord Jesus, and God poured rich blessings on them all. There was no one in the group who was in need. Those who owned fields or houses would sell them, bring the money received from the sale, and hand it over to the apostles; and the money was distributed to each one according to his need.

The word of the Lord.

Introduction to Gospel
Imagine the disciples. Their friend Jesus had been killed. They feared for their own safety and so locked themselves away. Maybe they thought back over the good times, when together with Jesus they travelled spreading the Good News of God's love for everyone. Our Gospel reading takes us to the evening of the Sunday following the Crucifixion.

Gospel
A reading from the holy Gospel according to John (20:19-31)

It was late that Sunday evening, and the disciples were gathered together behind locked doors, because they were afraid of the Jewish authorities. Then Jesus came and stood among them. 'Peace be with you.' After saying this, he showed them his hands and his side. The disciples were filled with joy at seeing the Lord. Jesus said to them again, 'Peace be with you. As the Father sent me, so I send you.' Then he breathed out on them and said, 'Receive the Holy Spirit. If you forgive people's sins, they are forgiven; if you do not forgive them, they are not forgiven.'

The Gospel of the Lord.

Dramatisation of Gospel
See Appendix III, p. 215.

Homily Suggestions

- Refer to the demonstration of water mixed with food colouring. Reiterate that through our Baptism, we have become children of God. God is in us. We cannot pick out which part of us is God – God is in every part of our hearts, minds and actions.

- Explain the banner 'Give Witness'. Mention common associations of 'witness' to trials, e.g. someone who saw an event and can testify to its truth. Emphasise the word 'give' as an action. Reflect on how the disciples 'gave witness' to God – they acted out the teachings of Jesus. They preached, and lived as they preached.

- Bring attention to the banner 'Together'. In the First Reading, we see the disciples huddled together in fear. Fear can bring people together but usually the focus is only on self-protection. Contrast this to the Gospel – the love and peace of the Risen Christ brings the disciples together also, but in a way that they are empowered to go out and share the Good News – together.

- Reiterate how God permeates all creation, and most especially how through the Sacraments of Initiation we are united with God. Extend this to how we are united to each other in a common bond.

- Offer some moments for quiet reflection on how we give witness to God in our daily lives, and how we express the togetherness exemplified by the disciples.

Prayer of the Faithful

We pray for our families. May love always keep us together, even if we live in different places.

We pray for unity in our Church. Help us to focus and build on what we have in common with our brothers and sisters in faith.

We pray for our leaders. Help them to heal the divisions in countries torn apart by civil unrest. May they work towards peace, justice and equality.

We pray for anyone who feels frightened, alone and without purpose. Help them to know they are welcome in our Church and that God is always with them.

We pray for our parish family. May God's Spirit strengthen our efforts to build and maintain a happy and faithful community.

Reflection/Thinking Prayer

As we believe in God

God believes in us.

As the Father sent Jesus

We are sent to spread the Good News.

God is at work in our hearts, minds and hands

Wanting us to bring love, peace and justice to all.

Help us to allow God to work through us.

Help us to put aside our selfishness.

We pray that we will always remember that we are called to live as children of God.

Giving witness together.

This week's Easter Challenge

At home, chat with some family or friends about your experience of Lent.

- Has it changed you?
- Are you more like the person Jesus knows you can be and wants you to be?

Just because Lent is over, it doesn't mean we stop trying! This week, identify some actions you can undertake that let you express that God is in you. In other words, find some ways to give witness to God this week, together with your family/friends.

✠

Our Family Mass Resources for the Family Sunday Liturgy **Year B**

Third Sunday of Easter

Colour White

Suggested Décor Images from readings

Theme Recognising the Risen Christ

Entrance Procession Candles, image of an open hand, spectacles

Gospel Procession Candles, Lectionary

Welcome
Welcome to our Family Mass. Let's take a moment to get ready to be in the full presence of God together as we celebrate the Eucharist.

Theme
Have you ever witnessed an event, or saw someone and were so astonished that you found it almost impossible to believe it was real? We bring a pair of spectacles to the altar. Today is about recognising Jesus. The Risen Christ is all around us. We might spend our time looking for God, but fail to recognise that God is right here all the time. These spectacles represent our need to see God, through using our eyes to look all around us, our ears to listen carefully and our hearts to feel God's presence.

We bring an image of an open hand. We offer an open hand to someone when we shake their hands. It is a sign of welcome and of invitation. Listen to our First Reading. Work out what this sign of welcome has to do with what you hear.

An open hand is touchable. We can feel it. It's real. Listen carefully to our Gospel today and find out what this symbol means to you.

Introduction to First Reading
Peter was talking to a crowd of Jews. He goes into detail about who Jesus was and how his death came about – that the Jews chose to put the innocent Jesus to death and to free a murderer instead. However, Peter's teaching emphasises the words of Jesus himself when Jesus, nearing death, said of his persecutors, 'Forgive them, they know not what they do.' As Jesus extended the hand of friendship and God's love to everyone regardless of their past behaviours, Peter does the same. Let's listen.

First Reading
A reading from the Acts of the Apostles (3:13-15, 17-19)

Peter said to the people: 'The God of Abraham, Isaac and Jacob, the God of our ancestors, has given divine glory to his servant Jesus. But you handed him over to the authorities, and you rejected him in Pilate's presence, even after Pilate had decided to set him free. He was holy and good, but you rejected him, and instead you asked Pilate to do you the favour of turning loose a murderer. You killed the one who leads to life, but God raised him from death, and we are witnesses to this. And now my brothers, I know what you and your leaders did to Jesus was due to your ignorance. God announced long ago through all of the prophets that his Messiah had to suffer; and he made it come true in this way. Repent then, and turn to God, so that he will forgive your sins.'

The word of the Lord.

Introduction to Gospel
Our Gospel passage today begins with two disciples explaining their recent encounter with the Risen Christ to the rest of their group. These two had travelled along a road, chatting about all that had happened in Jerusalem, to someone they thought was just another traveller – a stranger. Only when this 'stranger' broke bread with them that evening they recognised that it was in fact did Jesus, the Risen Christ. Just after they told their friends about their meeting with Jesus, another amazing event occurs. Let's listen.

Gospel
A reading from the holy Gospel according to Luke (24:35-48)

The disciples explained to them what had happened on the road, and how they had recognised the Lord when he broke the bread. While the two were telling them this, suddenly the Lord himself stood among them and said to them, 'Peace be with you.' They were terrified, thinking that they were seeing a ghost. But he said to them, 'Why are you alarmed? Why are these doubts coming up in your mind? Look at my hands and feet, and see that it is I myself. Feel me, and you will know, for a ghost doesn't have flesh and bones, as you can see I have.' He said this and showed them his hands and feet. They still could not believe, they were so full of joy and wonder; so he asked them, 'Have you anything here to eat?' They gave him a piece of cooked fish, which he took and ate in their presence.

The Gospel of the Lord.

Song 'Jacob's Ladder' (from *Alive-O*)[3]

Homily Suggestions
- Refer to the focal object of the open hand. Ask the congregation to think about Peter. He offered his hand of friendship and God's invitation to the Jews, in spite of how they had chosen Barabbas to be freed over Jesus. Peter does not seek revenge. Instead he practises what he preaches and extends the open hand of God's friendship. Invite the congregation to pause for a few moments and reflect on their daily lives – how quick are they to seek revenge or to offer the hand of friendship? What can they learn from Peter?

- Move on to how the focal object of the hand represents the realness of God. Emphasise how you know the person next to you is there because you can feel them. For example, if you shake their hand, it 'proves' to you that they are present. Relate this to the presence of Christ in the Eucharist (citing how both the Journey to Emmaus and today's Gospel passage end with the recognition of Christ through the breaking of bread). Emphasise that the presence of God in the Eucharist is a mystery, but that the same Christ from the Gospel is right here with us when we celebrate the Eucharist.

- Bring attention to the spectacles. Mention some times when we might feel it is easy to be aware of God's presence, e.g. a birth, happy occasions, in nature (as if we are wearing the 'right' spectacles). Also refer to the difficult times when we find it hard to believe that God is present (as if we do not have the 'right' spectacles). Emphasise that God is always present, most especially in the sacraments of the Church. We might think that if we had the 'right' spectacles, we could see this for ourselves. But spectacles only work on our eyesight. The presence of God goes beyond this. Sometimes we might be aware of God's presence within the stillness of our hearts and minds, or through the actions of others.

Prayer of the Faithful
We pray for our mammies, daddies and all our families. Help us to recognise the goodness of Christ in each other and to treat each other with forgiveness and respect.

We pray for our Church. May the celebration of the Eucharist fill the hearts of all the faithful with the real presence of the Risen Christ.

We pray for our leaders. Help them to work towards making our world a place of forgiveness and peace.

We pray for those who for some reason do not feel God's presence. Help them to know the closeness of God in their lives, and the love of God in their hearts.

We pray for our parish family. Help our community to be a place of forgiveness and welcome that reflects the presence of God.

Reflection/Thinking Prayer
If God said 'BOO!'
What would you do?
Would you scream and run off scared?
Well, here's the thing…
God always says 'BOO!' when you're least prepared.
When you think you've gotten away
With that thing you knew you shouldn't do.
You can guarantee in no time at all
God will come along and surprise you – 'BOO!'
It's not that God wants to get you in trouble
For whatever wrong you've done
It's just that when God says 'BOO!'
To me, to you, to everyone –
He's reminding us he's there.
Always was, is and will be.
And whenever we recognise him,
We won't hear 'BOO!' but 'YIPPEE!'

This week's Easter Challenge
Go out and find Christ! Better still, take some quiet time to go inside yourself and find Christ.

Take note of times when you are aware of the presence of God and share this with your family and friends.

---
[3] Finbar O'Connor, from *Alive-O 8 Teacher's Book* (Veritas, Dublin, 2004), p. 295.

Our Family Mass Resources for the Family Sunday Liturgy **Year B**

Fourth Sunday of Easter

Colour White

Suggested Décor Images from readings

Theme The Good Shepherd

Entrance Procession Keystone, shepherd's staff or toy sheep

Gospel Procession Candles, Lectionary

Welcome
Welcome to our Family Mass. Let's take a moment to remember that we are in a special place for a special reason. We are God's family, come to worship together. We will hear the Word of God and celebrate the Eucharist together as Jesus asked. Let's do our best to listen and take part.

Theme
We bring a shepherd's staff/toy sheep to the altar. A shepherd looks after a flock of sheep whatever the weather, when they are sick and when they are well. A shepherd knows each and every one of the sheep and loves them all equally. Today we will listen as Jesus describes himself as the Good Shepherd, and we, his followers, are his flock.

We bring a particular stone to the altar. We call it a keystone. It does not look like a brick you would see in the buildings around us. You would imagine it could be difficult to build a tower with a brick like this. It might wobble and collapse. You could understand why builders might throw it away.

Introduction to First Reading
Let's take another look at our keystone. It is oddly shaped, not regular like a brick. However, if you were to imagine it as the very top of an arch way (like an upside-down letter 'u') then it is the most important stone of all – the keystone. In our First Reading, we hear about a lame man who was healed. Like the keystone differs from other stones, he was different from other people. He was not as healthy. But God saw him to be just as special as everyone else. But if we were to think of a person as THE keystone – the most important person of all, who do you think that would be? Let's listen to the Word of God and find out.

First Reading
A reading from the Acts of the Apostles (4:8-12)

Peter, full of the Holy Spirit, answered them, 'Leaders of the people and elders: if we are being questioned today about the good deed done to the lame man and how he was healed, then you should all know that this man stands here before you completely well through the power of the name of Jesus Christ of Nazareth – whom you crucified and whom God raised from death. Jesus is the one of whom the Scripture says, 'The stone that you the builders despised turned out to be the most important of all.

'Salvation is to be found through him alone; in all the world there is no one else whom God has given who can save us.'

The word of the Lord.

Introduction to Gospel
Do you know what a shepherd is? It's a person whose job is to look after sheep. The sheep might wander over hills in search of food and sometimes the shepherd might be away from home for days, looking after the sheep because he loves them like family. When Jesus taught his disciples, there was no electricity, no computers to do work for you; you had to do all the work by yourself. And being a shepherd was hard work. Listen to how Jesus explained about the shepherd caring for his sheep and what it had to do with Jesus' job too.

Gospel
A reading from the holy Gospel according to John (10:11-18)

'I am the good shepherd who is willing to die for the sheep. When the hired man, who is not a shepherd and does not own the sheep, sees a wolf coming, he leaves the sheep and runs away; so the wolf snatches the sheep and scatters them. The hired man runs away because he is only a hired man and does not care about the sheep.

'I am the good shepherd. As the Father knows me and I know the Father, in the same way I know my sheep and they know me. And I am willing to die for them. There are other sheep which belong to me that are not in this sheepfold. I must bring them, too; they will listen to my voice, and they will become one flock with one shepherd.

'The Father loves me because I am willing to give up my life, in order that I may receive it back again. No one takes my life away from me. I give it up of my own free will. I have the right to give it up, and I have the right to take it back. This is what my Father has commanded me to do.'

The Gospel of the Lord.

Dramatisation of Gospel
See Appendix III, p. 219.

Homily Suggestions
- Refer to the focal object of the keystone with regard to the First Reading. Emphasise how appearances can deceive. That which seems trivial and unimportant, even useless, can be the most essential thing of all. A lame person might be excluded from a team because of their disability but that same person could be the best manager! Jesus was mocked and crucified but he was in fact the Son of God!
- Develop this into two strands (connecting it to the Good Shepherd motif also):
  - Everything and everyone is special in their own way. God loves each of us regardless of looks or ability
  - Jesus is at the heart of our lives. Jesus is our keystone. Every thought, action and feeling we have should take into account the endless and selfless love that Jesus has for us. Everything we do should be with the effort of returning that unending love.
- Explain the life of a shepherd at the time (refer to the focal object of the staff/sheep). Think about how lonely yet responsible a job it was. Refer to how the relationship develops between shepherd and sheep ... almost like family: getting to know when someone is sad, upset, sick etc. Most importantly, the shepherd knows each sheep (wouldn't we find it hard to tell one sheep from another?)
- Develop this into Jesus knowing each one of us because Jesus is like our parent, sibling and closest friend all in one, yet much more. (Note: The *Alive-O* programme has lots of material on the theme of the Good Shepherd if you wish to look for additional resources with which school children in particular would be familiar.)
- Ask the congregation to think about all the work and love the shepherd gives to the sheep. What can the sheep do for the shepherd in return? What can we do for the Good Shepherd, Jesus, in return?
- Consider elaborating on the final passage of the Gospel. Invite the congregation to imagine how they think a good shepherd would treat his sheep. Would he beat them into moving where he wanted? Or force feed them? No. He would be there when needed and treat them with respect. Relate this to the motif of freedom and choice that is mentioned in the final passage. Love brings freedom. Jesus, our Good Shepherd, loves us so that we can be free.

Prayer of the Faithful
We pray for our mammies and daddies. Bless them for looking after us so well.

We pray for our Church. We are the family of God. Help us to look after each other like the Good Shepherd looks after his sheep.

We pray for our leaders. Be with them as they work towards building a more loving and peaceful world.

We pray for those who feel left out or forgotten. Help them to know that you, the Good Shepherd, know them, care for them and will look after them.

We pray for our community. Bless all the carers who look after others who are sick, in need or elderly. Help them to know their work is appreciated.

Reflection/Thinking Prayer
Dear Jesus,
I'm so glad you care about me
It makes me feel very special
It's lovely to know that you think about me so much
And that you keep me safe and healthy.

It's great that you know how I feel
Even when I don't know the words to explain it myself!
Like the sheep who follow the Good Shepherd
I will follow you.

This week's Easter Challenge

Who looks after you? Your mammy/daddy, grandparents, teachers and so on. Think about how they care about you. Think of times they looked after you. Thank that person this week in a special way. Perhaps make them a card, sing their favourite song or give them a hug.

✠

Our Family Mass Resources for the Family Sunday Liturgy **Year B**

Fifth Sunday of Easter

Colour White

Suggested Décor Images from readings, Banners reading 'I am the Vine, you are the branches'

Theme 'I am the Vine and you are the branches'

Entrance Procession Bunch of grapes, flowering plant

Gospel Procession Candles, Lectionary

Welcome
Welcome to our Family Mass. We all belong here. Each one of us has a role to play, some singing, some reading, some praying, some listening. Let's take a moment to prepare ourselves to celebrate our love for God together.

Theme
We bring some grapes to the altar. In our Gospel, we will hear Jesus talk about vines and branches. In hot climates, such as where Jesus lived, there are fields called vineyards, where vines grow. Vines are plants that produce fruit, just like these grapes.

We also bring a flowering plant. The flowers are beautiful, aren't they? The flowers grow because they are nourished by the goodness that travels through the branches, from the roots in the soil. If we were to cut off those flowers and put them in a vase, they would look pretty. Have you ever seen real flowers in a vase? Do they last forever?

Introduction to First Reading
Saul was a Pharisee, not a follower of Jesus. In fact he hunted down anyone who declared their belief in Jesus. Saul was responsible for many arrests, tortures and deaths of early Christians. But something amazing happened to Saul. The Risen Lord appeared to him and asked him, 'Saul, Saul, why do you persecute me?' Saul was forever changed. He believed in Jesus and became one of the greatest missionaries of Christianity. Later, he became known as Paul.

First reading
A reading from the Acts of the Apostles (9:26-31)

Saul went to Jerusalem and tried to join the disciples. But they would not believe that he was a disciple, and they were all afraid of him. Then Barnabas came to his help and took him to the apostles. He explained how Saul had seen the Lord on the road and that the Lord had spoken to him. He also told them how boldly Paul had preached in the name of Jesus in Damascus. So Saul stayed with them and went all over Jerusalem, preaching boldly in the name of the Lord.

The word of the Lord.

Introduction to Gospel
A vine is a type of plant that produces fruit. The farmer, or vine grower, looks after the vine giving it water and making sure the soil is healthy. The vine is rooted in the soil and grows branches. On these branches grow fruit, like grapes or strawberries. In our Gospel, we will listen to Jesus describing himself as a vine, God as the vine grower and us as the branches. Listen carefully: what does Jesus mean?

Gospel
A reading from the holy Gospel according to John (15:1-8)

I am the vine and my Father is the vine grower. He breaks off every branch in me that does not bear fruit, and he prunes every branch that does bear fruit, so that it will be clean and bear more fruit. Remain united to me and I will remain united to you. You cannot bear fruit unless you remain in me. I am the vine and you are the branches. Whoever remains in me, and I in him, will bear much fruit, for you can do nothing without me. Whoever does not remain in me is thrown out like a dead branch and dries up. If you remain in me and my words remain in you, then you will ask for anything you wish, and you shall have it.

The Gospel of the Lord.

Dramatisation of Gospel
See Appendix III, p. 216.

Homily Suggestions

- Highlight how Paul in the First Reading is the same Paul who wrote so many of the letters in the New Testament. Emphasise the importance of Saul's conversion and how it underlines that nothing is impossible to God.

- Bring attention to the focal objects of the flowering plant and grapes. Mention how flowers and fruit bring happiness. Some might be used as medicine, some as food and others just for their beauty. Explain how the fruits contain seeds that can grow and spread the vine further.

- Invite the congregation to reflect on how they are capable of bringing happiness, of teaching others, of protecting others. In this way, we produce our own type of 'fruit'. We 'sow seeds' of love.

- Explain that our ability to bring happiness and love into the world around us comes from that one source of love, i.e. God. Because we are united to God through our baptism, we can both experience and spread this love. Compare this to the image of the vine-grower, vine and fruit-bearing branches.

- Invite the congregation to think about when branches are cut off. They wither and die. They do not grow because they are no longer connected to the rest of the vine. Compare this to us. We need to always remain connected to God because God is the source of everything.

Prayer of the Faithful

We pray for our mammies and daddies. Bless them for looking after us so well, providing us with food, love and protection.

We pray for our Church. As the family of God, help us to stay united and strong in our faith.

We pray for our leaders. May they keep the Gospel at the heart of their policies and reach out to those most in need.

We pray for anyone who feels isolated and alone. May they know that there is always a place for them in your heart.

We pray for our parish. Like the branches of the vine, help us to stay connected to you, to draw strength from you and to work towards spreading your love in our community.

Reflection/Thinking Prayer

You are the vine. We are the branches.
You are the shepherd. We are the sheep.
We thank you for all the love that you give us.
A special place in our lives for you we will keep.

We live because you gave us life.
We grow because you give us food.
We breathe because you give us air.
All we have is because of you.

So today we promise to keep you close
To talk to you every day.
To think of you when we make our decisions.
When we work and when we play.

✠

Our Family Mass Resources for the Family Sunday Liturgy **Year B**

Sixth Sunday of Easter

Colour White

Suggested Décor Images from readings, banner reading 'God loves us all'

Theme God loves us all

Entrance Procession Small group of children holding hands, banner 'God loves us all'

Gospel Procession Candles, Lectionary

Welcome
Welcome to our Family Mass. Let's take a moment to remember that we are in a special place. Let's try to listen and take part as best as we can.

Theme
As we begin our celebration today, you see that a group are standing in front of you holding hands. Each person is special. Imagine the love of God as a thread being passed from person to person. Just as they are joined by holding hands, the love of God joins them too. Each of us is loved by God, no matter where we come from or what age we are. God loves us all.

Introduction to First Reading
You might think that St Peter was one of these people who seemed to know everything, but when he led the disciples in their mission after the Resurrection of Jesus, Peter still had a lot of learning to do. He used to think that some people were more deserving of God's love than others. He soon learned that God loves us all equally. Listen to our First Reading about the time Peter met Cornelius, someone Peter would not originally have thought to be as worthy of God's love as others.

First Reading
A reading from the Acts of the Apostles (10:25-26, 34-35, 44-48)

As Peter was about to go in, Cornelius met him, fell at his feet, and bowed down before him. But Peter made him rise. 'Stand up,' he said; 'I myself am only a man.' Peter began to speak: 'I now realise that it is true that God treats everyone on the same basis. Whoever worships him and does what is right is acceptable to him, no matter what race he belongs to.' While Peter was still speaking, the Holy Spirit came down on all those who were listening to his message. The Jewish believers who had come from Joppa with Peter were amazed that God had poured out his gift of the Holy Spirit on the Gentiles also. For they heard them speaking in strange tongues and praising God's greatness. Peter spoke up: 'These people have received the Holy Spirit, just as we also did. Can anyone, then, stop them from being baptised with water?' So he ordered them to be baptised in the name of Jesus Christ. Then they asked him to stay with them for a few days.

The word of the Lord.

Introduction to Gospel
Jesus gives his disciples a simple but very strong message. This message is the main job that they are to do, and the main job that we also must do. Let's listen to hear what that is.

Gospel
A reading from the holy Gospel according to John (15:9-17)

Jesus said to his disciples: 'I love you just as the Father loves me; remain in my love. If you obey my commands, you will remain in my love, just as I have obeyed my Father's commands and remain in his love. I have told you this so that my joy may be in you and that your joy may be complete. My commandment is this: love one another, just as I love you. The greatest love a person can have for his friends is to give his life for them. And you are my friends if you do what I command you. This, then, is what I command you: love one another.'

The Gospel of the Lord.

Song 'We're All God's Children' by Alan Jackson.

Homily Suggestions

- Jesus' command is to 'love one another'. Give examples of how we can do this:
    - Caring/sharing/welcoming/listening/not being selfish and so on.
- Refer to how Jesus said, 'Love one another, just as I love you.' Ask the congregation to think about what Jesus did (so that we might follow his example).
    - He included everyone; shared meals (table fellowship); prayed; showed kindness.
- Focus on the equality of God's love. God has no favourites. We are all loved by God and though we have favourites in a sense (our closest family, our pets and so on), we should not see anyone as more or less deserving of God's love than anyone else. We are all loved the same.
- Present the figure of St Peter. Invite the congregation to take solace from how Peter recognised his previous errors (perhaps reminding them of the cock crowing three times), but he was persistent and learned from his mistakes, strengthening his relationship with God. Ask the congregation to reflect on how they can learn from Peter's example of humility.
- Focus on the central message 'love one another'. Dispel any idea that this might be easy – remind the congregation that Jesus was always being 'told off' for going against the normal trends in society, e.g. he mixed and dined with the so-called 'wrong' people. When we are asked to 'love one another', emphasise that this can be difficult, for example peer pressure, times when we might not 'get along' with others, fear, hurt and so on.

Prayer of the Faithful

We pray for our families. Help us to love one another as Jesus asks us.

We pray for our Church. Bless all the clergy, the religious orders and laypeople who work together to show your love to our world.

We pray for our leaders. May they bring peace to our world.

We pray for victims of injustice. May they experience love and equal treatment.

We pray for our parish community, especially for all those who receive the Sacraments of Baptism and Confirmation during this year. May the Holy Spirit be with them on their special journey.

Reflection/Thinking Prayer
God loves us all

I'm no better than you
Just as you're no better than me
In fact there isn't an 'I' or 'You';
In God's eyes, there is just 'We'.

We are all God's children.
God loves us all the same.
No matter where we come from.
No matter what our name.

The hardest thing for us to do
Is to see each other as God sees us
But we must try to love one another
As we are all equally loved by Jesus.

This week's Easter challenge

Jesus said, 'Love one another, just as I love you.' Jesus was a kind and loving person. He spent time with everyone and left no one out. Jesus prayed. He helped the sick and the poor.

This week, do something that will make a difference to someone else, in the way Jesus asks us. Maybe you could offer to help with the shopping. Or you could invite a new person to play in your group. Perhaps you could spend some extra time with a sick or older relative.

⊕

Our Family Mass Resources for the Family Sunday Liturgy **Year B**

The Ascension of the Lord

Colour White

Suggested Décor Images from readings

Theme The Ascension of Jesus, Be Not Afraid

Entrance Procession Crown, double-sided image of question mark/'Come Holy Spirit'

Gospel Procession Candles, Lectionary

Welcome
Welcome to our Family Mass. It's good to be together to celebrate the Good News in this special place.

Theme
Today marks the time that Jesus returned to heaven to take his rightful place as our king. We bring a crown to the altar.

Imagine how his friends must have felt – amazed at the vision, but afraid of being left alone without their leader, full of questions of what would happen. We show this with a question mark. But today we celebrate how Jesus' return was a wonderful event. He returned to heaven so that his Spirit could be sent to be with us always. The Holy Spirit is with us right here. We turn around our image of a question mark to reveal our prayer 'Come, Holy Spirit'.

Introduction to First Reading
For some time, Jesus had asked his friends to prepare themselves for his departure. Naturally, they were nervous about how they would feel when Jesus had returned to heaven. They were uncertain and full of questions. Let's listen.

First Reading
This reading requires three participants.
A reading from the Acts of the Apostles (1:1-11)

Narrator When the apostles met together with Jesus they asked him this question.

Apostle Lord, will you at this time give the Kingdom back to Israel?

Jesus The times and occasions are set by my Father's own authority, and it is not for you to know when they will be. But when the Holy Spirit comes upon you, you will be filled with power, and you will be witnesses for me in Jerusalem, in all Judaea and Samaria, and to the ends of the earth.

Narrator After saying this, he was taken up to heaven as they watched him, and a cloud hid him from their sight.

The word of the Lord.

Introduction to Gospel
For some time, the Apostles stayed in a room in Jerusalem, still afraid to go out in fear for their safety. Listen to what Jesus thought of that.

Gospel
A reading from the holy Gospel according to Mark (16:15-20)

Jesus appeared to the eleven disciples as they were eating. He scolded them, because they did not have faith and because they were too stubborn to believe those who had seen him alive. He said to them, 'Go throughout the whole world and preach the Gospel to all mankind. Whoever believes and is baptised will be saved; whoever does not believe will be condemned. Believers will be given the power to perform miracles: they will drive out demons in my name; they will speak in strange tongues; if they pick up snakes or drink any poison they will not be harmed; they will place their hands on sick people, who will get well.'

After the Lord Jesus had talked with them, he was taken up to heaven and sat at the right side of God. The disciples went and preached everywhere, and the Lord worked with them and proved that their preaching was true by the miracles that were performed.

The Gospel of the Lord.

Dramatisation of Gospel
See Appendix III, p. 216.

Homily Suggestions

- Ask the congregation to remember what it was like when they did something by themselves for the first time, for example riding a bike with no stabilisers, going to/from school alone and so on. These might conjure up the mixed feelings of fear and excitement, comparable to the feelings of the Apostles after the Ascension.

- Explain the word 'Ascension' as coming from the verb 'to ascend', for example to ascend the stairs = to go up the stairs. Jesus went back up to heaven. Refer to the focal object of the crown.

- Emphasise the request of Jesus to spread the news all over the world and baptise people. Ask the congregation to think about how big the Church has grown – all over the globe.

- Mention the different people in the world and different ways the Good News is spread; clergy, religious orders, families; reading the Bible, praying, chatting about God …

- Refer to the focal object of the question mark, 'Come Holy Spirit'. Emphasise that we can experience times of uncertainty, and at such times we can pray for the help of the Holy Spirit, just as Jesus promised that the Spirit would come to the aid of his frightened Apostles.

Prayer of the Faithful

We pray for our families. May we all know that our friend Jesus is always with us.

We pray for our Church. Bless all the clergy, religious orders and everyone who spreads the Good News.

We pray for our leaders. May they spread Jesus' message of love and peace.

We pray for those who face difficult decisions or who are anxious or worried about themselves and loved ones. We pray that their faith will be strengthened by the Holy Spirit.

We pray for our parish. Bless all the parents, teachers, priests and religious orders who help to spread your Good News in our community.

Reflection/Thinking Prayer

Remember, remember
All I have taught you.
I will watch over you.
Be not afraid.
I will send you my Spirit.
To guide you. To help you.
You will not be alone.
Be not afraid.

⊕

Our Family Mass Resources for the Family Sunday Liturgy **Year B**

✝ Seventh Sunday of Easter

Colour White

Suggested Décor Images from readings, pictures of groups/families, artwork of hands joined together in prayer

Theme Togetherness and Prayer

Entrance Procession Candles, photo of group/family/team, images of hands joined in prayer

Gospel Procession Candles, Lectionary

Welcome
Thank you for coming to our Family Mass today. You are all welcome. Today we will celebrate how we gather together in prayer.

Theme
We bring a photo of group/family/team to the altar. Friends are very important. We can have friends in our families, in our street, in our schools and in our workplaces. When we feel excited, we like to share our happiness with our friends. When we are worried, we can share our problems with our friends.

We bring an image of hands joined together in prayer. Friends pray for each other. Together, we pray as one family of God.

Togetherness in prayer – it's wonderful!

Introduction to First Reading
The apostles were like a family. When they lost Judas from their group, they wanted to add a new member. Let's listen to how they did this in our First Reading.

First Reading
A reading from the Acts of the Apostles (1:15-17, 20-26)

One day Peter stood up to speak. 'My brothers,' he said, 'Judas was the guide for those who arrested Jesus. He was a member of our group, for he had been chosen to have a part in our work. So then, someone must join us as a witness to the resurrection of the Lord Jesus. He must be one of the men who were in our group during the whole time that the Lord Jesus travelled about with us, beginning from the time John preached his message of baptism until the day Jesus was taken up from us to heaven.' So they proposed two men: Joseph, who was called Barabbas (also known as Justas), and Matthias. Then they prayed, 'Lord, you know the thoughts of everyone, so show us which of these two you have chosen to serve as an apostle in the place of Judas, who left to go to the place where he belongs.' Then they drew lots to choose between the two men, and the one chosen was Matthias, who was added to the group of eleven apostles.

The word of the Lord.

Introduction to Gospel
Jesus loved his friends very much. He promised them that they would not be left alone. In our Gospel, we listen to how Jesus knew that his friends were special, chosen by God. He knew that they believed in him and he prayed for them. He especially prayed that they would be safe after he was gone, and that they would hold onto that determination and faith he had shared with them. Let's listen to the Word of God together.

Gospel
A reading from the holy Gospel according to John (17:11-19)

'Father!'

'Keep them safe by the power of your name, the name you gave me, so that they may be one just as you and I are one. While I was with them, I kept them safe by the power of your name. I protected them, and not one of them was lost, except the man who was bound to be lost. I gave them your message, and the world hated them. I do not ask you to take them out of the world, but I do ask you to keep them safe from the Evil One. Dedicate them to yourself by means of the truth; your word is truth. I sent them into the world just as you sent me into the world. And for their sake I dedicate myself to you, in order that they, too, may be truly dedicated to you.'

The Gospel of the Lord.

Song 'Circle of Friends' from *Alive-O*.[4]

---

[4] By Finbar O'Connor, from *Alive-O 8 Teacher's Book* (Veritas, Dublin, 2004), p. 275.

Homily Suggestions

- Invite the congregation to think about their friends. What do they enjoy doing together? What do they like to talk about? Why are they friends? How can you be a good friend? – listening, sharing, caring, etc.

- Ask the congregation to think about their families. Remember that your family are your friends also – invite the congregation to think about how they might make a better effort to be good *friends* with their families.

- In reference to the First Reading, possibly include a brief recap of events from previous liturgies regarding the Ascension; after Jesus left, his friends may have felt ill at ease at being left to 'pick up the pieces'. They gained comfort from being together and wanted to protect that togetherness by adding to their group (replacing the loss of Judas). Ask the congregation to think about anyone they know who might have recently suffered loss, bereavement and loneliness. Invite them to reach out to each other in the spirit of togetherness.

- Refer to the Gospel: Jesus prayed for his friends. Suggest how wonderful that is, that Jesus prays for us! Emphasise how special Jesus thinks we are. Suggest that we ought to thank Jesus for this, that we should pray for our friends too and share the Good News as Jesus asked.

Prayer of the Faithful

We pray for our families and friends. Help us to always be good friends to each other.

We pray for our Church. May the prayers of Jesus strengthen the Church in her mission of spreading the Good News.

We pray for our leaders. May all leaders around the world work together towards a peaceful future for everyone.

We pray for the sick, the bereaved, the lonely and those who are away from home. May your friendship help them to feel the healing warmth of togetherness.

We pray for our parish. May we be good friends to each other and always be aware that you are with us.

Reflection/Thinking Prayer

A group of children could stand around the altar, joining hands.

We thank God for our friends.
Together, we can have fun.
Together, we can be safe.
Together, we can learn.
Together, we can laugh and play.
Together, we can pray.

Jesus said that wherever there are two or three gathered in his name, he is there also.

Jesus, we welcome you as our friend.

The group of children now join their own hands in prayer.

We pray for our friends, as you prayed for yours.

Jesus, help us to remember that you are always our friend.

Help us to spread your Good News so that everyone will know of your love and friendship.

Amen.

This week's Easter challenge

Try out one or more of the following:

- If there is someone often on their own in the playground, invite them to play.

- At home, try to spend time all together; eating a meal; saying a prayer …

- Smile at and greet the people you meet.

Our Family Mass Resources for the Family Sunday Liturgy **Year B**

Pentecost Sunday

Colour Red

Suggested Décor Images from readings, artwork of cards wishing 'Happy Birthday to the Church', lists of fruits of the Holy Spirit

Theme The Fruits of the Holy Spirit

Entrance Procession Candle, scroll naming the fruits of the Holy Spirit, birthday card for the Church

Gospel Procession Candles, Lectionary

Welcome
Welcome to our Family Mass. Let's take a moment to quieten ourselves and get ready to listen carefully to the Word of God.

Theme
Today we celebrate the birthday of the Church. On the day of Pentecost, the Holy Spirit came upon the disciples, just as Jesus promised. This same Spirit is within each one of us from the moment of our baptism. He teaches about God, helps us to spread the Good News and gives us the grace and assistance we need to be the best people we can be.

Today we bring some special items to the altar:

- A birthday card: today is the birthday of our Church family – Happy Birthday!
- A candle: sometimes fire is used to represent the coming of the Holy Spirit – welcome, Holy Spirit!
- A scroll with a list of qualities to which we all aspire: with the help of the Holy Spirit, we can become the best people we can be. Then we can say that we are or have these qualities. They are love, patience, kindness, goodness, faithfulness, humility and self-control. After the Gospel, we will try to explain each of these qualities more clearly.

Introduction to First Reading
Each of us is special and deserves love and respect. Sometimes though we can become too wrapped up in ourselves – 'I want', 'I need', 'What about me?', 'What's in it for me?' – do these phrases sound familiar? The Holy Spirit constantly reminds us, and helps us, to think of the good of others too. St Paul taught about this in our First Reading. Let's listen.

First Reading
A reading from Paul's letter to the Galatians (5:16-25)

Let the Spirit direct your lives and you will be in no danger of yielding to self-indulgence. Self-indulgence is the opposite of the Spirit. These two are enemies, and this means that you cannot do what you want to do.

What self-indulgence does is quite plain. It shows itself in immoral, filthy and indecent actions, in worship of idols and witchcraft. People become enemies and they fight; they become jealous, angry, and ambitious. They separate into parties and groups; they are envious, get drunk, have orgies, and do other things like these. Those who do these things will not possess the kingdom of God.

But the Spirit produces love, joy, peace, patience, kindness, goodness, faithfulness, humility and self-control. Those who belong to Jesus Christ have to put to death all self-indulgent passions and desires.

Let us be directed by the Spirit.

The word of the Lord.

Introduction to Gospel
We bless ourselves in the name of the Father, the Son and of the Holy Spirit. In our Gospel today, Jesus tells his disciples about the Spirit. Listen carefully to find out more about the Holy Spirit.

Gospel
A reading from the holy Gospel according to John (15:26-27; 16:12-15)

Jesus said to his disciples:

The Helper will come – the Spirit, who reveals the truth about God and who comes from the Father. When the Spirit comes who reveals the truth about God, he will lead you into all the truth. He will not speak on his own authority, but he will speak of what he hears, and he will tell you of things to come. He will give me glory, because he will take what I say and give it to you. All that my father has is mine; that is why I said that the Spirit will take what I give him and tell it to you.

The Gospel of the Lord.

Song 'Come Holy Spirit' (from *Alive-O*).[5]

Homily Suggestions
- Refer to the focal object of the candle. Explain how the flame of a candle seems to reach upwards, how a candle gives out light and heat. A candle spreads its gift of light and heat, not keeping it all to itself. We are called to do the same – reach out to others, give of ourselves to others. That is the essence of Church, whose birthday we celebrate today. The Holy Spirit nourishes the Church to help us in this outreach.

- Refer to how we bless ourselves. The Holy Spirit is the same Spirit from our readings today. It is the same Spirit urging us on in our daily lives to be the best people we can be (refer to the focal object of the scroll).

- Invite the congregation to think of the Apostles huddled in their room who then spread outwards in their mission of bringing the Gospel, baptising and preaching. Compare their small beginnings to our lives. Pentecost helps to remind us that the little 'outreaches' we make to family, friends and neighbours are very important and can have a ripple effect.

Prayer of the Faithful
We pray for our families. May they be filled with the Holy Spirit.

We pray for our Church. May the Holy Spirit continue to help the Church spread the Good News.

We pray for our leaders. May the Holy Spirit guide them to a world of peace and justice.

We pray for the sick, in mind and body. May the Holy Spirit bring them healing.

We pray for our parish. May the Holy Spirit always be at the heart of our community.

Reflection/Thinking Prayer[6]
Holy Spirit, I want to do what is right.

Help me.

Holy Spirit, I want to live like Jesus.

Guide me.

Holy Spirit, I want to pray like Jesus.

Teach me. Amen.

Task in preparation for next week's liturgy
Look out for things in threes: a shape with three sides, a children's tricycle, a sporting event of swimming, cycling and running. Try to remember their names and we will mention them at next week's Family Mass.

⊕

---

[5] Bernard Sexton, from *Alive-O 8 Teacher's Book* (Veritas, Dublin, 2004), p. 278.

[6] From *Alive-O 8 Teacher's Book* (Veritas, Dublin, 2004), p. 43.

V. Ordinary Time

An Overview

There is nothing 'ordinary' about Ordinary Time! Simply named to mark the remaining part of the liturgical year outside the seasons of Advent, Christmas, Lent and Easter, Ordinary Time consists of thirty-three to thirty-four Sundays. Therefore, it is the longest period of the Church's year. The liturgical colour of Ordinary Time is green.

The readings of this season focus on the life and ministry of Jesus. Our everyday lives (you could call them 'ordinary', if you wish!) can be enlightened by the wisdom of the actions, teachings and miracles of Jesus, many of which we encounter in our Scripture readings during Ordinary Time.

Understandably, summer time and other school holidays may affect the practicalities of organising family liturgies, so a selected sequence of Sundays might be a pragmatic alternative. There are a number of themes and key images throughout Ordinary Time. This might be of help if you wish to celebrate a short number of family liturgies on a particular topic. Also, you might consider simply including parts of the liturgies offered, or the resources from the Appendices, in your main parish Mass.

A Thematic Approach to the Sacraments
Ordinary Time can provide us with the opportunity to present the Sacraments in such a way that reinforces their centrality to our faith and our everyday lives. Catholicism embraces the sacramentality of everyday life, rather than focusing on a one-off celebration of a particular sacrament. This can be especially true of the Eucharist. The day of one's First Holy Communion is indeed a special occasion, but a deeper study of the Eucharist could encourage the congregation to see the wonderful event that is every experience of the Eucharist. For those who have not attended a Baptismal ceremony for a long time, for example, it would be nice to provide a display with images and information on the elements of the Baptismal Rite. The same is true for all the sacraments. Consider organising a sacred space focusing on a sacrament for a series of Sundays. The homilies could include a teaching aspect in relation to particular elements or actions that are involved in the chosen sacrament. The following is an example of groups of Sundays this year that particularly lend themselves to such an approach. You may well choose an alternative sequence, depending on your local circumstances:

Baptism   The Seasons of Christmas and Easter
                  Ordinary Time Sundays: 2, 3, 13, 14, 15, 21, 22, 23, 24

Eucharist   Passion Sunday, The Season of Easter
                  The Feast of the Body and Blood of Christ
                  Ordinary Time Sundays: 18–20

Confirmation The Season of Easter, Pentecost Sunday
                  Ordinary Time Sundays: 5, 10, 13, 14, 15, 24, 25

Sacraments of Healing *(Penance and Reconciliation, Anointing of the Sick)*
     The Seasons of Advent and Lent
     Ordinary Time Sundays: 6–8

Sacraments of Vocation *(Matrimony, Holy Orders)*
     These do not specifically match with particular liturgies but should feature at some point perhaps depending on local circumstances.

Think about it!

Several liturgies during Ordinary Time address two specific themes:

a. The Person of Jesus

b. The Body of Christ

Think about setting up a display of images and information that also invites contributions from members of the congregation and local groups.

a. The Person of Jesus

Examples of subjects for study include:

- Jesus the Healer

- Jesus the Son of God and Son of Mary

- Jesus the friend and Saviour of all

- Jesus the Good Shepherd (featuring concepts of authority, integrity, kingship and leadership)

- The Head of the Body of Christ.

b. The Body of Christ

Examples of aspects for study include:

- Local charities and support groups

- The roles of members of the parish. For example, Parish Pastoral Council, Ministers, Sacristan, altar servers, musicians and so on

- Catholic Relief Services – local, national and worldwide

- The Host – where it is made, the Eucharistic Rite, the Tabernacle, the Chalice and Ciborium.

A number of motifs occur across some liturgies. These include:
- Wisdom
- Love
- Miracles
- Parables
- Leadership
- Trust.

Important feast days occur during Ordinary Time. The Feasts of the Lord in Ordinary Time are included in this section:
- The Most Holy Trinity (p. 106)
- The Body and Blood of Christ (p. 108)
- Our Lord Jesus Christ, Universal King (p. 176).

Some other major feasts are included in the last section:
- Feast of Saint Patrick (p. 178)
- Feast of the Assumption (p. 182)
- Feast of All Saints (p. 184).

To Note The *Columba Lectionary* places the liturgy for the Baptism of the Lord in the Christmas section, after the Epiphany. It is also the First Sunday in Ordinary Time.

Our Family Mass Resources for the Family Sunday Liturgy **Year B**

Feasts of the Lord in Ordinary Time

The Most Holy Trinity (Sunday after Pentecost)

Colour White

Suggested Décor Symbols of the Trinity*

Theme Three Persons in one God: Father, Son and Holy Spirit

Entrance Procession Three candles

Gospel Procession Candles, Lectionary

Welcome
Welcome to our Family Mass. Though we are different in many ways, together we make up the Body of Christ – God's family. Let's take a moment to prepare to celebrate the Sacred Mysteries together.

Theme
Today we celebrate the most Holy Trinity. You might think that you don't know what this word 'Trinity' means, but we actually talk about it every time we bless ourselves – in the name of the Father, and of the Son and of the Holy Spirit. Three in one.

When we light each of our three candles, they have their own beautiful flame. Three flames. When we join them together (*an acolyte can demonstrate*) we see one wonderful united flame: three in one.

When we think about God, we know there is one God, but we also think about God like a loving Father, a caring Son and a Holy Spirit: three in one.

Introduction to First Reading
The message in our First Reading is very simple. There is one God whose unconditional offer of love and life is given to all that exists. Let's listen.

First Reading
A reading from the book of Deuteronomy (4:32-34, 39-40)

Moses said to the people, remember today and never forget: the Lord is God in heaven and on earth. There is no other God. Obey all his love that I have given you today, and all will go well with you and your descendants. You will continue to live in the land which the Lord your God is giving you to be yours forever.

The word of the Lord.

Introduction to Second Reading
We will hear about many ways in which we differ. Some of us are sons. Others are daughters. We will also hear three special names: 'God', 'Father' and 'Spirit'. We also hear how together, despite all difference, we are all God's children. That togetherness is so important when trying to understanding today's theme of the Trinity.

Second Reading
A reading from Paul's letter to the Romans (8:14-17)

Those who are led by God's Spirit are God's sons and daughters. For the Spirit that God has given you does not make you slaves and cause you to be afraid; instead, the Spirit makes you God's children, and by the Spirit's power we cry out to God, 'Father! My Father!'

The word of the Lord.

Introduction to Gospel
Our Gospel passage is so important. The Risen Christ gives the remaining apostles their big job – to go out into the world and continue his work in the way he taught them. Listen for a particular phrase that may be very familiar to you.

Gospel
A reading from the holy Gospel according the Matthew (28:16-20)

The eleven disciples went to the hill in Galilee where Jesus had told them to go. When they saw him, they worshipped him, even though some of them doubted. Jesus drew near and said to them, 'I have been given all authority in heaven and on earth. Go, then, to all peoples everywhere and make them my disciples; baptise them in the name of the Father, the Son, and the Holy Spirit, and teach them to obey everything I have commanded you. And I will be with you always to the end of the age.'

The Gospel of the Lord.

Song 'Gloria' (from *Alive-O*)[1]

---

1 Mary Amond-O'Brien, *Alive-O 8 Teacher's Book* (Veritas, Dublin, 2004), p. 289.

Homily Suggestions

- Refer to the symbolic use of the three candles to emphasise the doctrine of the Trinity. Perhaps extend this with another symbol of your choice.

- Elaborate on the terms 'Father', 'Son' and 'Holy Spirit' to the more inclusive terms of 'loving parent', 'child' and 'Love'. Emphasise genderlessness of God in preference for the message of 'love'.

- Talk about how the sign of the cross is prolific in our rituals – blessings, use during the mass, prayers at home and school, shape of the cross etc.

- Examine the word 'Trinity' – similar to 'three', 'triangle', 'tricycle', etc. to make it easier for younger children to comprehend.

- Suggest to the younger members of the congregation that when they next hug their mother and father, they are like the Trinity – love of a parent, love of a child and the love between them: three in one. Emphasise that God is present too.

- Stress the significance of the formula 'In the name of the Father, and the Son, and of the Holy Spirit' in the Sacrament of Baptism. It also highlights how the Word of God remains present in our everyday practices now, even beyond the Sacrament of Baptism to the use of the same formula in blessing ourselves, for example.

Prayer of the Faithful

We pray for our families. Just like our three candles shone brighter together, may we enjoy a togetherness that will keep our families strong, loving and caring.

We pray for our Church. May she be like a loving parent to all her members, and may your Spirit guide her in her mission.

We pray for our leaders. May they follow your example and treat everyone equally as family.

We pray for all those who need your forgiveness, compassion and love. Bless them.

We pray for our parish, for all our adults, our young people and the love that brings us all together.

Reflection/Thinking Prayer

A woman and two children take turns in stepping forward holding up one of the three lit candles. At the end they hold their candles together to make one united flame.

What can we learn about the Trinity today?
Woman steps forward

God is like a loving parent.

We pray that we will be responsible, that we look after those younger than us, and that we care for our environment.

First child steps forward

Jesus is our friend.

We pray that we will be friendly to each other, that we share and that we forgive each other for any hurt we may cause.

Second child steps forward

God's love brings us together.

We pray that we will see goodness in other people, that we will invite others to join in our playtime and that we will remember to be thankful for everything that other people do for us.

Three candles join together.

By doing our best, we pray that we will become the very best people we can be.

Sign of the Cross
* Examples of symbols of Trinity

- Triquetra (interlocking Celtic triangle)
- Shamrock
- Rublev's Icon of the Trinity

Our Family Mass Resources for the Family Sunday Liturgy **Year B**

The Body and Blood of Christ

Colour White

Suggested Décor Images of chalice, ciborium, bread and wine of Holy Communion

Theme The Body and Blood of Christ

Entrance Procession Banners reading 'This is my Body', 'This is my Blood', candles, image of chalice and ciborium if unable to bring up actual items

Gospel Procession Candles, Lectionary

Welcome
Welcome to our Family Mass. Every week we come together to listen to the Word of God and celebrate the Eucharist – Holy Communion. But what does it mean when the priest says, 'This is my Body' and 'This is my Blood'. Take a few moments to think about it, while we prepare for this wonderful occasion.

Theme
Our banners read 'This is my Body' and 'This is my Blood'.

The ciborium (*or image of ciborium*) holds the bread we receive at Holy Communion. When blessed or consecrated this becomes the Body of Christ.

The chalice (*or image of chalice*) is used for the wine that when blessed or consecrated becomes the Blood of Christ.

At every Mass, we celebrate the Eucharist. At every Mass, we can receive the real Jesus into our bodies to fill us with goodness and God's love. It can be difficult to understand. But it is the greatest gift God has given us.

As we go through our Mass today, listen for those words 'Body' and 'Blood'. Allow God to help you understand.

Introduction to First Reading
The Eucharist is the central part of our Mass – when we receive the bread and wine which has become the Body and Blood of Christ, as the priest says. In our reading today we will hear how Moses performs a ritual using real animal blood. Listen and see what parts might remind you of how we celebrate the Eucharist, and what parts are different.

First Reading
A reading from the book of Exodus (24:3-8)

Moses went and told the people all the Lord's commands and all the ordinances, and all the people answered together, 'We will do everything that the Lord has said.'

Moses wrote down all the Lord's commands.

Early the next morning he built an altar at the foot of the mountain and set up twelve stones, one for each of the twelve tribes of Israel. Then he sent young men, and they burnt sacrifices to the Lord and sacrificed some cattle as fellowship-offerings. Moses took half of the blood of the animals and put it in bowls; the other half he threw against the altar. Then he took the book of the covenant, in which the Lord's commands were written, and read it aloud to the people. They said, 'We will obey the Lord and do everything that he has commanded.'

Then Moses took the blood in the bowls and threw it on the people. He said, 'This is the blood that seals the covenant which the Lord made with you when he gave all these commands.'

The word of the Lord.

Introduction to Gospel
Remember how Moses in our First Reading said, 'This is the blood that seals the covenant which the Lord made with you.' Listen to our Gospel. What does Jesus say that sounds familiar?

Gospel
This reading requires two participants.
A reading from the holy Gospel according to Mark (14:12-16, 22-26)

Narrator The disciples went to the city and prepared the Passover Meal. While they were eating, Jesus took a piece of bread, gave a prayer of thanks, broke it and gave it to his disciples.

Jesus Take it; this is my body.

Narrator Then he took a cup, gave thanks to God, and handed it to them, and they all drank from it.

Jesus This is my blood which is poured out for many, my blood which seals God's covenant. I tell you I will never again drink this wine until I drink the new wine in the Kingdom of God.

The Gospel of the Lord.

Homily Suggestions
- Allow some time to reflect on the connections made between the readings and refer to the banners reading 'This is my Body', 'This is my Blood'.
- Invite the congregation to think about times during the Mass that they will hear, 'This is my Body' and 'This is my Blood'. Ask them to pay special attention to sounds and actions during this part of the Mass.
- Address the pre-Communion children; invite them to come up at the time of Communion and be blessed by the Ministers. Emphasise that this is very special too.
- Address those who will receive Communion. Ask them to think back to their First Holy Communion and reclaim that special feeling that was associated with the day, because every time we receive Communion, it is 'a big deal': we receive Jesus and our whole bodies, minds, souls and spirits are refreshed.
- Consider giving a brief explanation of where the Holy Communion bread is made.

Prayer of the Faithful
We pray for our mammies, daddies and all those who buy us our food, cook our meals and prepare our lunches. May we remember to be grateful to them.

We pray for our Church. Every time we share Holy Communion, may we remember that we are all part of your family.

We pray for our leaders. May they work to bring an end to hunger and famine across the world.

We pray for anyone who goes hungry or who does not have enough to drink. May they receive what they need and may their faith be strengthened at such difficult times.

We pray for our parish. May we make sure that everyone in our community has enough to eat, and may your love, that we receive in Holy Communion, fill our homes with joy.

Reflection/Thinking Prayer
Song 'I am the Bread' (from *Alive-O*).[2]
(Alternatively, the lyrics could be read out as a poem/reflection)

Lyrics
Jesus said: 'I am the bread.

Blessed and broken, work of God spoken.'

Jesus said : 'I am the bread.

My body I give. Eat and live.'

We your people gather round your table to be fed.

'Do this in memory of me.

Take this my body, my bread.'

We your people gather round your table to be fed.

Thank you for your presence in the world,

In people, in priest, in bread.

'I am the Bread, Bread of Life'.

⊕

---

[2] From *Prayer Services for 4–12 Year Olds* (Veritas, Dublin, 2005), pp. 72–73.

Our Family Mass Resources for the Family Sunday Liturgy **Year B**

Sundays in Ordinary Time
Second Sunday in Ordinary Time

Colour Green

Suggested Décor Images from readings, names and titles as featured in the Gospel

Theme Recognising God, the significance of names

Entrance Procession Candles, magic markers, name tag

Gospel Procession Candles, Lectionary

Welcome
Welcome to our Family Mass. We are in the presence of God. Each one of us is a good person, filled with God's love. Let's take a moment to remember and recognise that, and to prepare to celebrate Mass together.

Theme
In today's readings we will listen to how people in our faith's history came to recognise God and realise God had been there with them all along. We bring magic markers to the altar. In our playtime, we might draw a picture or write a message. It is there but invisible unless you use the magic marker to reveal it. The magic marker makes you realise what had been there all along. We bring a name tag. Names are important: they help us to identify each other, to call one another's attention and to be friendly. Our names are special to us and tell others about who we are. We will hear a lot of names in our reading.

Introduction to First Reading
Samuel was a young boy. In our reading we will listen to how God was calling him but Samuel did not recognise God's voice. He thought someone else was beckoning him and he kept getting up and going to see why. Let's listen to what happened.

First Reading
A reading from the first book of Samuel (3:3-10, 19)

The boy Samuel was sleeping in the sanctuary, where the sacred Covenant Box was. Before dawn, while the lamp was still burning, the Lord called Samuel. He answered, 'Yes, sir!' and ran to Eli and said, 'You called me. Here I am.' But Eli answered, 'I didn't call you; go back to bed.' So Samuel went back to bed. The Lord called Samuel again. The boy did not know that it was the Lord, because the Lord had never spoken to him before. So he got up and went to Eli, and said, 'You called me, and here I am.' But Eli answered, 'My Son, I didn't call you; go back to bed.' The Lord called Samuel a third time, he got up and went to Eli and said, 'You called me, and here I am.' Then Eli realised that it was the Lord who was calling the boy, so he said to him, 'Go back to bed; and if he calls you again, say, "Speak, Lord, your servant is listening."' So Samuel went back to bed. The Lord came and stood there, and called as he had before, 'Samuel! Samuel!' Samuel answered, 'Speak Lord; your servant is listening.'

As Samuel grew up, the Lord was with him and made everything that Samuel said come true.

The word of the Lord.

Introduction to Gospel
Our Gospel reading today features a lot of names. So get ready to concentrate! As we read, the names will be explained. Listen carefully.

Gospel
This reading requires five participants.
A reading from the holy Gospel according to John (1:35-42)

Narrator John was standing with two of his disciples, when he saw Jesus walking by.

John There is the Lamb of God!

Narrator The two disciples heard him say this and went with Jesus. Jesus turned, saw them following him, and asked:

Jesus What are you looking for?

Disciples Where do you live, Rabbi?

Narrator This word means 'Teacher'.

Jesus Come and see.

Narrator It was then about four o'clock in the afternoon. So they went with him and saw where he lived, and spent the rest of the day with him. One of them was Andrew, Simon Peter's brother. At once he found his brother Simon and told him:

Andrew We have found the Messiah.

Narrator This word means 'Christ'. Then he took Simon to Jesus. Jesus looked at him and said:

Jesus Your name is Simon son of John, but you will be called Cephas.

Narrator This is the same as Peter and means 'a rock'.

Reader The Gospel of the Lord.

Song 'Sanctus' (from *Alive-O*).

Homily Suggestions
- Refer to First Reading – caution listeners against thinking that Samuel became magical: 'God made everything Samuel said come true.' Encourage them to seek the deeper meaning.
- Ask the congregation to think of times when their names were called but they were otherwise distracted or not paying attention. Allow for a moment of quiet reflection on times when God is perhaps calling to them but they are not being attentive.
- Refer to the Gospel and the focal object of the name tag. Invite the congregation to think about the importance of their names and how names carry a meaning. Recount the names mentioned in the Gospel (Lamb of God, Rabbi, Christ, Messiah, Cephas/Rock) and give a brief explanation of each.
- Connect the two readings. Emphasise that God knows each and every one of us by name and we are all special to God. Consider quoting Isaiah 40:26.

Prayer of the Faithful
We pray for our families and friends. Help us to use each other's names with love and respect and to pay attention when our names are called.

We pray for our Church. Bless her in her mission of baptising people in your holy name.

We pray for our leaders. Help them to remember that every person in society is special and deserves attention, justice and respect.

We pray for those who feel unseen and unheard as if they have no name. Bless them with loving friendships.

We pray for our parish family in the name of the Father, the Son and the Holy Spirit.

Reflection/Thinking Prayer
When we bless ourselves

We say 'In the name of the Father, and of the Son, and of the Holy Spirit'.

When we start each day

As we go to bed each night

Help us to remember that we are praying in your name.

Help us to treasure your name

To be inspired by your name

To be guided by your name.

May the goodness of your name live in our hearts, our minds and our souls.

Always and forever.

Amen.

⊕

Our Family Mass Resources for the Family Sunday Liturgy **Year B**

Third Sunday in Ordinary Time

Colour Green

Suggested Décor Images from readings, posters of names mentioned in Gospel

Theme Putting our trust in God and taking action ourselves

Entrance Procession Bible, box of assorted 'tools' (for example a spanner, paintbrush, pencil, spatula)

Gospel Procession Candles, Lectionary

Welcome
Welcome to our Family Mass. Each of us has an important part to play in our celebration. Listening, reading, praying, welcoming God. Let's take a moment to prepare ourselves in silence.

Theme
We bring a Bible to the altar. It is God's Word to us. Reading and listening to the Word of God guides us on our journey through life. In our readings today, taken from the Bible, we will hear how people from our faith's history listened to the Word of God, placed their trust in him and took action to change their lives.

We bring a box of tools (*list the selected tools*). This reminds us that we have a responsibility to take action for own our lives. While we placed our trust in God, we must do our job, whatever that might be, to make our lives and our world a better place.

Introduction to First Reading
Jonah was a prophet, chosen by God to relate God's message to the people of his time. Once, God instructed Jonah to remind the people of Ninevah of their promise to follow God and lead good lives. You see, they had forgotten their responsibilities to God and had become selfish. Do you think they listened to Jonah and changed their ways? Let's find out.

First Reading
A reading from the prophet Jonah (3:1-5, 10)

The Lord spoke to Jonah. He said, 'Go to Nineveh, that great city, and proclaim to the people the message I have given you.' So Jonah obeyed the Lord and went to Nineveh, a city so large that it took three days to walk through it. Jonah started through the city, and after walking a whole day, he proclaimed, 'In forty days Nineveh will be destroyed!' The people of Nineveh believed God's message. So they decided that everyone should fast, and all the people, from the greatest to the least, put on sackcloth to show that they had repented. God saw what they did; he saw that they had given up their wicked behaviour. So he changed his mind and did not punish them as he had said he would.

The word of the Lord.

Introduction to Gospel
It was an ordinary day for the fishermen at Galilee. Simon and his brother Andrew were fishing just like they did every day. A little further on, two other brothers called James and John were doing their work too. But this was to be no ordinary day. Listen to discover why.

Gospel
A reading from the holy Gospel according to Mark (1:14-20)

As Jesus walked along the shore of Lake Galilee, he saw two fishermen, Simon and his brother Andrew, catching fish with a net. Jesus said to them, 'Come with me, and I will teach you to catch men.' At once they left their nets and went with him. He went a little farther on and saw two other brothers, James and John, the sons of Zebedee. They were in their boat getting their nets ready. As soon as Jesus saw them, he called them; they left their father Zebedee in the boat with the hired men and went with Jesus.

The Gospel of the Lord.

Dramatisation of Gospel
See Appendix III, p. 216.

Homily Suggestions

- Refer to the First Reading. Acknowledge that we can all be a little selfish and forgetful of our responsibilities at times. We need to be reminded of what is the right thing to do. Invite the congregation to make time to take stock and ask, 'Is this what God would want me to do?'

- Encourage the congregation to place their trust in God. We might not like 'not being in control' all the time but it is God who sees the 'bigger picture'. Especially when things are not going well for us, when we are worried or sick, it is then that we must be brave and place our trust in God.

- In reference to the Gospel, elaborate on how the disciples must have been so inspired by Jesus to place all their trust in him and leave their jobs and families – everything they knew – just to follow Jesus. Allow some time for the congregation to reflect on how massive an undertaking that was!

- Briefly explain the meaning of the phrase 'to catch men' in order to dispel any literal connotations.

- Emphasise the duality of placing our trust in God but also taking responsibility ourselves and taking actions. Offer suggestions of social justice, neighbourly care, charitable events and so on.

Prayer of the Faithful

We pray for our mammies and daddies. Help us to remember that they want what is good for us, and even though we might not understand why, we need to follow their advice and trust their judgement.

We pray for our Church. In recent times, some people have been betrayed by those in positions of trust. May we experience healing, renewal and a rebuilding of trust.

We pray for our leaders. May they be responsible in their work and take action to improve the lives of those in need.

We pray for anyone who feels that they don't count. Help them to remember that God loves each and every one of us and that we can all make a difference to our world in our own unique way.

We pray for our parish family. Bless all those in positions of trust who care for us, teach us and keep us safe.

Reflection/Thinking Prayer
Trust in me

Will you believe me when I say
That I have your best interests at heart?
Especially when things seem a mess
When everything's falling apart.

And also when you forget about me
And just do whatever you please.
When everything's going swimmingly
When the whole world seems at your knees.

Put your trust in me.
I will look after you.
But remember you must do your part as well.
Because I have placed my love in you.

☩

Our Family Mass Resources for the Family Sunday Liturgy **Year B**

Fourth Sunday in Ordinary Time

Colour Green

Suggested Décor Images from readings

Theme Authority and integrity

Entrance Procession Bible, cross, empty frame (to represent a window)

Gospel Procession Candles, Lectionary

Welcome
Welcome to our Family Mass. We are lucky to be able to gather together to celebrate God's love in this special place. Let's try to look and listen as best as we can.

Theme
Today we will hear a lot about authority. People in authority are those we think of as being in positions of trust and power – our parents, teachers, clergy and police, for example. However, power and authority in our faith is a little different and very special. We learn about this from the Word of God – the Bible which we bring to the altar today.

Jesus is the Word of God. Jesus talked the talk and walked the walk – he spread the Good News but lived by it too. Jesus taught about love for others and, on his cross, he gave his life for our sake. We bring a cross to the altar.

How can we view Jesus as a figure of authority? This frame might help explain. Think of it as a window. We will come back to it later in the Mass and talk about it some more.

Introduction to First Reading
Moses was the leader of the Israelites. They followed his advice. They placed their trust in him. He was their authority figure. God spoke to Moses about the future, when he would send another authority figure. Let's listen.

First Reading
A reading from the book of Deuteronomy (18:15-20)

Moses said, 'He will send you a prophet like me from among your own people, and you are to obey him.

'On the day that you were gathered on Mount Sinai, you begged not to hear the Lord speak again or to see his fiery presence any more, because you were afraid you would die. So the Lord said to me, "They have made a request. I will send them a prophet like you from among their own people; I will tell him what to say, and he will tell the people everything I command. He will speak in my name, and I will punish anyone who refuses to obey him. But if any prophet dares to speak a message in my name when I did not demand him to do so, he must die for it, and so must any prophet who speaks in the name of other gods."'

The word of the Lord.

Introduction to Gospel
Jesus taught about God. Others taught about God too and had done for many years. These teachers, Rabbis, were the Jewish teachers and as such were figures of authority. So what was different about Jesus? Let's listen.

Gospel
This reading requires six participants.
A reading from the holy Gospel according to Mark (1:21-28)

Narrator Jesus and his disciples came to the town of Capernaum, and on the next Sabbath Jesus went into the synagogue and began to teach. The people who heard him were amazed at the way he taught. He taught with authority. Just then a man with an evil spirit in him came into the synagogue and screamed.

Evil Spirit What do you want with us, Jesus of Nazareth? Are you here to destroy us? I know who you are – you are God's holy messenger!

Narrator Jesus ordered the spirit to be quiet, and come out of the man.

Jesus Be quiet, and come out of the man!

Narrator The evil spirit shook the man hard, gave a loud scream, and came out of him. The people were all amazed that they started saying to one another:

Person 1 What is this?

Person 2 Is it some kind of new teaching?

Person 3 This man has authority to give orders to the evil spirits, and they obey him!

Narrator And so the news about Jesus spread quickly everywhere in the province of Galilee.

The Gospel of the Lord.

Song 'Sayen and Dooen' (from *Alive-O*).[3]

Homily Suggestions

- Refer to the focal objects, emphasising the empty frame/window. Explain how when you look through a window, you see clearly. There is nothing blocking your view. What you see is what you get. Compare this to Jesus's teaching: he practiced what he preached to the point of giving himself up for our sake. Invite the congregation to reflect on how honest and full of integrity Jesus was. His authority came from the fact that he was the Truth; with Jesus, too, what you see is what you get.

- Mention the common and sometimes negative associations we can have with the word 'authority'; for example being told what to do is not always enjoyable. Also refer to the mistakes made by some figures of authority; for example being nasty instead of understanding and being compassionate. Focus on the authority of Jesus coming from his integrity. Jesus taught us and lived out his message too. We can always trust Jesus.

- Give the congregation a challenge for the week: invite them to pay attention to what they say and compare it to what they actually do. Give some examples such as saying that you should share and play fairly, and then actually doing so.

Prayer of the Faithful
We pray for our parents. Help them to be good parents and help us to be loving children.

We pray for our Church leaders. May they always keep the integrity of Christ as the example of how they should lead others.

We pray for our Government. Help them to be honest in their work.

We pray for those who misuse and abuse their authority. Help them to see the right and just way to lead.

We pray for our parish. Bless all those in positions of authority in our community.

Reflection/Thinking Prayer
Jesus, we thank you for your incredible love

So strong that you gave yourself up on the cross for our salvation.

Help us to always recognise you in the Word and in the Eucharist.

Help us to be inspired by your example of practising what you preach.

Amen.

✠

---

[3] Geraldine Doggett, *Alive-O 4 Teacher's Book* (Veritas, Dublin, 1999), p. 109.

Our Family Mass Resources for the Family Sunday Liturgy **Year B**

Fifth Sunday in Ordinary Time

Colour Green

Suggested Décor Images from readings, similar images to objects in entrance procession

Theme Only in the darkness do we see the light

Entrance Procession First aid kit, candle

Gospel Procession Candles, Lectionary

Welcome
Welcome to our Family Mass. A special welcome to those who have made the effort to come here today even though you are sick or feeling upset. We are here to listen to God's Word and celebrate the Eucharist together. May we experience some healing today.

Theme
For the next number of Sundays, we will hear readings about people who are sick in different ways. We too can get ill sometimes. Some sicknesses can be helped with a hug, some rest, medicine or a plaster. We might get better quickly; other illnesses can be more serious. We bring a first aid kit to the altar.

We bring a candle. When does the flame of a candle seem brightest? In the darkness. Have you ever brought in a birthday cake and dimmed the lights so you can see the candles shine brightly? It's only in the darkness that we can see the light at its brightest. When we experience pain and sickness, the world around us can seem dark. It is then that Jesus shines even more brightly for us. Our candle represents Jesus – the light of our world.

Introduction to First Reading
Our reading sounds very depressing indeed. Job, a prophet, felt very sad. He worked tirelessly trying to tell people about God, but many people did not want to listen. They made his work very difficult. In our reading, we can hear just how horrible Job felt. Let's listen.

First Reading
A reading from the book of Job (7:1-4, 6-7)

Human life is like forced army service, like a life of hard manual labour, like a slave longing for cool shade; like a worker waiting for his pay. Month after month I have nothing to live for; night after night brings me grief. When I lie down to sleep, the hours drag; I toss all night and long for dawn. My days pass by without hope; pass faster than a weaver's shuttle. Remember, O God, my life is only my breath; my happiness has already ended.

The word of the Lord.

Introduction to Gospel
Soon after Jesus gathered his first disciples, he went to the house of one of them – Simon. Simon's mother-in-law was very sick. Things were different in those days. There were no ambulances to call in an emergency or chemists around the corner. People did not have medicines or the knowledge to help people recover like we do nowadays. Let's listen to the Word of God to hear what happened.

Gospel
A reading from the holy Gospel according to Mark (1:29-39)

Jesus and his disciples, including James and John, left the synagogue and went straight to the home of Simon and Andrew. Simon's mother-in-law was sick in bed with a fever, and as soon as Jesus arrived, he was told about her. He went to her, took her by the hand, and helped her up. The fever left her, and she began to wait on them.

After the sun had set and evening had come, people brought to Jesus all the sick and those who had demons. Jesus healed many who were sick with all kinds of diseases and drove out many demons. He would not let the demons say anything, because they knew who he was.

Very early the next morning, long before daylight, Jesus got up and left the house.

The Gospel of the Lord.

Dramatisation of Gospel
See Appendix III pp. 216.

Homily Suggestions

- Ask the congregation to think of a time when they were sick. Remind them of the services and help that we get nowadays from many people to help us get better. Offer thanks for those in the healing and caring profession.

- Refer to the first-aid kit. Highlight that there are many different types of sickness – some can be easily healed, others are more difficult. Similarly some sicknesses are easy to recognise, for example we can see the chickenpox or broken bones, but we cannot see inside a person who is depressed or suffering from Alzheimer's.

- Refer to the horrible feeling that we associate with sickness – pain, fear and worry. Compare it to the dark. Now focus attention on the candle. In the darkness, the light shines brightest.

- Mention the healings carried out by Jesus. Encourage the congregation against thinking of it as magical. Instead, emphasise the healing power of God. In addition, acknowledge the reference in the Gospel to demons. Keep the emphasis on the light of Jesus casting away the darkness that accompanies sickness.

- Encourage the congregation to look to Jesus especially when they or a loved one is sick. Invite them to offer prayers. Perhaps mention the Sacrament of the Sick in brief.

Prayer of the Faithful

We pray for our parents. We thank them for their love and care especially when we are sick.

We pray for our Church. Bless all those who are ill and receiving the Sacrament of the Sick during this time.

We pray for our leaders. Help them to put the care of the sick at the centre of their policies.

We pray for the sick, in mind and body. May they experience your healing presence.

We pray for our parish. Be with all those who are sick, and those who care for them.

Reflection/Thinking Prayer

A cold, toothache, a fractured bone
An argument, cancer, feeling alone
Different sicknesses
Different types of pain
Feeling lost in the darkness
Broken again.

Jesus, be our light.
In the dark, be our guide
Help us be strong
And keep your loving light inside.

Inside our hearts, our minds and our souls.
Dispelling the darkness.
To feel once again whole.

⊕

Our Family Mass Resources for the Family Sunday Liturgy **Year B**

Sixth Sunday in Ordinary Time

Colour Green

Suggested Décor Images from readings

Theme Jesus the Healer

Entrance Procession First aid kit, image of hands to represent touch

Gospel Procession Candles, Lectionary

Welcome
Welcome to our Family Mass. We especially welcome all those who are sick, or worried about loved ones who are ill. Together we will listen to the Word of God and celebrate the Eucharist. We pray that we will experience the healing presence of God.

Theme
Again, we bring to the altar the first aid kit. Our readings today also concern those who are ill and how they are treated. When you are sick, who looks after you? When others are sick, how do you treat them?

We bring an image of hands. In our Gospel, we will hear how Jesus healed a sick person by reaching out to him with his hand. Sometimes, as we will hear in our First Reading, sick people are neglected or left alone. We might want to stay away from them because they are sick – how do you think this makes them feel?

Introduction to First Reading
The Book of Leviticus, from which our First Reading comes, is full of rules and regulations. One rule is explained here: what to do if someone in the community becomes sick with a skin disease. Let's listen.

First Reading
A reading from the book of Leviticus (13:1-2, 44-46)

The Lord gave Moses and Aaron these regulations. If anyone has a sore on his skin or a boil or an inflammation which could develop into a dreaded skin-disease, he shall be brought to the Aaronite priest.

The priest shall pronounce him unclean, because of the dreaded skin-disease on his head.

A person who has a dreaded skin-disease must wear torn clothes, leave his hair uncombed, cover the lower part of his face, and call out, 'Unclean, unclean!' He remains unclean as long as he has the disease and he must live outside the camp, away from others.

The word of the Lord.

Introduction to Gospel
When Jesus walked this earth, he acted in a new way. He taught in a new way. When someone was sick, Jesus welcomed them instead of sending them away. He reached out his hand and offered the sick his healing touch. Let's listen to the Word of God.

Gospel
A reading from the holy Gospel according to Mark (1:40-45)

A man suffering from a dreaded skin-disease came to Jesus, knelt down, and begged him for help. 'If you want to,' he said, 'you can make me clean.'

Jesus was filled with pity, and stretched out his hand and touched him. 'I do want,' he answered. 'Be clean!'

At once the disease left the man, and he was clean. Then Jesus spoke sternly to him and sent him away at once, after saying to him, 'Listen, don't tell anyone about this. But go straight to the priest and let him examine you; then in order to prove to everyone that you are cured, offer the sacrifice that Moses ordered.'

But the man went away and began to spread the news everywhere. Indeed, he talked so much that Jesus could not go into a town publicly. Instead, he stayed out in lonely places, and people came to him from everywhere.

The Gospel of the Lord.

Dramatisation of Gospel
See Appendix III, pp. 216–217.

Homily Suggestions

- Refer to the First Reading, acknowledge that it appears strict. Highlight that Jesus did not come to overturn the Law, but to emphasise the need to put the worth of the human being first – stressing the importance of reaching out, rather than pushing away.

- Mention the use of the words 'clean' and 'unclean'. Offer brief explanation of its usage.

- Compare the two readings: the First Reading sees the sick person sent off alone; the Gospel sees Jesus, the healer, going away to find some peace. Offer the congregation some time to reflect on the two readings and what God might be trying to say to them today.

- Invite the congregation to think about how we treat the sick. Do we reach out to them in help and comfort, or do we push them away in fear? Acknowledge that at times doctors recommend that a sick person be kept separate for good reason, i.e. prevention of infection, contagions and so on.

Prayer of the Faithful

We pray for our families. May they be blessed with health, and in times of sicknesses may we look after each other.

We pray for our Church. May those who are sick always know that the Church can be a place of healing for them.

We pray for our leaders. Guide them to building a just and fair society with quality health care for all people.

We pray for medical staff and care workers everywhere. We thank them for their bravery, kindness and generosity of spirit.

We pray for our parish. Help us to reach out to each other especially in times of sickness.

Reflection/Thinking Prayer
A Healing Touch

Hold out your hand
I will keep you from falling
Hold out your hand
Can't you hear me calling?

Calling your name
I will not abandon you.
Whether you are healthy or sick
I will be right beside you.

Offering my hand
My healing touch
To you, yes you,
Because I love you very much.

✠

Our Family Mass Resources for the Family Sunday Liturgy **Year B**

✝ Seventh Sunday in Ordinary Time

Colour Green

Suggested Décor Images from readings

Theme Persistence and faith

Entrance Procession First aid kit, banner reading 'Faith' using letters that look like bricks

Gospel Procession Candles, Lectionary

Welcome
Welcome to our Family Mass. It is good to recognise that we have taken the time to leave whatever else is happening in our lives to come together in faith to celebrate the sacred mysteries.

Theme
Once again, we bring a first aid kit to the altar. Our Gospel reading today features a very sick man who was paralysed. He could not move by himself and needed people to carry him from place to place. Imagine how awful that must be. When things are so bad we can be close to giving up on God altogether! But God never gives up on us. Today we are reminded of this.

Our banner reads 'Faith'. The letters look like bricks. Bricks are strong and solid, which is just what our faith needs to be, especially when things look very bad.

Introduction to First Reading
Have you ever heard someone constantly moaning, whinging and giving out? Never with a good word to say, forgetting to be nice to you or doing kind things for you? How would you treat them? The people of Israel became like that, neglecting to worship God, to thank God for all God did for them. Our First Reading tells us how God responded to Israel's behaviour.

First Reading
A reading from the prophet Isaiah (43:18-19, 21-22, 24-25)

The Lord says, 'But you were tired of me, Israel; you did not worship me. You didn't buy incense for me or satisfy me with the fat of your animals. Instead you burdened me with your sins; you wore me out with the wrongs you committed. And yet, I am the God who forgives your sins, and I do this because of who I am. I will not hold your sins against you.'

The word of the Lord.

Introduction to Gospel
There are two important features to listen out for in today's Gospel. Firstly, what happens when a paralysed man, who cannot move without the help of others, wants to be healed by Jesus, in whom he has great faith. Secondly, how the teachers of the Law, who were important figures in society, reacted to how Jesus dealt with the paralysed man.

Gospel
A reading from the holy Gospel according to Mark (2:1-12)

Later Jesus went back to Capernaum, and the news spread that he was at home. So many people came together that there was no room left, not even out in front of the door. Jesus was preaching the message to them when four men arrived, carrying a paralysed man to Jesus. Because of the crowd, however, they could not get the man to him. So they made a hole in the roof right above the place where Jesus was. When they had made an opening, they let the man down, lying on his mat. Seeing how much faith they had, Jesus said to the paralysed man, 'My son, your sins are forgiven.' Some teachers of the Law who were sitting there thought to themselves, 'How does he dare to talk like this? This is blasphemy! God is the only one who can forgive sins!' At once Jesus knew what they were thinking, so he said to them, 'Why do you think such things? Is it easier to say to this paralysed man, "Your sins are forgiven," or to say, "Get up, pick up your mat, and walk"? I will prove to you, then, that the Son of man has authority on earth to forgive sins.' So he said to the paralysed man, 'I tell you, get up, pick up your mat, and go home!' While they all watched, the man got up, picked up his mat, and hurried away. They were all completely amazed and praised God, saying, 'We have never seen anything like this!'

The Gospel of the Lord.

Dramatisation of Gospel
See Appendix III, p. 217.

Homily Suggestions
- Refer to the First Reading; acknowledge that our hardships can be overwhelming. We are right to complain and vent our feelings. Encourage the congregation to distinguish between airing our frustrations and needless whining. Ask them to imagine how annoying it can be to hear such moaning, that we are likely to want to avoid contact with that person. Ask them if this is what God would do?

- Invite them to become more aware of the extent to which they 'moan at God', or how they might only think of God when they want something. Emphasise that God's love is so deep and unconditional that he never gives up on us. Challenge the congregation to be as loving and forgiving as God is in our First Reading.

- Refer to the Gospel. Connect with previous Gospels that featured Jesus healing. Focus on the strength of the paralysed man's faith and the support this man had. Despite his paralysis, he, with the help of his friends, persisted and managed to get into the room where Jesus was. Refer to the banner and the significance of the bricks. Suggest that this man's faith was so strong and his friends' support so powerful that we could compare this strength to the solidity of the bricks. Offer the congregation some time to reflect on how the strength of their faith compares to that in the Gospel.

- Mention the incredulity of the Teachers of the Law, briefly referring back to how we talked about 'authority' a few Sundays ago.

- Explain how the amazing event of a paralysed man walking allows us to somewhat grasp just how big a deal the forgiveness of sins really is. It is much more than words. Forgiveness of our sins changes our lives, allowing us to get up and walk from whatever had been paralysing us. Allow some time for meaningful reflection on forgiveness in our lives, both asking for forgiveness as well as forgiving others who have hurt us.

Prayer of the Faithful
We pray for our families, especially our mammies and daddies. Throughout all our ups and downs we pray that we will always be a strong support to each other.

We pray for our Church. We thank you for the gift of the Sacrament of Reconciliation.

We pray for our leaders. Guide them in their work for the health care of all. May they work together with a sense of purpose for the good of all in their duty of care.

We pray for those whose faith has faltered due to bereavement, grave illness and other serious issues. Grant them strength.

We pray for our parish family. May our community be loving and forgiving.

Reflection/Thinking Prayer
We have taken this brief time from the rest of our day to come together and celebrate the sacred mysteries.

We pray that the experience and wisdom we have gained from Our Family Mass today will remain with us throughout the coming days and weeks.

We pray that our faith will grow stronger and stronger.

We pray that we will be forgiving to others, as we ask forgiveness too.

We pray that we will keep on going when the road ahead seems bleak and dark.

We pray that we will always be aware of your loving and forgiving presence.

We ask this through Christ our Lord.

Amen.

✠

Our Family Mass Resources for the Family Sunday Liturgy **Year B**

Eighth Sunday in Ordinary Time

Colour Green

Suggested Décor Images from readings, storyboards representing 'A Fresh Start'

Theme A fresh start

Entrance Procession Banner reading 'A Fresh Start'; new item of clothing with a hole, along with a piece of old material

Gospel Procession Candles, Lectionary

Welcome
Welcome to our Family Mass. What a wonderful way to start off a fresh week, coming together to listen to the Word of God and celebrate the beautiful sacrament of the Eucharist. Let's take a moment to remember we are in a sacred space, in the presence of God.

Theme
We all make mistakes. We can all be selfish at times and forget about other people's needs and their feelings. Sometimes we might even forget about all that God has given to us. Our precious gift of life, our families and friends, our whole world. The beautiful truth we can learn today is that God is always willing to welcome us back, to give us another chance, to allow us to make a fresh start. Our banner this week reads 'A Fresh Start'.

We also bring some cloth to the altar. Here we see some new material, but unfortunately it was torn and now there is a hole in it. Here is some tattered and worn-out cloth. Should we use this old cloth to patch up the hole, or would it be better to find a newer piece of material to mend it? As we celebrate our Mass today, we might find out just what to do.

Introduction to First Reading
Remember last week we listened to how God's love knows no limits. God kept on loving those who had grown selfish and neglected their relationship with him. In our reading today, we can imagine God as a husband to Israel, his wife. God explains that just as a husband might rekindle his relationship, showing love, honour and respect to his wife, so too will God show his love for Israel. Perhaps this will help the Israelites truly realise the depth of God's love.

First Reading
A reading from the prophet Hosea (2:16-17, 21-22)

I am going to take her into the desert again; there I will win her back with words of love. She will respond to me there as she did when she was young, when she came from Egypt. Israel, I will make you my wife; I will be true and faithful; I will show you constant love and mercy and make you mine forever. I will keep my promise and make you mine, and you will acknowledge me as Lord.

The word of the Lord.

Introduction to Gospel
Jews at the time of Jesus loved their faith. They abided by the rules of the Law very strictly. So much so, that if Jesus, who was Jewish himself, was seen to do anything different such as not fasting when others fasted, people used this as an excuse to ridicule him and make him look like a liar or charlatan. But Jesus came to teach a simple message in a new way. Let's listen to how Jesus explained this.

Gospel
A reading from the holy Gospel according to Mark (2:18-22)

On one occasion the followers of John the Baptist and the Pharisees were fasting. Some people came to Jesus and asked him, 'Why is it that the disciples of John the Baptist and the disciples of the Pharisees fast, but yours do not?' Jesus answered, 'Do you expect the guests at a wedding party to go without food? Of course not! As long as the bridegroom is with them, they will not do that. But the day will come when the bridegroom will be taken away from them, and then they will fast. No one uses a piece of new cloth to patch up an old coat, because the new patch will shrink and tear off some of the old cloth, making an even bigger hole. Nor does anyone pour new wine into used wineskin, because the wine will burst the skins, and both the wine and the skins will be ruined. Instead new wine must be poured into fresh wineskins.'

The Gospel of the Lord.

Song 'Try Again' (from *Alive-O*).[4]

---

[4] Fran Hegarty, Patricia Hegarty and Mary Nugent, from *Alive-O 8 Teacher's Book* (Veritas, Dublin, 2004), p. 328.

Homily Suggestions

- Give some brief background to the First Reading, reminding how fervently the Israelites worshipped after their liberation from Egypt, to the time of Hosea when Hosea felt that they had turned their backs on God and so on.

- Compare the First Reading to our own relationships – they must be worked at, and we must continue to make an effort to show our love for each other. Using the banner 'A Fresh Start', provide some time for reflection on how attentive we are in our own relationship with God, as well as relationships in general – do we need a fresh start in any area?

- Refer to the Gospel and how we can get a sense of Jesus being scrutinized and reprimanded if he appeared to do or say something that went against the status quo. Emphasise how Jesus, a good Jew, was highlighting the simple message of 'love one another' and that this took precedence over all 'rules and regulations'.

- Highlight how Jesus was radical – he did things in a new way. Stress that underneath it is the same message throughout all salvation history – the unconditional love of God and our duty to love one another as God loves us. Recount the examples from today's Gospel that emphasise newness.

Prayer of the Faithful

We pray for our families. Help us to be ready to forgive each other and grow as a loving family.

We pray for our Church. May she always welcome those who have neglected their faith for any reason, especially through the Sacrament of Reconciliation.

We pray for our leaders. May their work be influenced by the importance of family and the loving relationships that are at the heart of every society.

We pray for anyone making a fresh start – in family life, in their work or through moving house. Bless them always and keep them safe.

We pray for our parish family. We especially pray for those receiving the Sacrament of Marriage in our community this year.

Reflection/Thinking Prayer
A Fresh Start

A new way of thinking

A new way of living

Where 'ifs', 'buts' or 'maybes' hold no sway.

Not ruled by 'dos' and 'don'ts'

Just simply have a go

God will be with you every step of the way.

✠

Our Family Mass Resources for the Family Sunday Liturgy **Year B**

Ninth Sunday in Ordinary Time

Colour Green

Suggested Décor Images from readings

Theme The Sabbath and common sense

Entrance Procession Banner reading 'common sense', poster of the days of the week with Sunday highlighted

Gospel Procession Candles, Lectionary

Welcome
Welcome to our Family Mass. Each Sunday, we make the effort to gather together to listen to the Word of God and celebrate the Sacrament of the Eucharist together. Let's take a moment to reflect on how important it is for us to do this.

Theme
We bring a poster of the days of the week to the altar. Sunday is highlighted, marked out as different to the rest. The Jewish people continue to observe the Sabbath, which starts from Saturday night until Sunday night. During this time, they fast and rest, spending time thinking about their relationship with God. In our Mass today, we will hear about the Sabbath, and we will be invited to think about how we treat our Sundays. Is Sunday just like any other day? Or is there something special about Sunday?

Introduction to First Reading
When God revealed the Ten Commandments to Moses, he instructed the Israelites on how best to live their lives, always keeping God and God's will to the forefront of their thoughts and actions. One of the commandments, or guidelines for living, was to keep holy the Sabbath day.

First Reading
A reading from the book of Deuteronomy (5:12-15)

The Lord said, 'Observe the Sabbath and keep it holy, as I, the Lord your God, have commanded you. You have six days in which to do your work, but the seventh day is a day of rest dedicated to me. On that day no one is to work – neither you, your children, your slaves, your animals, nor the foreigners who live in your country. Your slaves must rest just as you do. Remember that you were slaves in Egypt, and that I, the Lord your God, rescued you by my great power and strength. That is why I command you to observe the Sabbath.'

The word of the Lord.

Introduction to Gospel
As a Jew, Jesus was expected to follow all the aspects of Jewish Law regarding the Sabbath. In our Gospel today we will hear about a time when Jesus did not follow this Law. Pharisees, a group of people who were especially critical of Jesus, challenged him about this. Let's listen to what Jesus said.

Gospel
A reading from the holy Gospel according to Mark (2:23-28)

Jesus was walking through some cornfields on the Sabbath. As his disciples walked along with him, they began to pick the ears of corn. So the Pharisees said to Jesus, 'Look, it is against our Law for your disciples to do that on the Sabbath!' Jesus answered, 'Have you never read what David did that time when he needed something to eat? He and his men were hungry, so he went into the house of God and ate the bread offered to God. This happened when Abiathar was the High Priest. According to our Law only the priests may eat this bread – but David ate it and even gave it to his men.' And Jesus concluded, 'The Sabbath was made for the good of man. Man was not made for the Sabbath. So the Son of Man is Lord even of the Sabbath.'

The Gospel of the Lord.

Song 'This is the Day' (from *Alive-O*).[5]

---

[5] Mary Amond O'Brien, *Alive-O 8 Teacher's Book* (Veritas, Dublin, 2004), p. 325.

Homily Suggestions
- Briefly explain the Jewish Sabbath and the connection to the Christian understanding of Sunday as the day of rest.

- Invite the congregation to think about their Sundays. Are they the same as other days? Do they do anything special on a Sunday? Do they take time out for themselves as a family?

- Emphasise the importance of rest in terms of our health, mental and physical, as well as providing us with time for pure fun. Suggest that the congregation be proactive in planning rest/fun activities on a Sunday such as doing something fun together – going for a walk. Emphasise the importance of putting aside specific time on a Sunday for God, beyond just attendance at Mass, such as praying together at home or reading some Scripture. Even some quiet time can be a way of intentionally spending time in the presence of God.

- Refer to the Gospel. Highlight how Jesus put the needs of the person before the rules and regulations. Imagine if Jesus had followed the rules and regulations, then perhaps he and his friends would have become ill from hunger (similarly in the example of David that Jesus cited).

- Stress the importance of the person over the rule as a means of explaining 'The Sabbath was made for the good of man. Man was not made for the Sabbath.' Encourage the congregation to put the needs of people before bureaucracy.

Prayer of the Faithful
We pray for our families. Help us to make the effort to put aside some special time on Sundays just to spend together and be grateful for one another.

We pray for our Church. Bless all those who work so hard to spread the Good News. May they also enjoy time to themselves to be quiet in the presence of God.

We pray for our leaders. Bless them with good health, and guide them in making policies that cater for the well-being of all people.

We pray for those who are overworked, anxious about financial commitments and those who have little time for leisure and rest through no fault of their own. Grant them peace and respite.

We pray for our parish, especially all those involved in the provision of respite care for the parents and guardians of children with special needs.

Reflection/Thinking Prayer
Common Sense

We work hard all week

At school, at home, in offices.

Help us to remember that we are more than what we do.

We are people first, workers second.

Help us to look after our health, our families, our relationships.

Help us to relax, take time out

And be grateful for all our blessings.

Help us to spend more time with those we love

And allow ourselves to really listen to God speaking to us in the ordinary events of our lives.

Help us to have the common sense not to lose sight of what is really important in life – each other.

We ask this through Christ our Lord.

Amen.

✢

Our Family Mass Resources for the Family Sunday Liturgy **Year B**

Tenth Sunday in Ordinary Time

Colour Green

Suggested Décor Images from readings

Theme Faithful to the truth

Entrance Procession Banner reading 'Truth', building blocks/Lego

Gospel Procession Candles, Lectionary

Welcome
Welcome to our Family Mass. We gather in this sacred space to spend some special time with God and with each other as God's children. Let us prepare to listen carefully to the Word of God and to reverently celebrate the Sacrament of the Eucharist.

Theme
We bring building blocks to the altar. Imagine each block as part of your life. Wouldn't you like those blocks to be linked strongly so that you could build a big, solid tower, not one that is wobbly and likely to collapse? Likewise, we would all like to become the best people we can be – brave, trustworthy and loving. We would like our lives to be secure and safe.

Today we will listen to the Word of God where we will hear about truth and how truth can keep people together, building strong connections and bonds. We show the word 'Truth' on our banner. Can you see the connection between our banner 'Truth' and our building blocks? Listen carefully to the Word of God and you might discover the link.

Introduction to First Reading
Do you know the account of Adam and Eve in the Garden of Eden? In the Bible, we read that Adam and Eve lived in perfect harmony and peace in the Garden of Eden. Their relationship with God was wonderful. God had one request – that Adam and Eve not eat the fruit from one particular tree. Can you guess what happened? Let's find out.

First Reading
A reading from the book of Genesis (3:9-15)

The Lord God called out to the man, 'Where are you?' He answered, 'I heard you in the garden; I was afraid and hid from you, because I was naked.' 'Who told you that you were naked?' God asked. 'Did you eat the fruit that I told you not to eat?' The man answered, 'The woman you put here with me gave me the fruit, and I ate it.' The Lord God asked the woman, 'Why did you do this?' She replied, 'The snake tricked me into eating it.' Then the Lord God said to the snake, 'You will be punished for this; you alone of all the animals must hear this curse: From now on you will crawl on your belly, and you will have to eat dust as long as you live. I will make you and the woman hate each other; her offspring and yours will always be enemies. Her offspring will crush your head, and you will bite their heel.'

The word of the Lord.

Introduction to Gospel
Jesus spent his days travelling, teaching and healing. Sometimes he was so busy he missed his meals. Not everyone was impressed by him: some were frightened and claimed that an evil spirit was at work through Jesus. Listen to Jesus's response to such a claim.

Gospel
A reading from the holy Gospel according to Mark (3:20-35)

Jesus went home. Again such a large crowd gathered that Jesus and his disciples had no time to eat. When his family heard about it, they went out to take charge of him, because people were saying, 'He's gone mad!' Some teachers of the Law who had come from Jerusalem were saying, 'He has Beelzebub in him! It is the chief of the demons who gives him the power to drive them out.' So Jesus called them to him and spoke to them in parables: 'How can Satan drive out Satan? If a country divides itself into groups which fight each other, that country will fall apart. If a family divides itself into groups which fight each other, that family will fall apart and come to an end.'

The Gospel of the Lord.

Song 'Connected' (from *Alive-O*).[6]

[6] Fr Peter O'Reilly, from *Alive-O 8 Teacher's Book* (Veritas, Dublin,

Homily Suggestions

- Refer to the song 'Connected' – where the verse ends 'it's love', suggest that we could substitute 'it's truth'.

- Refer to the First Reading. Acknowledge how we all make mistakes, not follow instructions and find it difficult to own up. Offer some anecdotes such as excuses for not having homework done, for example, 'The dog ate it'. (The children's book *Tiddler*, by Julia Donaldson, is relevant here and children may be familiar with it.)

- Extend this to compare 'little lies' to 'big lies'. Encourage the congregation to think about the 'big lies/big truths' in their lives. Invite them to reflect on times when they get 'gut feelings' that can guide them in being truly honest with themselves. Encourage the congregation to be brave and embrace the truth.

- Emphasise the importance of truth in relationships. Connect this with the Gospel passage. Jesus spoke about divisions within countries and families and how those divisions ultimately break down the whole unit. Focus on the converse, that truth can bind families and countries together.

- Make reference to the focal objects of the banner and blocks – the best connections in life are based on truth.

Prayer of the Faithful

We pray for our families. May our homes be places of trust and truthfulness.

We pray for our Church. May all the faithful live their lives truthfully according to the Gospel message.

We pray for our leaders. Help them to work towards a world of peace and justice.

We pray for anyone caught up in war, family separations and disputes of any kind. May the truth set them free.

We pray for our parish. Help us enrich our community with a spirit of truth and respect.

Reflection/Thinking Prayer
Building Blocks of Life

Build your life on what is true
And your connections will be strong.
Be honest. Tell the truth.
Telling fibs is just plain wrong!

Truth keeps people together.
It creates trust and happiness.
Without truth, our lives break down.
Fall apart and make a mess.

We all make mistakes
It might not even be our fault.
Still we must live by the truth.
Just as Jesus taught.

✠

Our Family Mass Resources for the Family Sunday Liturgy **Year B**

Eleventh Sunday in Ordinary Time

Colour Green

Suggested Décor Images from readings, seeds, seedlings and plants

Theme The Parable of the Mustard Seed

Entrance Procession Seed, young sapling, bigger plant or bouquet of flowers

Gospel Procession Candles, Lectionary

Welcome
Welcome to our Family Mass. Each and every one of us belongs here. The time we spend together today listening to God's Word and celebrating the Sacrament of the Eucharist is very important. Take a moment to prepare to listen carefully and take part as best as you can.

Theme
We bring a seed to the altar. It is tiny. It doesn't look like much now does it? But with some love and care … well let's see, shall we?

Here is a sapling. Love and care in the form of water, sunlight and healthy soil has allowed the tiny seed to grow. The sapling is like a child, still small, still young, but full of potential.

Next we present a beautiful plant/bouquet. Isn't it magnificent? And all this beauty, that brings such pleasure to us, sometimes even used in medicine or food, came from a tiny little seed.

Introduction to First Reading
Our First Reading mentions a tree called a cedar. Think of the seed, the sapling and the plant/bouquet we showed you earlier. Listen to the Word of God and see if you can make a connection between them.

First Reading
A reading from the prophet Ezekiel (17:22-24)

This is what the Sovereign Lord says: 'I will take the top of a tall cedar and break off a tender sprout; I will plant it on a high mountain. It will grow branches and bear seed and become a magnificent cedar. Birds of every kind will live there and find shelter in its shade.'

The word of the Lord.

Introduction to Gospel
Jesus also spoke about the potential that is in a tiny seed. Jesus chose the tiniest of seeds in this famous passage from the Gospel of Mark. It is called the Parable of the Mustard Seed.

Gospel
A reading from the holy Gospel according to Mark (4:26-34)

'What shall we say the Kingdom of God is like?' asked Jesus. 'What parable shall we use to explain it? It is like this. A man takes a mustard seed, the smallest seed in the world, and plants it in the ground. After a while it grows up and becomes the biggest of all plants. It puts out such large branches that the birds come and make their nests in its shade.'

The Gospel of the Lord.

Dramatisation of Gospel
See Appendix III, p. 217.

Homily Suggestions
Referring to the focal objects, emphasise the hope that runs through both readings. From the tiniest seed grows a great tree/plant.

Compare it to:

- The significance of every single individual amongst the millions of people who inhabit the earth
- The significance of even the smallest gesture or word that can make someone else's day, for example. Talk about the ripple effect of our actions.

· Encourage the congregation to be thankful for all the little things that people do. Emphasise the importance of saying thank you for even those small gestures that can sometimes go unnoticed.

· Give the example of St Thérèse of Lisieux and her 'Little Way'. Invite the congregation to find out more about this Saint.

· Highlight the importance of environmental care. We have the responsibility to care for nature and wildlife. Suggest that in the coming week, the congregation could find ways of being more environmentally friendly.

Prayer of the Faithful
We pray for our mammies and daddies. We thank them for all the little things they do for us, especially those we have not shown appreciation for. Bless them.

We pray for our Church. Bless all her members for the efforts they make, no matter how big or small, to spread the Good News.

We pray for our leaders. May they work towards a society that provides equal opportunities for everyone.

We pray for those who feel worthless and unimportant. Help them to remember that everyone is special as a child of God.

We pray for our parish, especially all our children and young people. Bless them as they go through life, making decisions and facing challenges.

Reflection/Thinking Prayer
From the smallest seed can grow the biggest tree.

From the gentle ripple grows the mighty wave.

From one kind word can grow a beautiful friendship.

A shy little child becomes a hero or heroine – brave.

Everything we do can make a difference

Even when it doesn't seem like much

Tall or small, young or old, you're important

God loves each and every one of us very much.

⊕

Twelfth Sunday in Ordinary Time

Colour Green

Suggested Décor Images from readings

Theme Calm in the storm

Entrance Procession Seascape, banner reading 'Calm in the Storm'

Gospel Procession Candles, Lectionary

Welcome
Welcome to our Family Mass. Let's take a moment to remember we are in a sacred space. Quieten ourselves, allow ourselves to be more open to the presence of God as we prepare to celebrate the Liturgy of the Word and the Sacrament of the Eucharist together.

Theme
We present a seascape. The sea can be calm in good weather and rough in bad weather. We travel by sea and swim in it too. Many creatures and plants live in the sea. It is full of life. This life comes from God. God creates and God protects.

Our banner reads 'Calm in the Storm'. As we celebrate our Mass together today, its meaning will become clearer.

Introduction to First Reading
Imagine the creation of everything – in particular water. Endless water gushing everywhere with nothing to stop it … well, perhaps … let's listen to the First Reading.

First Reading
A reading from the book of Job (38:1, 8, 11)

Who closed the gates to hold back the sea when it burst from the womb of the earth? It was I who covered the sea with clouds and wrapped it in darkness. I marked a boundary for the sea and kept it behind bolted gates. I told it, 'So far and no farther! Here your powerful waves must stop.'

The word of the Lord.

Introduction to Gospel
Jesus and the Apostles set out across the lake. Suddenly there is a storm. The Apostles panic – will their boat overturn? Will they all die? What's more, Jesus is just sleeping! Based on our First Reading, what do you expect will happen?

Gospel
A reading from the holy Gospel according to Mark (4:35-41)

On the evening of that same day Jesus said to his disciples, 'Let us go across to the other side of the lake.' So they left the crowd; the disciples got into the boat in which Jesus was already sitting, and they took him with them. Other boats were there too. Suddenly a strong wind blew up, and the waves began to spill over into the boat, so that it was about to fill with water. Jesus was in the back of the boat, sleeping with his head on a pillow. The disciples woke him up and said, 'Teacher, don't you care that we are about to die?' Jesus stood up and commanded the wind, 'Be quiet!' and he said to the waves, 'Be still!' The wind died down, and there was a great calm. Then Jesus said to his disciples, 'Why are you frightened? Have you still no faith?' But they were terribly afraid and said to one another, 'Who is this man? Even the wind and the waves obey him!'

The Gospel of the Lord.

Song 'Do Not Be Afraid' (from *Alive-O*).[7]

---

[7] Gerard Markland, *Alive-O 8 Teacher's Book* (Veritas, Dublin, 2004), p. 283.

Homily Suggestions
- Dispel misconceptions of illusionist/magician tricks of stopping water and so on.
- Focus on God as the source of all life, including water and all its life-giving properties. God is both creator and protector of all life.
- Refer to the Gospel reading. Invite the congregation to imagine themselves on the boat. Would they panic or not?
- Elaborate on this theme to focus on the 'stormy' moments in our lives, such as times when we are overwhelmed, unable to cope and afraid. Do we see Jesus sleeping as if he does not care? If so, what can today's Gospel teach us?
- Suggest that we must trust in God. God is with us in the calm and in the storm.

Prayer of the Faithful

We pray for our families. In good times and bad, may we keep together and provide support and love for each other.

We pray for our Church. May she remain strong through all the scandals and difficulties she faces.

We pray for our leaders. Help them to bring peace and calm to troubled parts of the world.

We pray for those who suffer from panic, self-doubt and fear. Bring them peace and strength.

We pray for our parish family, especially those who work or travel by sea. May they be safe always.

Reflection/Thinking Prayer
Stormy Times

The floodgates open
The troubles begin
Soon hope seems lost
Might as well give in.

The floodgates open
Then Jesus stands tall
Saying 'Peace. Be Calm.
I'm with you through it all.'

Life is not easy
It has its ups and downs
Some days filled with smiles
Others with frowns.

Remember this truth
Be it stormy or calm
You are always in my reach
Held lovingly in my palm.

⊕

Our Family Mass Resources for the Family Sunday Liturgy **Year B**

Thirteenth Sunday in Ordinary Time

Colour Green

Suggested Décor Images from readings, contrasting images of light/darkness

Theme God of Life

Entrance Procession Banner reading 'God of Life', candles

Gospel Procession Candles, Lectionary

Welcome
Welcome to our Family Mass. A special welcome to those who mourn the loss of a loved one and also to anyone who is worried about a sick friend or relative. In our deepest suffering, we need to be together as God's family to comfort one another and welcome God's grace as we celebrate the Sacred Mysteries.

Theme
God is the God of Life. All life comes from God. Our candles that we bring to the altar today represent the light of God that dwells in each one of us. This light is alive within us. When we die, our light joins with the light of Christ as we join God in heaven. (*Each candle flame should be joined with that of the Paschal Candle and then placed on the altar.*) Death does not separate us, but unites us with God in a special way. Together with God, our loved ones who have gone before us shine their light on us too.

Introduction to First Reading
God is the source of all life. When death extinguishes a life, we can question whether God really loves us at all. If God loved us, why is there death? It is okay to ask these questions. They can be difficult to answer. Let's listen to the First Reading and allow God to help us understand.

First Reading
A reading from the book of Wisdom (1:13-15; 2:23-24)

God did not invent death, and when living creatures die, it gives him no pleasure. He created everything so that it might continue to exist, and everything he created is wholesome and good. There is no deadly poison in it. No, death does not rule this world, for God's justice does not die. When God created us, he did not intend that we should die; he made us like himself. It was the devil's jealousy that brought death to the world, and those who belong to the devil are the ones who will die.

The word of the Lord.

Introduction to Gospel
Has anyone close to you been very ill, near death even? It is a very scary and upsetting experience. Our Gospel today features a man called Jairus, an official of the local synagogue. He sees Jesus arrive at the lakeside and this is where we join the events.

Gospel
This reading requires five participants.
A reading from the holy Gospel according to Mark (5:21-24, 35-43)

Narrator Jesus went back across the other side of the lake. There at the lakeside a large crowd gathered round him. Jairus, an official of the local synagogue, arrived, and when he saw Jesus he threw himself down at his feet and begged him earnestly:

Jairus My little daughter is very ill. Please come and place your hands on her, so that she will get well and live!

Narrator Then Jesus started off with him. So many people were going along with Jesus that they were crowding him from every side. Some messengers came from Jairus' house and told him:

Messengers Your daughter has died. Why bother the Teacher any longer?

Narrator Jesus paid no attention to what they said, but told him:

Jesus Don't be afraid, only believe.

Narrator Then he did not let anyone else go on with him except Peter and James and his brother John. They arrived at Jairus' house, where Jesus saw the confusion and heard all the loud crying and wailing. He went in and said to them:

Jesus Why all this confusion? Why are you crying? The child is not dead – she is only sleeping!

Narrator They laughed at him, so he put them all out, took the child's father and mother and his three disciples, and went into the room where the child was lying. He took her by the hand and said to her:

Jesus Talitha, Koum.

Narrator Which means, 'Little girl, I tell you to get up!' She got up at once and started walking around. When this happened, they were completely amazed. But Jesus gave them strict orders not to tell anyone, and he said:

Jesus Give her something to eat.

Reader The Gospel of the Lord.

Song 'The Cloud's Veil' (from *Alive-O*)[8] or 'Do Not Be Afraid' (from *Alive-O*).[9]

Homily Suggestions

- Acknowledge the suffering of those who mourn for friends, family and pets. Empathise with the difficulty of maintaining faith when faced with such pain and suffering.

- Emphasise how those who have died now enjoy the full presence of God in heaven. It can help to think of the happiness they now enjoy with God, no longer in pain or suffering.

- Refer to the candles (and the demonstration from the theme today). They can represent those who are sick or who have died. They now join with the light of Christ, which gives light and life to the whole world.

- Highlight that God is the God of life. Referring to the Gospel, Jesus gave life to the daughter of Jairus when all hope seemed lost. Dispel images of reanimation or magic. Instead, emphasise that God's love and gift of life is open to all and knows no bounds.

Prayer of the Faithful

We pray for our families especially those who are sick. May they be healed.

We pray for our Church. Bless all those who minister to the sick in your name.

We pray for our leaders. May they create policies that look after those most in need in our society and for those who care for the sick and dying.

We pray for the sick. May they experience comfort and peace through your Sacraments of Healing.

We pray for our parish family. Bless all those in our community whose job is to look after those who are ill or in need in any way.

Reflection/Thinking Prayer

'Help me please, my daughter's sick

Come to her, healer! Come to her, quick!'

Jesus looked at his face – it was fraught with worry.

He looked into his eyes – they pleaded him to hurry.

'Please, healer, please. I know I don't deserve it.

But my daughter's going to die, I simply cannot bear it.

Help her, healer, please, not for my sake but for hers.

No one else can save her, not a doctor, not a nurse.'

Jesus smiled: 'Go inside,' he said. 'Your daughter is healed –

No matter what your beliefs, to me you appealed.'

He turned to his disciples. 'This man, please observe:

He has what many people lack, this man – he has nerve!

Do you really think following rules and regulations is enough?

You've got to do it, not just say it. You must be made of sterner stuff.

It didn't matter where Jairus came from.

It didn't matter what he thought.

What matters is that he came to me.

That kind of faith can't be bought.'

✠

---

[8] Liam Lawton, *Alive-O 8 Teacher's Book* (Veritas Dublin, 2004), p. 321.

[9] Gerard Markland, *Alive-O 8 Teacher's Book* (Veritas, Dublin, 2004), p. 283.

Our Family Mass Resources for the Family Sunday Liturgy **Year B**

✝ Fourteenth Sunday in Ordinary Time

Colour Green

Suggested Décor Images of the locality

Theme God is right here

Entrance Procession A selection of items representing the locality

Gospel Procession Candles, Lectionary

Welcome
Welcome to our Family Mass. We know each other from work, school or play. But gathering here is not like going to the cinema together. Every single time we celebrate Mass, it is special. Extraordinary. Let's take a moment to remember that we are in a sacred space, in the presence of God.

Theme
We bring (*a selection of items representing the locality*). We might see the same people and places every day. We might not take much heed of them, thinking them to be normal and ordinary. If these items were from a Hollywood film set, we might say 'wow' and think they are really special. But, no, these are from our everyday lives and the places we see every day.

In today's Mass, we will learn that the ordinary is in fact extraordinary. Listen carefully and open your heart to God. Let him explain it to you.

Introduction to First Reading
God knew that his people were being unfaithful to him – not living as they had promised, even forgetting about God entirely. So God chose an ordinary man called Ezekiel to go and tell his people that God is among them. Let's listen.

First Reading
A reading from the prophet Ezekiel (2:2-5)

While the voice was speaking, God's spirit entered me and raised me to my feet, and I heard the voice continue. 'Mortal man, I am sending you to the people of Israel. They have rebelled and turned against me and are still rebels, just as their ancestors were. They are stubborn and do not respect me, so I am sending you to tell them what I, the Sovereign Lord, am saying to them. Whether those rebels listen to you or not, they will know that a prophet has been among them.'

The word of the Lord.

Introduction to Gospel
The events of today's Gospel could take place anywhere. Imagine your next door neighbour visited your house. Now imagine that a famous person visited your house. Which one would seem more exciting? Who would you pay more attention to? We know now just how special and important Jesus was. But to his neighbours, Jesus was just a normal, ordinary person – just Jesus.

Gospel
A reading from the holy Gospel according to Mark (6:1-6)

Jesus went back to his home town, followed by his disciples. On the Sabbath he began to teach in the Synagogue. Many people were there; and when they heard him, they were amazed. 'Where did he get all this?' they asked. 'What wisdom is this that has been given him? How does he perform miracles? Isn't he the carpenter, the son of Mary, and the brother of James, Joseph, Judas and Simon? Aren't his sisters living here?' And so they rejected him. Jesus said to them, 'A prophet is respected everywhere except in his own home town and by his relatives and his family.' He was not able to perform any miracles there, except that he placed his hands on a few sick people and healed them. He was greatly surprised, because the people did not have faith.

The Gospel of the Lord.

Dramatisation of Gospel
See Appendix III, p. 217.

Homily Suggestions

- Remind the congregation of the focal objects being from the locality. Ask them: if they were from a Hollywood film set, would they seem more interesting and exciting? Mention how 'exclusives' and 'one-off specials' generate excitement and greater attention. Contrast this to the seeming ordinariness of the focal objects.

- Invite the congregation to reflect on the desire of many people to be famous, to 'be somebody'. Is this necessary in order to realise your worth, value, how special you are?

- Emphasise that God is in the ordinary and everyday, in people we know and people we might not think are special. Consider some references to Ignatian spirituality.

- Refer once again to the focal objects. The fact that they are ordinary while being special is not a disappointment but a joy. It reminds us that God is for everyone, in everyone, offers God's love to everyone. We just have to be ourselves and God still loves us.

Prayer of the Faithful

We pray for our families. Help us to recognise the worth of each other, and to be grateful for all the things we do for each other that we sometimes take for granted.

We pray for our Church. May she continue to be 'catholic' in the truest sense of the word – 'for all', 'all-welcoming' and 'universal'.

We pray for our leaders. May they listen to the voices of everyone in society and address the needs of all in a spirit of equality and justice.

We pray for anyone who feels unloved, unwanted or alone. Help them to realise their value and uniqueness. May they come to love themselves as you already love them.

We pray for our parish. Help us to be more considerate of everyone in our community as we continue to work on creating a vibrant community spirit.

Reflection/Thinking Prayer
Just Jesus

That's only the guy from down the road.
You know Joseph and Mary's son.
Sure, he's just a carpenter, not a rabbi or leader.
There's something fishy going on with this one.

How can he know what he knows?
How can he speak with such power?
He's just the guy next door, he's nothing special.
But he gathers more and more followers by the hour.

Is he just Jesus or is he something more?
Something just doesn't sit right.
I admit there's something about him.
Something of power and might.

But I always knew him as 'just Jesus'.
'Just Jesus' from next door.
Not the preacher, the teacher, the healer,
The saviour of the sick and the poor.

Who is he to you?
Have you even given it thought?
Is he 'just Jesus' or not?
Is he something more – the Son of God,
With whose life our salvation was bought?

⊕

Fifteenth Sunday in Ordinary Time

Colour Green

Suggested Décor Images from readings

Theme God's love is free

Entrance Procession Basket of price tags, large label reading 'For Free'

Gospel Procession Candles, Lectionary

Welcome
Welcome to our Family Mass. We will listen to the Word of God and celebrate the Sacrament of the Eucharist together. This is a special time for us. In this sacred space, let us take a moment to prepare to listen well and take part as best as we can.

Theme
We present a basket of price tags. From houses to holidays, books to bread, it seems everything comes at a cost. This can be worrying for a lot of people who can struggle to pay the bills. It seems nothing comes for free.

But here is where today's readings will show us something wonderful. We present a large label that reads 'For Free'. Get ready to listen carefully, and through the Scripture readings, our music, prayer and homily, allow God to explain to you just what is 'for free', for us all.

Introduction to First Reading
Amos used to be a shepherd. He was good at taking care of his sheep. He did it out of love, not for the money. Shepherds did not get paid much after all. So Jesus chose Amos to teach others about God. Amos travelled from his home in Judah to Bethal, doing just as God asked. He taught about God out of love for God, not expecting to be paid lots of money. Let's join in the events when Amaziah, a person of authority in Bethel, speaks to Amos.

First Reading
A reading from the prophet Amos (7:12-15)

Amaziah then said to Amos, 'That's enough, prophet! Go on back to Judah and do your preaching there. Let them pay you for it. Don't prophesy here at Bethal any more. This is the king's place of worship, the national temple.' Amos answered, 'I am not the kind of prophet who prophesies for pay. I am a herdsman, and I take care of fig-trees. But the Lord took me from my work as a shepherd and ordered me to come and prophesy to his people of Israel.'

The word of the Lord.

Introduction to Gospel
Jesus gave his disciples instructions on how best to go about spreading the Good News. In particular, Jesus told them to bring nothing with them on their mission, and not to accept any payment. All they needed was the Good News. Let's listen.

Gospel
A reading from the holy Gospel according to Mark (6:7-13)

Jesus called the twelve disciples together and sent them out two by two. He gave them authority over the evil spirits and ordered them, 'Don't take anything with you on your journey except a stick – no bread, no beggar's bag, no money in your pockets. Wear sandals, but don't carry an extra shirt.' He also said, 'Wherever you are welcomed, stay in the same house until you leave that place. It you come to a town where people do not welcome you or will not listen to you, leave it and shake the dust off your feet. That will be a warning to them!' So they went out and preached that people should turn away from their sins. They drove out many demons, and rubbed olive-oil on many sick people and healed them.

The Gospel of the Lord.

Song 'Let Them Grow' (from *Alive-O*).[10]

---

[10] Finbar O'Connor, *Alive-O 8 Teacher's Book* (Veritas, Dublin, 2004), p. 299.

V. Ordinary Time

Homily Suggestions

- Refer to the focal objects of the price tags. Reiterate the costs that surround us. Everything must be paid for – our clothes, our food, our books. Emphasise that not everyone has enough money to pay for these things. Invite the congregation to offer a silent prayer for those in financial difficulty at this time.

- Refer to the readings. Amaziah expected that Amos's work came at a cost. Highlight how we also have this expectation – we assume we will have to pay for all services and goods. Generosity can be a surprise. Give the congregation a moment to reflect on how sad a reality this can be. Generosity should be the norm, should it not?

- Both readings emphasise the necessity of the Good News and the willingness to carry out God's will. They stress that material goods and payment are not as important.

- Suggest that we might learn from these readings that:
  - To be a giving person, without expecting anything in return, is an attribute that Jesus wants us to embrace
  - We can look for goodness in others, unlike Amaziah who assumed Amos had an ulterior motive (i.e. payment) for his preaching.

- Refer to the focal object of the label reading 'for free'. State that the unconditional love of God is offered freely to us all. Similarly, we are called upon to spread this Gospel to each other, freely, with no expectation of anything in return.

- Provide some time for quiet reflection on this challenge.

Prayer of the Faithful

We pray for our families. Bless all those who are struggling to make ends meet. Help us to be supportive of each other and to always be generous with that one free gift we have to share – our love.

We pray for our Church. Bless all those who give freely of their time and talents to be part of our Church family in so many different ways.

We pray for our leaders. Help them to focus on the welfare of all people as they create their laws and policies.

We pray for those who are struggling financially and also those who are blinded by greed. May they all come to a greater understanding of what is important in life and be comforted by your unconditional love.

We pray for our parish family. Bless all those who carry out volunteer work for the benefit of the sick, the elderly and those in need in our community.

Reflection/Thinking Prayer

Father in heaven,
As your children
We have a lot to learn.

Help us to learn the true value of those around us,
The value of life itself.

Keep us from being distracted with material goods and the illusion of wealth.

Help us to remember what really matters in life.

We pray that we learn from today's Scripture readings.

We pray that we become more generous people.

We pray that we learn not to always expect something in return.

We pray that our hearts be filled with your unconditional love,
And that we learn how to give that love freely to others in all areas of our lives.

We ask this through Christ our Lord.

Amen.

✠

Our Family Mass Resources for the Family Sunday Liturgy **Year B**

Sixteenth Sunday in Ordinary Time

Colour Green

Suggested Décor Images from readings, symbols of kings and shepherds

Theme The True King – the Good Shepherd

Entrance Procession Crown, shepherd's staff

Gospel Procession Candles, Lectionary

Welcome
Welcome to our Family Mass. We are in a sacred space. Let us take a few moments to quieten ourselves, open our eyes, our ears and our hearts as we prepare to celebrate the Sacred Mysteries together as God's family.

Theme
We bring a crown to the altar. What is your idea of a good king or queen? What kind of person would they be? How would they treat their people? Imagine you are a king: what would you do? In our First Reading we will hear about some of the attributes of kings, those which please God and those which do not.

We present a shepherd's staff. It is a long stick used by a shepherd to help him climb over difficult terrain as he tends to his sheep on the mountains. Shepherding is not an easy job. It is not very glamorous or well paid. A shepherd does his work for the love of his sheep.

Introduction to First Reading
Our First Reading comes from the prophet Jeremiah. He lived at a time when the rulers and kings treated their people badly. The rulers made their lives so miserable that many people left their homes out of fear or were forced to leave as punishment. God spoke through Jeremiah to explain how God felt about these rulers and kings and what God would do about it.

First Reading
A reading from the prophet Jeremiah (23:1-6)

How terrible will be the Lord's judgement on those rulers who destroy and scatter his people! This is what the Lord, the God of Israel, says about rulers who were supposed to take care of his people: 'You have not taken care of my people; you have scattered them and driven them away. Now I am going to punish you for the evil you have done. I will gather the rest of my people from the countries where I have scattered them, and I will bring them back to their homeland. They will have many children and increase in number. I will appoint rulers to take care of them. My people will no longer be afraid or terrified, and I will not punish them again. I, the Lord, have spoken.' The Lord says, 'The time is coming when I will choose as king a righteous descendant of David. That king will rule wisely and do what is right and just throughout the land. When he is king, the people of Israel will live in peace. He will be called "The Lord Our Salvation".'

The word of the Lord.

Introduction to Gospel
Do you remember the shepherd's staff? Listen for the reference to a shepherd in the Gospel. It begins by explaining how Jesus and his disciples were going to a quiet place to rest from all their hard work and to eat.

Gospel
A reading from the holy Gospel according to Mark (6:30-34)

The apostles returned and met with Jesus, and told him all they had done and taught. There were so many people coming and going that Jesus and his disciples didn't even have time to eat. So he said to them, 'Let us go off by ourselves to some place where we will be alone and you can rest for a while.' So they started out in a boat by themselves for a lonely place. Many people, however, saw them leave and knew at once who they were; so they went from all the towns and ran ahead by land and arrived at the place ahead of Jesus and his disciples. When Jesus got out of the boat, he saw this large crowd, and his heart was filled with pity for them, because they were like sheep without a shepherd. So he began to teach them many things.

The Gospel of the Lord.

Dramatisation of Gospel
See Appendix III, pp. 217–218.

Homily Suggestions

- Refer to the focal objects of the crown and shepherd's staff: invite the congregation to compare and contrast them in terms of wealth, power, authority, leadership and so on. Ask them to reflect on which role most appeals.

- Compare the societal problems in the First Reading to modern times. How are people treated in our world? Is there justice and equality? Do our leaders look after us all well?

- Emphasise that we are always on a journey to achieve the kind of leadership that God wishes. Provide some time for reflection on how we can become better leaders in all our positions of authority, for example as older siblings, parents, teachers, employers and so on.

- Ask the congregation to think about the bad king described in the First Reading: if they could ask him who he put first in his life, himself or his people, what might be his answer? Then extend this to the description of 'The Lord Our Salvation' as well as Jesus' actions in the Gospel: who did Jesus put first – he and his disciples who were tired and hungry, or his followers who desired more teaching?

- Allow the congregation to think about how important it is for us to be considerate of the needs of others, in our daily relationships, and more widely as a community and global human family.

- Once again, ask them to reflect on the significance of the focal objects and which one could teach them more about the kind of people God wishes us to be.

Prayer of the Faithful

We pray for our mammies, daddies, grandparents and older brothers and sisters. Help them to be considerate and wise in how they look after those in their care.

We pray for our Church. We especially pray for our Pope, bishops and all the clergy. Help them to follow the example of the Good Shepherd.

We pray for our leaders. Guide them to build a world of justice and peace with a special care for the poor and marginalised.

We pray for all people in positions of power. May they be strengthened in their work by your Spirit.

We pray for our parish. Bless all those who work for the welfare of others in our community.

Reflection/Thinking Prayer

Jesus, our friend,

You put us first.

You cared for us and taught us how to care for each other.

For the times we have failed or been selfish – we are sorry.

Help us to be better people by recognising the value and importance of each other.

We pray that we will be caring and considerate like you.

Amen.

☩

Our Family Mass Resources for the Family Sunday Liturgy **Year B**

Seventeenth Sunday in Ordinary Time

Colour Green

Suggested Décor Images from readings

Theme Miracle of the loaves and fishes

Entrance Procession Candles, empty basket, cardboard cut-outs of two fish and five loaves

Gospel Procession Candles, Lectionary

Welcome
Welcome to our Family Mass. Let's take a moment to remember that we are in a special place. We come here to celebrate our love for God, and God's love for us. Together, we will hear the Word of God – let's try to listen as best as we can.

Theme
We are always hungry for something – our next meal, extra playtime, one more story before bedtime … no matter what we receive, we always seem to want more. We bring an empty basket to the altar to remind us that the things we have, the food we eat, the stuff we buy, they never really satisfy us. It's as if our 'basket of life' is never as full as we would like it to be. There's always something we feel we do not have enough of.

We also bring images of fish and loaves of bread. In our Gospel today we will hear how Jesus fed thousands of people – as many as all the fans at a big football match – with just two fish and five loaves of bread, and still had some left over afterwards!

After we have listened to the Word of God, and after we have celebrated the Eucharist, we will think back on today's Mass and look again at our 'basket of life'.

Introduction to First Reading
Our First Reading gives an account of a meal. Elisha gave his servant some food to give to the prophets but the servant worried that they did not have enough for everyone. Let's listen.

First Reading
A reading from the second book of the Kings (4:42-44)

A man came from Baal Shalishah, bringing Elisha twenty loaves of bread made from the first barley harvested that year, and some freshly cut ears of corn. Elisha told his servant to feed the group of prophets with this, but he answered, 'Do you think this is enough for a hundred men?' Elisha replied, 'Give it to them to eat, because the Lord says that they will eat and still have some left over.' So the servant set the food before them, and, as the Lord had said, they all ate and there was still some left over.

The word of the Lord.

Introduction to Gospel
The events in the First Reading are very like what follows in our Gospel reading today. Jesus was given just five loaves of bread and two fish to feed about five thousand people. Would it be enough? Let's find out.

Gospel
This reading requires five participants.
A reading from the holy Gospel according to John (6:1-15)

Narrator Jesus went across Lake Galilee. A large crowd followed him, because they had seen his miracles of healing those who were ill. Jesus went up a hill and sat down with his disciples. The time for the Passover Festival was near. Jesus looked around and saw that a large crowd was coming to him. He turned to Philip.

Jesus Philip, where can we buy enough food to feed all these people?

Philip For everyone to have even a little, it would take more than two hundred silver coins to buy enough bread.

Narrator Another of his disciples, Andrew, who was Simon Peter's brother, spoke.

Andrew There is a boy here who has five loaves of barley bread and two fish. But there will certainly not be enough for all these people.

Jesus Make the people sit down.

Narrator So all the people sat down; about five thousand of them. Jesus took the bread, gave thanks to God and distributed it to the people who were sitting there. He did the same with the fish and they all had as much as they wanted. When they were all full Jesus spoke to his disciples:

Jesus Gather the pieces left over; let us not waste any.

Narrator So they gathered them all up and filled twelve baskets with the pieces left over from the five barley loaves which the people had eaten.

Voice from the crowd Surely this is God's prophet who has come into the world.

Narrator Jesus knew that they were about to come and seize him in order to make him King by force; so he went off again to the hills by himself.

The Gospel of the Lord.

Song 'Happy in the Presence' (from *Alive-O*).[11]

Homily Suggestions
- Caution against thinking of Jesus as a magician who 'magically' fed thousands of people with a small amount of food. Name this event as a miracle – something that happens but only God knows how or why. (There were other miracles too that we will hear about at other times.)
- Bring attention to the empty basket. Refer to it as 'basket of life'. Ask the congregation to think of the different things they can hunger for:
  - Food and drink for our bodies
  - Knowledge and stories for our minds
  - Friendship and love for our hearts.
- Bring attention to the cardboard cut-outs of fish and loaves. In our Gospel, Jesus fed with these. Everyone was satisfied and no one was left hungry.
- Compare how people in both readings worried that they did not have enough food. Similarly, we worry about not having enough time, enough holidays, enough money and so on. Provide some time for the congregation to reflect on what they have, the importance of which they may not realise, such as their health.
- Refer to how Jesus gave thanks before distributing the food; compare this to the Eucharist at Mass. Emphasise how Jesus continues to feed us through the Eucharist.

- Combine the focal object of the 'basket of life' with the reference to Jesus continuing to feed us through the Eucharist. Our belief in God, our love for Jesus and God's love for us in return is the food for our bodies, minds and hearts together. Only God can satisfy our hunger.
- Perhaps suggest (and explain the relevance of) the St Augustine quote: 'Our hearts are restless 'til they rest in you.'

Prayer of the Faithful
We pray for our mammies and daddies who provide us with our meals. Thank you.

We pray for our Church. May our celebrations of the Eucharist nourish our spirits and souls.

We pray for our leaders. Help them to work together to rid the world of hunger and famine.

We pray for those whose lives feel empty. May your Good News fill their hearts, minds and bodies with new life.

We pray for our parish. Help us to be grateful for the gifts in our community, our people and our talents.

Reflection/Thinking Prayer
We look again at our 'basket of life' and reflect on what we have listened to today.

What do we really need in order to live the best lives possible so that our 'basket of life' can be filled? (*Pause for a few moments.*)

When we comment that we don't have enough of something, is that always true?

We pray that God will help us to be satisfied and happy with what we have.

We pray that God will help us to realise what we really need is love.

We pray that we will always welcome God's love in our lives.

We thank God for the love that fills our hearts, our minds and our bodies – that fills our 'basket of life'.

Amen.

⊕

---

[11] Bernard Sexton, *Alive-O 4 Teacher's Book* (Veritas, Dublin, 1999), p. 325–326.

Our Family Mass Resources for the Family Sunday Liturgy **Year B**

✝ Eighteenth Sunday in Ordinary Time

Colour Green

Suggested Décor Images from readings

Theme Jesus is the Bread of Life

Entrance Procession Bread, poster depicting the Host

Gospel Procession Candles, Lectionary

Welcome
Welcome to our Family Mass. The Word of God and the Eucharist nourish us in a very special and unique way. Let's prepare ourselves to welcome God by listening, looking and taking part as best we can.

Theme
We bring some bread. Our bodies need energy to grow and to play. This bread represents all food and drink – breakfast, lunch, dinner, snacks and treats.

We present the Host. This is an image of the bread used at Holy Communion. When blessed it becomes the Body of Christ. The priest or minister holds it to us and says 'Body of Christ', to which we answer 'Amen'.

In our Mass today, we will begin to learn why the Bread of Holy Communion is so special.

Introduction to First Reading
When Moses freed the Israelites from slavery in Egypt, they travelled in the wilderness for a long time. Food was scarce. They began to starve. Many complained that God was not providing for them and looking after them. Some even thought they would be better off back in Egypt. Let's listen to what happened.

First Reading
A reading from the book of Exodus (16:2-4, 12-15)

The whole Israelite community began to complain to Moses and Aaron and said to them, 'We wish that the Lord had killed us in Egypt. There we could at least sit down and eat meat and as much other food as we wanted. But you have brought us out into this desert to starve us all to death.' The Lord said to Moses, 'Now I am going to make food rain down from the sky for all of you. The people must go out every day and gather enough food for that day. In this way I can test them to find out if they will follow my instructions. I have heard the complaints of the Israelites. Tell them that at twilight they will have meat to eat, and in the morning they will have all the bread they want. Then they will know that I, the Lord, am their God.' In the evening a large flock of quails flew in, enough to cover the camp, and in the morning there was dew all round the camp. When the dew evaporated, there was something thin and flaky on the surface of the desert. It was as delicate as frost. When the Israelites saw it, they didn't know what it was and asked each other, 'What is it?' Moses said to them, 'This is the food that the Lord has given you to eat.'

The word of the Lord.

Introduction to Gospel
Listen carefully. In our Gospel today you will hear Jesus talk about the exact events we just heard about in our First Reading. He begins to explain the difference between the nourishment and goodness that we get from everyday food and drink to the nourishment and life we receive from Jesus.

Gospel
A reading from the holy Gospel according to John (6:24-35)

When the crowd saw that Jesus was not there, nor his disciples, they got into those boats and went to Capernaum, looking for him. When the people found Jesus on the other side of the lake, they said to him, 'Teacher, when did you get here?' Jesus answered, 'I am telling you the truth: you are looking for me because you ate the bread and had all you wanted, not because you understood my miracles. Do not work for the food that goes bad; instead, work for the food that lasts for eternal life. This is the food which the Son of Man will give you, because God, the Father, has put his mark of approval on him.' So they asked him, 'What can we do in order to do what God wants us to do?' Jesus answered, 'What God wants you to do is to believe in the one he sent.' They replied, 'What miracle will you perform so that we may see it and believe you? What will you do? Our ancestors ate manna in the desert just as the Scripture says, "He gave them bread from heaven to eat".' 'I am telling you the truth,' Jesus said. 'What Moses gave you was not bread from heaven; it is my Father who gives you the real bread from heaven. For the bread that God gives is he who comes down from heaven and gives life to the world.' 'Sir,' they asked him, 'give us this bread always.' 'I am the bread of life,' Jesus told them. 'He who comes to me will never be hungry; he who believes in me will never be thirsty.'

The Gospel of the Lord.

Song 'Eat this Bread' (from *Alive-O*).[12]

Homily Suggestions
- Refer to the First Reading, especially how the Israelites soon resorted to complaining. Ask the congregation to think about times when they give out to God, feeling the whole world is against them. Recognise that we all have these moments of anger and fear and that it is part of life. We can relate to the plight of the Israelites.

- Elaborate on the unconditional love and mercy of God. Despite the moaning and complaining of the Israelites, God still provided for them. Consider providing an explanation for the phrase 'manna from heaven' in everyday life as 'unexpected good fortune'.

- Refer to the focal object of bread. Refer to our mealtimes: invite reflections on favourite foods and special meals. Recognise that food is essential for the nourishment of our bodies, providing nutrients just like plants need good soil, sunshine and water.

- Mention how this is the first of a series of Sunday liturgies that will revolve around the theme of 'Bread of Life'. Bring attention to the focal object of the image of the Host. Consider a brief explanation of how the bread is manufactured. Emphasise that during Mass over the next number of Sundays special attention will be brought to the elements of the Liturgy of the Eucharist. (*See Ordinary Time – An Overview.*)

- Explain that the Host is also bread, but emphasise how it is different to everyday bread. Refer to how Jesus in the Gospel referred to himself as 'the bread of life … he who comes to me will never be hungry; he who believes in me will never be thirsty'. At this stage, ask the congregation to think about the following question:

  • Why do they get out of bed in the morning – is it just to get breakfast or is it to live?

- Provide some time for reflection on the difference between just eating our meals and living our lives, and where does Jesus as the Bread of Life fit into our response?

Prayer of the Faithful
We pray for our mammies and daddies who provide us not just with our meals, but also with love, care and affection.

We pray for our Church. May she continue in her mission to nourish the hearts, souls and minds of all with the Gospel message.

We pray for world leaders. May they work for the benefit of those in developing countries devastated by famine.

We pray for those who hunger and thirst for justice and peace in our world. May their efforts be fruitful.

We pray for our parish family. Help us to take care of all in our community, especially those who are in need of help at this time in providing their own families with food, clothing and education costs.

Reflection/Thinking Prayer
Bread of Life

My tummy is rumbling,
Time for a snack,
A nice cool drink,
And then it will be back.

Back to the shops,
To buy more food and drink,
The cupboard is empty. Again.
Never-ending! Don't you think?

The satisfaction we get
Doesn't last, you see,
We'll get hungry again
And soon will be thirsty.

The kind of food and drink
That Jesus describes
Isn't just for our bodies,
It's for our whole lives.

Jesus, the Bread of Life
Quenches all hunger and thirst,
Our hearts, souls and minds
Will be replenished first.

---
12 Jacques Berthier, © Taizé, *Alive-O 4 Teacher's Book* (Veritas, Dublin, 1999), p. 383.

It is our hearts, souls and minds
What we ask Jesus to feed.
This Truth, the Bread of Life.
It's all we'll ever need.

Our Family Mass Resources for the Family Sunday Liturgy **Year B**

Nineteenth Sunday in Ordinary Time

Colour Green

Suggested Décor Images from readings

Theme Jesus is the Bread of Life

Entrance Procession Bread, poster depicting the Host, Rubik's cube

Gospel Procession Candle, Lectionary

Welcome
Welcome to our Family Mass. Ask yourself why are you here? Is it a habit? Or is it something more? Let's take a moment to remember that we are gathered together here in this wonderful sacred space for a reason.

Theme
Just as we did last week, we bring some bread. Our bodies need energy to grow and to play. This bread represents all food and drink – breakfast, lunch, dinner, snacks and treats.

We present the Host. This is an image of the bread used at Holy Communion. In our Mass today, we will continue to learn why the Bread of Holy Communion is so special.

We also bring a Rubik's cube. This is a children's puzzle. The aim is to get all colours matching on all sides. It is very tricky. Just when we think we have it solved, we find ourselves no better off than when we began. It is easy to get frustrated and give up.

In today's Mass we will hear about how followers of Jesus and even Elijah, the prophet, were frustrated and wanted to give up on God. We have our ups and downs, our frustrations and troubles too. Open your ears and hearts and allow God to teach you today.

Introduction to First Reading
Elijah was a great prophet of God. He listened to God and followed God's instructions to travel and spread the Good News of God's love. We might expect that people like Elijah had it easy – working for God would surely mean they would be looked after, not left to starve or not be treated badly by people, right? Well, let's listen.

First Reading
This reading requires three participants.
A reading from the first book of Kings (19:4-8)

Narrator Elijah walked the whole day into the wilderness. He stopped and sat down in the shade of a tree and wished he would die.

Elijah It's too much, Lord! Take away my life; I might as well be dead!

Narrator He lay down under the tree and fell asleep. Suddenly an angel touched him.

Angel Wake up and eat.

Narrator He looked round, and saw a loaf of bread and a jar of water near his head. He ate and drank, and lay down again. The Lord's angel returned and woke him up a second time.

Angel Get up and eat, or the journey will be too much for you.

Narrator Elijah got up, ate and drank, and the food gave him enough strength to walk forty days to Sinai, the holy mountain.

The word of the Lord.

Introduction to Gospel
In last week's Gospel reading, we listened to Jesus describing himself as the bread of life. He did not just do this once, he did it again and again. We hear it again today. Why do you think he repeatedly taught this message?

Gospel
A reading from the holy Gospel according to John (6:41-51)

The people started grumbling about him, because he said, 'I am the bread that came down from heaven.' So they said, 'This man is Jesus, son of Joseph, isn't he? We know his father and mother. How, then, does he now say he came down from heaven?' Jesus answered, 'Stop grumbling among yourselves. I am the bread of life. Your ancestors ate manna in the desert, but they died. But the bread that comes down from heaven is of such a kind that whoever eats it will not die. I am the living bread that came down from heaven. If anyone eats this bread he will live forever. The bread that I will give him is my flesh, which I give so that the world may live.'

The Gospel of the Lord.

Song 'I am the Bread' (from *Alive-O*).[13]

Homily Suggestions

- In both our readings today, just as we heard in last week's liturgy, people continue to complain and moan about the difficulties of their lives. We can relate to this too. It seems that we always find something to grumble about – not getting what we want, feeling that bad things keep happening to us. Refer to the Rubik's cube – just when we think our lives are stable, something can crop up and upset us. This often affects our faith. Provide some time to reflect on times this may have happened to us.

- Refer to other focal objects of bread and the image of Host. Reiterate how this liturgy is part of a series that focuses on the theme of Jesus as the Bread of Life. Invite the congregation to think about why Jesus repeated this message:
    - Why are we taught some lessons more than once?

- Suggest that the repetition is to get the message through so that we really believe it and truly remember it. Compare it to a skill, such as playing a sport: if we do not practise, we lose our competency.

- Refer to our First Holy Communion experiences. Highlight that this is a special occasion and that much celebration surrounds it. Focus on the word 'First' – reminding the congregation that the celebration of our First Holy Communion is just the beginning. When the ceremony that day is over, it is not the end of the special occasion, but the beginning of another wonderful aspect of our relationship with God. Just as Jesus repeated the message that he was the Bread of Life, we return to Mass to receive Holy Communion again and again. Provide some time for the congregation to reflect on the significance of receiving Holy Communion on a regular basis.

- Emphasise that during Mass over these number of Sundays special attention will be given to the elements of the Liturgy of the Eucharist. (*See Ordinary Time – An Overview, p. 102.*)

Prayer of the Faithful

We pray for our families. Help our love for each other support us during our good days and our bad days.

We pray for our Church. May a deeper understanding of the Sacrament of the Eucharist and the practice of Eucharistic Adoration strengthen the faithful.

We pray for our leaders. Be with them as they try to overcome the many difficulties and problems in the world.

We pray for those who despair and find it difficult to hold on to any hope in their lives. Through the Eucharist, may they find hope in you.

We pray for our parish family. May our shared experience of the Eucharist bring us together as the community of Christ.

Reflection/Thinking Prayer

Jesus, you are the Bread of Life.

Thank you for feeding us with your life and love.

Thank you for the gift of the Eucharist.

Help us to treat the Eucharist with love and respect.

It is you. You are the Bread of Life.

We love and adore you.

Amen.

⊕

---

[13] Clare Maloney, Mary Nugent, *Alive-O 4 Teacher's Book* (Veritas, Dublin, 1999), pp. 384–385.

Our Family Mass Resources for the Family Sunday Liturgy **Year B**

Twentieth Sunday in Ordinary Time

Colour Green

Suggested Décor Images from readings

Theme Jesus is the Bread of Life

Entrance Procession Bread, image of the Host, poster showing complex mathematical equation

Gospel Procession Candles, Lectionary

Welcome
Welcome to our Family Mass. Each week we gather here as the family of God to celebrate the Word and the Eucharist together. Although we may not understand everything that happens or all that is said, let's prepare to open our ears, eyes and hearts to God to allow him to teach us what we need to learn today.

Theme
For the third time, we bring some bread. We remember that our bodies need energy to grow and to play. This bread represents all food and drink – breakfast, lunch, dinner, snacks and treats.

For the third time, we present the Host. During this series of liturgies we hope that we are coming to a greater understanding of just how special the Eucharist, Holy Communion, really is.

We present this equation. To most of us it is just symbols, numbers and letters. Not only might we not understand it, but we might also think we could never understand something as complex and difficult as this.

In our Mass today, we will hear how Jesus yet again describes himself as the Bread of Life, and still his followers do not grasp what he means. We recognise that we might also find this, like the equation, really difficult to understand. That's okay. Let's try together.

Introduction to First Reading
To be wise is to know, not just answers to questions or solutions to puzzles, but to make sense of things. To be wise is not the same as being clever or brainy. In our reading, wisdom is presented as a woman who prepares a feast and invites ignorant people. Ignorant means not wise or knowing. Let's listen.

First Reading
A reading from the book of Proverbs (9:1-6)

Wisdom has built her house and made seven pillars for it. She has had an animal killed for the feast and laid the table. She has sent her servant-girls to call out from the highest places in the town: 'Come in, ignorant people!' And to the foolish man she says, 'Come, eat my food, and drink the wine that I have mixed. Leave the company of ignorant people, and live. Follow the way of knowledge.'

The word of the Lord.

Introduction to Gospel
Yet again, our Gospel features Jesus describing himself as the Bread of Life. His listeners question him. Isn't he just Jesus, Joseph's son? How could he be bread? What does he mean about eating the bread – he is made of flesh, does he mean we must eat his flesh, his skin, his muscles and organs? Let's listen to Jesus and allow his words to enlighten us.

Gospel
A reading from the holy Gospel according to John (6:51-58)

Jesus said to the crowd: 'I am the living bread that came down from heaven. If anyone eats this bread, he will live forever. The bread that I will give is my flesh, which I give so that the world may live.' This started an angry argument among them. 'How can this man give us his flesh to eat?' they asked. Jesus said to them, 'I am telling you the truth: if you do not eat of the flesh of the son of Man and drink his blood, you will not have life in yourselves. Whoever eats me will live because of me. This is the bread that came down from heaven. The one who eats this bread will live forever.'

The Gospel of the Lord.

Song 'Blessed Be God' (from *Alive-O*).[14]

---

[14] John McCann, *Alive-O 4 Teacher's Book* (Veritas, Dublin, 1999), p. 362.

Homily Suggestions

- Refer to the focal objects together. Empathise that just like the complexity of the equation, understanding what Jesus means by being the Bread of Life is very difficult. Reassure the congregation that not understanding is okay. Not understanding does not prevent us from receiving Jesus.

- Perhaps allude to Orthodox terminology of Sacred Mysteries for Sacraments as a means of highlighting 'mystery'. Refer to next week's liturgy where we will examine 'mystery' in more detail.

- Refer to the First Reading. Explain 'wisdom'. Emphasise how wisdom often comes from learning from our mistakes, and from life experience. Consider a blessing for our elderly whose wisdom can be overlooked in society. Encourage the children in the congregation to be more considerate of their older relations.

- Remind the congregation of the elements of the Liturgy of the Eucharist that we have examined in the two previous liturgies. (*See Ordinary Time – An Overview.*) Expand on this if necessary.

Prayer of the Faithful

We pray for our families, especially our older relations. Help us to treat them with respect and listen to their words of wisdom.

We pray for our Church. Bless all those who are Ministers of the Eucharist.

We pray for our leaders. Guide them in looking after the elderly in society and providing for the educational needs of people of all ages.

We pray for those with special needs. May their talents triumph over their difficulties.

We pray for our parish. Guide us in becoming a wise community.

Reflection/Thinking Prayer
Prayer after Communion[15]

Lord Jesus, I love and adore you.

You're a special friend to me.

Welcome, Lord Jesus, O welcome.

Thank you for coming to me.

Thank you, Lord Jesus, O thank you

for giving yourself to me.

Make me strong to show your love

wherever I may be.

Be near me, Lord Jesus, I ask you to stay

close by me forever and love me, I pray.

Bless all of us children in your loving care

and bring us to heaven to live with you there.

I'm ready now, Lord Jesus,

to show how much I care.

I'm ready now to give your love

at home and everywhere. Amen.

⊕

---

[15] From *Alive-O 8 Teacher's Book* (Veritas, Dublin, 2004), p. 46.

Our Family Mass Resources for the Family Sunday Liturgy **Year B**

Twenty-First Sunday in Ordinary Time

Colour Green

Suggested Décor Images from readings, images of long and winding roads

Theme You Alone Are Our God

Entrance Procession Banner reading 'You Alone Are Our God', skipping rope

Gospel Procession Candles, Lectionary

Welcome
Welcome to our Family Mass. We are in a sacred place to pray and celebrate the love of God together. Let's prepare to listen carefully and take part as best as we can.

Theme
We present a skipping rope. Imagine that it represents our lives of faith. You are at one end, God at the other.

(*Two children hold the rope straight*) Our journeys are not straightforward.

(*Two children allow the rope to slacken, making it full of twists; they can also make it 'wave' up and down*) Our lives are full of ups and downs, twists and turns, good days and bad days. Sometimes we might doubt that God is part of our journey, as if the twists and turns block him from our view.

We present our banner. It reads 'You Alone Are Our God'. We will hear this sentiment repeated in both readings today. Hopefully, as we listen to the Word and celebrate the Eucharist together, we can connect the message of our banner with the symbol of a 'long and winding road' – our skipping rope.

Introduction to First Reading
In our reading today, Joshua, a leader, gathers together lots of people. These people have experienced ups and downs, just like us. At times, they have lost sight of God, and followed other paths instead. Joshua wants them to think carefully and asks them just who is it they believe in. Who guides their lives?

First Reading
A reading from the book of Joshua (24:1-2, 15-18)

Joshua gathered all the tribes of Israel together at Shechem. He called the elders, the leaders, the judges, and the officers of Israel, and they came into the presence of God. Joshua said to all the people, 'If you are not willing to serve him, decide today whom you will serve, the gods your ancestors worshipped in Mesopotamia or the gods of the Amorites, in whose land you are now living. As for my family and me, we will serve the Lord.' The people replied, 'We would never leave the Lord to serve other gods! The Lord our God brought our fathers and us out of slavery in Egypt, and we saw the miracles that he performed. He kept us safe wherever we went among all the nations through which we passed. As we advanced into this land, the Lord drove out all the Amorites who lived here. So we also will serve the Lord; he is our God.'

The word of the Lord.

Introduction to Gospel
This reading requires four participants.

Jesus must have been a very patient person. Yet again in our Gospel today we encounter grumbles and complaints from people who do not understand Jesus' teaching. Even more significant is that Simon Peter, possibly Jesus' closest friend, also had his ups and downs with Jesus. Listen carefully. What can you hear that sounds like what we listened to in our First Reading? What does this tell you about Simon Peter?

Gospel
This reading requires four participants.

A reading from the holy Gospel according to John (6:60-69)

Narrator Many of Jesus' followers heard this doctrine and said:

Followers This teaching is too hard. Who can listen to it?

Narrator Without being told, Jesus knew that they were grumbling about this, so he said to them:

Jesus Does this make you want to give up? Suppose, then, that you should see the Son of Man go back up to the place where he was before? What gives life is God's Spirit; man's power is of no use at all. The words I have spoken to you bring God's life-giving Spirit. Yet some of you do not believe.

Narrator Many of Jesus' followers turned back and would not go with him anymore. So he asked the twelve disciples:

Jesus And you – would you also like to leave?

Narrator Simon Peter answered him:

Simon Lord, to whom would we go? You have the words that give eternal life. And now we believe and know that you are the Holy One who has come from God.

The Gospel of the Lord.

Song 'We Come to You, Lord Jesus' (from *Alive-O*).[16]

Homily Suggestions

- Refer to the First Reading, how Joshua gathered people together to encourage them to clarify who it is they are guided by. Ask the congregation to think of this Mass as a similar event. Invite them to think about their own response.

- Refer to the focal object of the skipping rope. It is full of twists and turns, just like our lives. Older members of the congregation could relate it to The Beatles' song 'The Long and Winding Road'. Emphasise that we all experience times during our lives when we are unsure where God is in our lives, or even if God is there at all, but just as the song says, 'The road always leads to your door'. Using this analogy, the door is God's welcoming embrace, and God's 'door' is always open to us.

- Mention the things in life that can distract us from God, such as getting carried away by our work, other people, our ambitions for success … highlight that these are just distractions. God is our source and our goal. Refer to the banner 'You Alone Are Our God'.

- Refer to Simon Peter in the Gospel. Allude to other examples from Scripture that show how Peter had ups and downs in his relationship with Jesus (for example Mark 8:31-33, Matthew 26:32-35, John 21:15-19). Suggest that the commitment of Peter is a great role model for us because his journey of faith was tumultuous yet he always returned to the one true God.

Prayer of the Faithful

We pray for our families. May God's love be at the heart of our family life supporting us through our difficulties.

We pray for our Church. May Jesus be the guiding light of truth through all the difficulties that the Church has recently faced.

We pray for our leaders. Help them to remain focused on serving the needs of all in society, especially the elderly, poor and sick.

We pray for those who have lost sight of God in their lives. May they realise the active presence of God in their lives.

We pray for our parish family. Bless all those who work to keep our Church a central feature of our community.

Reflection/Thinking Prayer
You Alone Are Our God

Ups and downs, twists and turns
Through the good times and the bad.
When we are healthy, fit and happy,
When we are ill, worried and sad.

Despite all the distractions that come our way
All the other paths we may have trod.
We hope that at the end of each day
We can honestly say 'You Alone Are Our God'.

⊕

---

[16] Maura Kitching, *Alive-O 4 Teacher's Book* (Veritas, Dublin, 1999), pp. 360–361.

Our Family Mass Resources for the Family Sunday Liturgy **Year B**

Twenty-Second Sunday in Ordinary Time

Colour Green

Suggested Décor Images from readings, symbol of Ten Commandments, quote from 1 Jn 4:19: 'We love because he first loved us'

Theme God Comes First

Entrance Procession Symbol of Ten Commandments (such as that from Jesse Tree), banner reading 'God Comes First'

Gospel Procession Candles, Lectionary

Welcome
Welcome to our Family Mass. Please take a few moments to forget about all the hustle and bustle of life, to forget about what we have done so far today and what is ahead of us later. We are here to focus on celebrating the Liturgy of the Word and of the Eucharist. Let's prepare to do our best.

Theme
We present the symbol of the Ten Commandments. These were given to Moses by God. The Ten Commandments were guidelines on how to live as God wished us to live. In any relationship we have agreements, expectations of how we should treat each other. In our relationship with God, the Ten Commandments formed the basis of how we should live in relationship with God.

We present our banner 'God Comes First'. In the Bible we are told, 'We love because he first loved us' (1 Jn 4:19). We need to remember that amongst everything else, all the busyness of our lives, God comes first. During our Mass today, we ask that God will reach out into our hearts and that we will embrace this simple truth: God comes first.

Introduction to First Reading
Just as Jesus taught the same message many times, we hear in our First Reading how Moses, who lived years before Jesus, and who led the Israelites out of slavery in Egypt, reminded them of the Ten Commandments. These were the guidelines of how to live in relationship with God. Moses tells the people just how important the Ten Commandments are. Let's listen.

First Reading
A reading from the book of Deuteronomy (4:1-2, 6-8)

Moses said to the people, 'Obey all the laws that I am teaching you, and you will live and occupy the land which the Lord, the God of your ancestors, is giving you. Do not add anything to what I command you, and do not take anything away. Obey the commands of the Lord your God that I have given you. Obey them faithfully, and this will show the people of other nations how wise you are. When they hear of all these laws, they will say, 'What wisdom and understanding this great nation has!' No other nation, no matter how great, has a god who is so near when they need him as the Lord our God is to us. He answers us whenever we call for help. No other nation, no matter how great, has laws so just as those that I have taught you today.'

The word of the Lord.

Introduction to Gospel
Centuries after Moses, many of the Israelites focused so much on the rituals and rules involved in following the Law that their actions became like empty habits. Have you ever done something so often that you forget why you do it in the first place? Jesus observes this empty behaviour and reminds the people that simply following God with all our hearts is the most important thing we can do. It is more important than any ritual or ceremony that we have invented.

Gospel
A reading from the holy Gospel according to Mark (7:1-8, 14-15, 21-23)

Some Pharisees and teachers of the Law who had come from Jerusalem gathered round Jesus. They noticed that some of his disciples were eating their food with hands that were ritually unclean – that is, they had not washed them in the way the Pharisees said people should. For the Pharisees, as well as the rest of the Jews, follow the teaching they received from their ancestors: they do not eat unless they wash their hands in the proper way; nor do they eat anything that comes from the market unless they wash it first. And they follow many other rules which they have received, such as the proper way to wash cups, pots, copper bowls, and beds. So the Pharisees and the teachers of the Law asked Jesus, 'Why is it that your disciples do not follow the teaching handed down by our ancestors, but instead eat with ritually unclean hands?' Jesus answered them, 'How right Isaiah was when he prophesied about you. You are hypocrites, just as he wrote: "These people, says God, honour me with their words, but their heart is really far away from me. It is no use for them to worship me, because they teach man-made rules as though they were God's laws!" You put aside God's command and obey the teachings of men.'

The Gospel of the Lord.

Dramatisation of Gospel
See Appendix III, pp. 218.

Homily Suggestions
- Invite the congregation to think about some of the following:
  - Why do they come to Mass?
  - Why do they bless themselves?
  - Why do they pray in the morning, at night, before/after meals?
  - Why do they value kindness, gentleness, truth, respect and so on?
- Encourage the congregation to be aware of whether their thoughts/behaviour are more of a habit than a meaningful action.
- Recount the Ten Commandments (a modern format version can be found in Appendix II, p. 205).
- Challenge the congregation to be mindful of putting God first during the coming week. When they are faced with a decision, consciously think about God and God's will first before making their choice. Encourage them to reflect upon the change in their lives afterwards.
- Focus on the Scripture quotation from 1 Jn 4:19. We love because God first loved us. All love comes from God. Everything and everyone has its source in God. This is so basic and essential that we can overlook its significance. Allow some time for the congregation to reflect on this. Highlight how it is our duty to put God first, just as God puts us first.

Prayer of the Faithful
We pray for our families. Help us to treasure each other, rather than taking each other for granted.

We pray for our Church. Help her in her mission to spread the simple truth that 'We love because God loved us first'.

We pray for our leaders. Help them to make laws and policies that deal directly with the most important needs of all people – health care, justice and education.

We pray for those who feel lost or without guidance in their lives. Help them to follow you in faith and love.

We pray for our parish. May we grow to recognise God in each other and build a real community with you at its heart.

Reflection/Thinking Prayer
Dear God,

We pray that we will remember how you loved us first.

We pray that we accept that all things have their origin in you.

Help us to think of you as we approach our decisions and choices.

This week, be with us as we try to really make the effort of putting you first in everything we say and do.

We ask this through Christ our Lord.

Amen.

✠

Our Family Mass Resources for the Family Sunday Liturgy **Year B**

Twenty-Third Sunday in Ordinary Time

Colour Green

Suggested Décor Images from readings

Theme God, Hope

Entrance Procession Baptismal candle, image of the Host, banner reading 'Hope'

Gospel Procession Candles, Lectionary

Welcome
Welcome to our Family Mass. Whether we also know each other from school or work, see each other in the shops or even if we don't recognise the people sitting here near to us, we are all here for one reason. We are all children of God. Together we make up the Body of Christ and because of our baptism we come here each Sunday to celebrate the Liturgy of the Word and the Eucharist together.

Theme
We bring a baptismal candle. The Sacrament of Baptism was our first step in becoming a member of the family of God. The light from this candle shines for all the days of our life, guiding us through our ups and downs, and focusing our attention on Jesus Christ always. During our readings today we will hear about certain actions and words that also happen during the Sacrament of Baptism.

We present an image of the Host. During Mass, the bread is blessed, or consecrated, and it becomes the Body of Christ. Each time we receive the Host, we renew our commitment to being the Body of Christ in the world. All that Jesus did for others in his life on this earth, we are called to do for one another now. This is a challenge, and our path as Christians is not always easy.

This brings us to our banner which reads 'Hope'. Both the light of our Baptismal Candle and the Host remind us that no matter how difficult our path in life may be, no matter what hardships we face, we can always hope in Jesus Christ. Our readings today will show us this joyous hope that Jesus offers to us.

Introduction to First Reading
The Prophet Isaiah wrote a lot about the coming of someone special, a messiah or saviour, who would bring us hope and help us to overcome our difficulties. This particular passage is full of hope and joy. Let's listen together.

First Reading
A reading from the prophet Isaiah (35:4-7)

Tell everyone who is discouraged, 'Be strong and don't be afraid! God is coming to your rescue, coming to punish your enemies. The blind will be able to see, and the deaf will hear. The lame will leap and dance, and those who cannot speak will shout for joy.'

The word of the Lord.

Introduction to Gospel
Think back on all the miracles we heard of in our First Reading. Our Gospel passage features one such miracle, performed by our Saviour Jesus. Pay close attention to the actions of Jesus and the words he speaks.

Gospel
A reading from the holy Gospel according to Mark (7:31-37)

Jesus left the neighbourhood of Tyre and went on through Sidon to Lake Galilee, going by way of the territory of the Ten Towns. Some people brought him a man who was deaf and could hardly speak, and they begged Jesus to place his hands on him. So Jesus took him off alone, away from the crowd, put his fingers in the man's ears, spat, and touched the man's tongue. Then Jesus looked up to heaven, gave a deep groan, and said to the man, 'Ephphatha,' which means, 'Open up!' At once the man was able to hear, his speech impediment was removed, and he began to talk without any trouble. Then Jesus ordered the people not to speak of it to anyone; but the more he ordered them not to, the more they spoke. And all who heard were completely amazed. 'How well he does everything!' they exclaimed. 'He even causes the deaf to hear and the dumb to speak!'

The Gospel of the Lord.

Song 'We are the Body of Christ' (from *Alive-O*).[17]

[17] Fr Peter O'Reilly, *Alive-O 6 Teacher's Book* (Veritas, Dublin, 2002), pp. 211–212.

Homily Suggestions

- Refer to the baptismal candle. Highlight the aspects of the Gospel that feature in the Sacrament of Baptism (Ephphetha). Consider a brief explanation of the elements of the Rite of Baptism.

- Stress the centrality of the Eucharist. This is the body and blood of Christ and we 'do this in memory of' him. Reiterate the challenge of being the Body of Christ in the world today. Empathise that it can be difficult to be openly Christian in today's society at times, but that the Eucharist strengthens us in our mission, with the assistance of the Holy Spirit.

- Dispel images of the healings and miracles from the First Reading and Gospel as works of magic, or indeed, that we are called upon to do such deeds either. Instead, highlight that nothing is impossible to God. Where there is darkness, God brings light, where there is despair God brings hope (refer to banner 'Hope')

Prayer of the Faithful

We pray for our families, especially those who are ill or feeling without hope at this time. Help us, as the Body of Christ, to bring a sense of togetherness and support to each other.

We pray for our Church. We especially pray for anyone who has received the Sacrament of Baptism this year, and for those receiving the Sacrament of the Sick.

We pray for our leaders. In times of darkness and difficulty, may they follow the guiding light of Jesus in the hope of justice and peaceful resolution.

We pray for those who are sick, in mind or body. May their spirits be lifted by hope in Jesus Christ. May they experience healing and peace in the presence of God.

We pray for our parish family. May we truly work together as the Body of Christ.

Reflection/Thinking Prayer

Open up our hearts,
Let the light of Jesus shine,
Healing, hope and happiness,
Into our bodies and minds.

Open up our ears
So we may listen to your Word.
Teach us how to live,
To be just, fair and good.

Open up our mouths
So that we can speak the Truth,
So that we can spread the Gospel message
And bear the Spirit's fruit.

✠

Our Family Mass Resources for the Family Sunday Liturgy **Year B**

Twenty-Fourth Sunday in Ordinary Time

Colour Green

Suggested Décor Images from readings, pictures of candles

Theme God is with us

Entrance Procession Banner reading 'God is with us', candle

Gospel Procession Candles, Lectionary

Welcome
Welcome to our Family Mass. You belong here. All of us together are the family of God. Let's take a moment to let go of anything that is on our mind, of the plans ahead of us, or troubles behind us. Let us simply be ourselves in the presence of God.

Theme
Our banner reads 'God is with us'. Maybe this is something we should remind ourselves of every day – as we wake, when we eat, as we fall asleep. On good days, when everything seems to go our way, it can be easy to remember that God is with us. We need to remember too that on bad days, God is still with us.

We present a candle. We light a candle to bring light to the darkness. In our Church, we might light a candle when praying for a particular intention or person. Sometimes, a candle in the window can be a sign of welcome for the baby Jesus at Christmas time. Overall, a candle tells us that God is present. Even the little flame of a candle can remind us of the massive Good News that God is with us.

Introduction to First Reading
In our First Reading, we hear about the hardships that came with being a prophet. Isaiah tells us how people make fun of him, even hurt him physically, all because he spoke for God. The one thing that kept Isaiah going through all these difficulties was his faith in God, knowing that God was with him always.

First Reading
A reading from the prophet Isaiah (50:5-9)

The Lord has given me understanding, and I have not rebelled or turned away from him. I bared my back to those who beat me. I did not stop them when they insulted me, when they pulled out the hairs of my beard and spat in my face. But their insults cannot hurt me because the Sovereign Lord gives me help. I brace myself to endure them. I know that I will not be disgraced, for God is near, and he will prove me innocent. Does anyone dare to bring charges against me? Let us go to court together! Let him bring his accusation! The Sovereign Lord defends me – who, then, can prove me guilty?

The word of the Lord.

Introduction to Gospel
Have you ever asked the question 'Who is Jesus?' Even Jesus himself asked his friends once. He asked, 'Who do people say that I am?' Then he asked for their own opinion, as his friends surely knew him better: 'Who do you say I am?' Let's listen to their answers together.

Gospel
A reading from the holy Gospel according to Mark (8:27-35)

Jesus and his disciples went away to the villages near Caesarea Philippi. On the way he asked them, 'Tell me, who do people say I am?' 'Some say that you are John the Baptist,' they answered; 'others say that you are Elijah, while others say that you are one of the prophets.' 'What about you?' he asked them. 'Who do you say I am?' Peter answered, 'You are the Messiah.'

The Gospel of the Lord.

Song 'Críost Liom' (from *Alive-O*).[18]

Homily Suggestions
- Refer to First Reading. Highlight that throughout history Christians have experienced difficulties. It has been hard to hold onto our faith when others ridicule us, for example, children might be made fun of for saying their prayers aloud, for going to Mass if it's not the 'done' thing and so on. When we suffer tragedies in our lives, it is difficult to maintain our faith. Point the congregation to Scripture for many instances in which prophets in particular had a tough time proclaiming the message given to them by God.

---

18 Bernard Sexton, *Alive-O 7 Teacher's Book* (Veritas, Dublin, 2003), p. 294.

- Give examples of times when we might be glad of some companionship, someone to hold our hand or give us a sense of security, for example, a first trip on a plane, going to the dentist, attending a funeral and so on. Refer to the poem 'Footprints in the Sand' to highlight the presence of God even when we might not be aware of it.
- Refer to the focal object of the candles. Emphasise the safety aspects surrounding the use of candles (battery-operated lights would be a suitable substitute if necessary). Suggest that as a family, together a candle could be lit for a period of time just to bring awareness to the presence of God among us, perhaps at the dinner table or for a time of quiet reflection and prayer.
- Refer to the Gospel. Briefly explain the term 'Messiah', the 'Anointed One'. Consider a short description of how Jesus was the Messiah, the Saviour, the 'Anointed One'. For example, when we light our candle, we could do so in recognition and acceptance of Jesus as the Messiah.

Prayer of the Faithful

We pray for our families, especially our mammies and daddies, who look after us, care for us, keep us safe and cheer us up.

We pray for our Church. In times of difficulty, may the faithful be assured by the light of the world – Jesus Christ our Saviour.

We pray for our leaders. Help them to be good leaders for all in their duty of care.

We pray for those who have lost their faith. May they find strength in their parish community and rekindle their relationship with God.

We pray for our parish. Help us to recognise that God is with us always, in and working through each other. May we always welcome God's presence.

Reflection/Thinking Prayer

Jesus, our friend and Saviour

You suffered. You experienced sadness, anxiety and pain. We do too.

But you overcame it all for us, because of your infinite love and trust in your Father.

Our Father.

Because of you, we can overcome our difficulties too.

You have given us the gift of the Spirit so that you are with us always.

We are your Body on this earth.

We can be for each other what you have been for us.

Friend and Saviour.

Thank you.

We promise to try our best to live like you.

For you and for one another.

Amen.

✠

Our Family Mass Resources for the Family Sunday Liturgy Year B

Twenty-Fifth Sunday in Ordinary Time

Colour Green

Suggested Décor Images from readings

Theme God – Reality of Faith

Entrance Procession Newspaper, Bible, image of the Host

Gospel Procession Candles, Lectionary

Welcome
Welcome to our Family Mass. Please take a moment to remember that you are in the presence of God. God loves us and wants us to be here to celebrate the sacred mysteries as his family.

Theme
We bring a newspaper. More often than not, our newspapers tell us about sad stories, bad news and tragedies from around the world. Good news does not seem to make the headlines. It gives the impression that life is full of troubles, worries and problems.

We bring the Bible. The Bible tells us about many people and places. They, too, suffered dreadfully. In it, we hear about wars, oppression, death and exile.

We present the Host. This is God. God the Creator is still with us. This image of the Host, the Body of Christ, reminds us that there is goodness in the world. There can be good news stories. The Bible teaches us that despite all the hardships throughout history, God has remained with us and goodness will continue to prevail. When we celebrate the Eucharist together, we affirm this Good News. Life can be difficult, but God is always with us. That is the reality of our faith.

Introduction to First Reading
Have you ever been made fun of for blessing yourself, saying a prayer, going to Mass or even talking about God? Nearly everyone has that experience. Being a Christian, a believer in God is not easy. Our First Reading comes from many years ago. Even then, people were trying to find ways to ridicule, insult and hurt those who believed in God. Let's listen.

First Reading
A reading from the book of Wisdom (2:12, 17-20)

The godless say to themselves, 'Righteous people are nothing but a nuisance, so let's look for chances to get rid of them. They are against what we do; they accuse us of breaking the law of Moses and violating the traditions of our ancestors. But we'll see if that's true. Let's see what will happen when it's time for them to die! If the righteous really are God's children, God will save them from their enemies. So let's put them to the test. We'll be cruel to them and torment them; then we'll find out how calm and reasonable they are! We'll find out just how much they can stand! We'll condemn them to a shameful death. After all, they say that God will protect them.'

The word of the Lord.

Introduction to Gospel
You have heard the phrase 'the Good News'. It's understandable that you would expect the 'Good News' to be all happy and joyful. It's understandable that the suffering and death of Jesus might not seem to fit in with your idea of 'Good News'. The disciples felt like that too. It is confusing. But that's okay. Faith is not easy. Let's listen to the Word of God and allow God to teach us to understand more clearly.

Gospel
A reading from the holy Gospel according to Mark (9:30-37)

Jesus and his disciples left that place and went on through Galilee. Jesus did not want anyone to know where he was, because he was teaching his disciples: 'The Son of Man will be handed over to men who will kill him. Three days later, however, he will rise to life.' But they did not understand what this teaching meant, and they were afraid to ask him.

The Gospel of the Lord.

Song
'Jesus, Be With Me' (from *Alive-O*).[19]

---

[19] Geraldine Doggett, *Alive-O 6 Teacher's Book* (Veritas, Dublin, 2002), p. 168.

Homily Suggestions

- Refer to the newspaper and the First Reading. Reiterate how bad news dominates the headlines. Empathise that we all have tough times in our lives and understandably our faith can be shaken.

- Emphasise that to hold on to faith is a challenge. Refer to the image of the Host. Highlight the centrality of the Eucharist to all life, especially in strengthening our faith in both good times and bad. Refer to the Bible and how it tells of salvation throughout a myriad of hardships.

- Invite the congregation to reflect upon the Gospel. Jesus, who initiated the Eucharist, in whose memory we gather today, exemplifies the reality of faith. Good triumphs. Encourage the congregation to place their faith in Jesus, especially through the Sacrament of the Eucharist. Life is not easy and neither is holding onto faith. Jesus and his disciples had this difficulty too. If they triumphed, then so can we.

Prayer of the Faithful

We pray for our families. Through good times and bad, may our faith remain strong and deeply rooted in Jesus Christ.

We pray for our Church. May the presence of the Holy Spirit, sent by Jesus to be with us always, help the Church overcome her many challenges.

We pray for our leaders. Be with them as they try to resolve the problems that face the world today.

We pray for those who find life difficult, who feel unsafe, unloved, hungry or afraid. Strengthen them in their hardship.

We pray for our parish. Help us to look after each other, to bring happiness and security to our community.

Reflection/Thinking Prayer
Be the Good News

Step up. Step up.
Take on the challenge.
Be the Good News
Do whatever you can manage.

Be it share a smile a day
Or say 'Well done you!'
Tell the truth, play fairly,
Remember Jesus is with you.

Life can be tough.
No one said it would be easy.
It's a hard job to be a Christian
And there's lots to keep us busy.

To bring peace where there is conflict.
To bring healing to the ill.
To bring an end to injustice.
To spread happiness and goodwill.

Whatever you can do.
However trivial it may appear.
To be Christian is to work hard at it
Every day of every year.

✠

Our Family Mass Resources for the Family Sunday Liturgy **Year B**

Twenty-Sixth Sunday in Ordinary Time

Colour Green

Suggested Décor Images from readings, images of teams

Theme God's Love is for Everyone

Entrance Procession Banner reading 'God's love is for everyone', poster with 'love' written in many languages, globe

Gospel Procession Candles, Lectionary

Welcome
Welcome to our Family Mass, one and all. Whether this is your first visit or you come here regularly, whether you live nearby or are a visitor, we welcome you to celebrate our Mass together today.

Theme
We present a poster. Written on it is the word 'love' in many different languages. In our world, many languages are spoken. There are many ways to say the same word 'love'.

Here is a globe. There are lots of countries in our world. The world is so big that our entire country only takes up a tiny space on the globe. Imagine how many people there are.

Our banner reads 'God's Love is for Everyone'. All the people in all the countries of the whole world, no matter what language they speak, God invites them all to join in his love. There is no special password or secret code we must solve, God simply offers God's love to everyone.

Introduction to First Reading
Have you ever been to a sports competition? Usually there are only prizes for the winners. In God's eyes, everyone deserves a prize. This prize is God's loving Spirit. In our First Reading, we hear how some people complain that God's Spirit should only belong to them and not to others. Let's listen.

First Reading
A reading from the book of Numbers (11:25-29)

The Lord came down in the cloud and spoke to Moses. He took some of the spirit he had given to Moses and gave it to the seventy leaders. When the spirit came on them, they began to shout like prophets, but not for long. Two of the seventy leaders, Eldad and Medad, had not stayed in the camp and had not gone out to the tent. There in the camp the spirit came on them, and they too began to shout like prophets. A young man ran out to tell Moses what Eldad and Medad were doing. Then Joshua son of Jun, who had been Moses' helper since he was a young man, spoke up and said to Moses, 'Stop them, sir!' Moses answered, 'Are you concerned about my interests? I wish that the Lord would give his spirit to all his people and make all of them shout like prophets!' Then Moses and the seventy leaders of Israel went back to camp.

The word of the Lord.

Introduction to Gospel
This Gospel reading is very similar to our First Reading. Here we see how Jesus is told that someone else seems to be doing God's work. Jesus' followers question him – this other person doesn't belong to their group, why should he be able to do God's work? How do you think Jesus responded?

Gospel
A reading from the holy Gospel according Mark (9:38-43, 47-48)

John said to him, 'Teacher, we saw a man who was driving out demons in your name, and we told him to stop, because he doesn't belong to our group.' 'Do not try to stop him,' Jesus told them, 'because no one who performs a miracle in my name will be able soon afterwards to say evil things about me. For whoever is not against us is for us. I assure you that anyone who gives you a drink of water because you belong to me will certainly receive his reward.'

The Gospel of the Lord.

Dramatisation of Gospel
See Appendix III, p. 218.

Homily Suggestions
- Refer to the focal objects. Emphasise how God's love is offered to everyone.

- Explain to younger members of the congregation that even if they move or travel to another place, they are still loved by God.

- Elaborate on what today's readings mean for our daily interactions with others: we must be more tolerant and welcoming, open to others and inclusive in our behaviours.
- Give some examples of activities to undertake this week: for example, invite other children to play, have a family get-together and so on.
- Highlight local initiatives that promote inclusivity and tolerance.
- If the reflection provided is to be used, consider offering St Francis as an example of someone who saw the 'togetherness' of everything in God, including nature.

Prayer of the Faithful

We pray for our families. Help us to recognise God in each other and to be loving and forgiving just as Jesus would want us to be.

We pray for our Church. Bless all the faithful all over the world.

We pray for our leaders. May they work together to build a global community of peace and justice.

We pray for anyone who feels left out or excluded. May they experience welcome and remember that they are very much loved by God.

We pray for our parish family. Bless all those who work for the good of our community, those who are involved in clubs and organisations that bring people together.

Reflection/Thinking Prayer

St Francis of Assisi believed that God was everywhere and God's love was offered to all. He saw his job as trying to live out that truth in his own life. Our reflection today is inspired by a prayer written by St Francis.

Lord, make us instruments of your peace.

Help us to do your work on earth.

Help us to bring people together.

Help us to teach others that God's love is for everyone.

Where there is hatred, let us sow love.

Where there is doubt, let us sow faith.

Where there is despair, help us to bring hope.

Where there is darkness, help us show your light.

Where there is sadness, help us to bring joy.

In giving, we receive.

Help us all to realise the happiness that comes from sharing your love.

Your love knows no boundaries or limits.

Help us to be as welcoming and inclusive as you are.

We ask this through Christ our Lord.

Amen.

✠

Twenty-Seventh Sunday in Ordinary Time

Colour Green

Suggested Décor Images from readings, artwork by children

Theme All of us are Children of God

Entrance Procession Child's blanket, banner reading 'We are the Greatest'

Gospel Procession Candles, Lectionary

Welcome
Welcome to our Family Mass. A special welcome to all children, toddlers and babies. We hope that together we will experience our celebration of the sacred mysteries with a childlike sense of wonder and awe.

Theme
Our Mass today celebrates the importance of children to God. Children are blessed with innocence, the ability to see the world in a special way, full of possibility and creativity. Children love unconditionally. Children trust. We bring a child's blanket to remind us that God sees us all as his children. God wants us to trust, love unconditionally and see the world around us with the joy and wonder of a child.

Our banner reads 'We are the Greatest'. This is the name of a song that celebrates what we will hear Jesus speaking about in our Gospel today. Join us in finding out more as we listen to the Word of God together.

Introduction to First Reading
We were all young once. The trees were seeds, the frogs were tadpoles, our grandparents were babies. Our First Reading gives us an account of Creation. Let's listen together.

First Reading
A reading from the book of Genesis (2:18-24)

The Lord God said, 'It is not good for the man to live alone. I will make a suitable companion to help him.' So he took some soil from the ground and formed all the animals and all the birds. Then he brought them to the man to see what he would name them; and that is how they all got their names. So the man named all the birds and all the animals; but not one of them was a suitable companion to help him. Then the Lord God made the man fall into a deep sleep, and while he was sleeping, he took out one of the man's ribs and closed up the flesh. He formed woman out of the rib and brought her to him. Then the man said, 'At last, here is one of my own kind – bone taken from my bone, and flesh from my own flesh. "Woman" is her name because she was taken out of man.' That is why a man leaves his father and mother and is united with his wife, and they become one.

The word of the Lord.

Introduction to Gospel
Sometimes we give introductions to our Gospel readings to help us understand it better. In this case, let us simply listen to the Word of God and allow Jesus to teach us something very special.

Gospel
A reading from the holy Gospel according to Mark (10:2-16)

Some people brought children to Jesus for him to place his hands on them, but the disciples scolded the people. When Jesus noticed this, he was angry and said to his disciples, 'Let the children come to me, and do not stop them, because the Kingdom of God belongs to such as these. I assure you that whoever does not receive the Kingdom of God like a child will never enter it.' Then he took the children in his arms, placed his hands on each of them, and blessed them.

The Gospel of the Lord.

Song
'We are the Greatest' (from *Alive-O*).[20]

Homily Suggestions
- Refer to the Gospel. Invite the congregation to think about what qualities of children Jesus could be pointing towards – innocence, trust, unconditional love, fun and so on. Remind the older members of the congregation that they were children too and really we are all still children, only older. Encourage all members of the congregation to have a 'childlike heart'.

- Refer to the First Reading. Emphasise that everything has its source in God. Mention how

---

[20] Clare Maloney and Fran Hegarty, *Alive-O 4 Teacher's Book* (Veritas, Dublin, 2004), p. 330.

this can be especially obvious when we are lucky enough to welcome a baby into the family or community. The birth of a child can remind us of the infinite love and power of God the Creator.

- Highlight how we must treasure and protect our children – they are the future.
- Address the children who have yet to make their First Holy Communion. Invite them to join in the celebration of the Eucharist and to come up to the Minister of the Eucharist/Priest for a blessing.

Prayer of the Faithful

We pray for our families, especially those with very young children. Bless them with health and happiness.

We pray for our Church, especially for our altar-servers, youth prayer groups and those who travel to World Youth Day.

We pray for our leaders. Help them to tend to the needs of our youth by providing quality education and job prospects for all.

We pray for families who have suffered the tragic loss of a child, and for those who have been unable to have children of their own. Grant them strength.

We pray for our parish family. Bless all our young people. Help them to grow up keeping you in their hearts and minds always.

Reflection/Thinking Prayer
Why is it, Lord?[21]

Why is it, Lord,
That parents see puddles and think wellies
And our children see magic mirrors
Waiting for a pebble-plop
To ripple into smiles?

Why is it, Lord,
That parents see snow and think gloves
And our children see sleds and slides
And the tingle of a snowflake's farewell kiss
Upon the palm?

Why is it, Lord,
That parents see toys and think tidy
And our children see the endless possibilities
For fantasy and play?

Why is it that when we were growing up
We somehow grew away?
Away from all the joy and wonder
In the everyday?
From carefree to careful,
From outgoing to anxious,
From confident to concerned?
And unless we regain our vision of God
In the here and now
How shall we ever know Him then?

Help us to be humble.
To be led by our children
Into the small joys and special moments
Where miracles abound,
So that hand in hand
We may enter with them
The Kingdom of Heaven.
Amen.
By Christy Kenneally

⊕

---

21 From *Prayer Services for 4–12 Year Olds* (Veritas, Dublin, 2005), p. 29.

Our Family Mass Resources for the Family Sunday Liturgy **Year B**

Twenty-Eighth Sunday in Ordinary Time

Colour Green

Suggested Décor Images from readings

Theme Wisdom: The Parable of the Rich Young Man

Entrance Procession Bag of money (pretend coins or a bag with a money symbol), an empty box

Gospel Procession Candles, Lectionary

Welcome
Welcome to our Family Mass. Let us take a moment to put aside our plans for today, any worries or problems we may have. Let us simply enjoy being here together as we prepare to celebrate the sacred mysteries. Let us try to listen and watch carefully as we allow God to teach us.

Theme
We bring a bag of money. In our Gospel today, we will hear about a rich young man. He was a good man who treated people well and tried his best at whatever he did. The bag of money represents all the stuff in our lives, our games consoles, our treats, our luxuries – things we love. But do we really need them?

We bring an empty box. Have you ever longed for a particular toy or present? When you got it, were you happy forever after? Or did something else catch your attention and you wanted that instead? Our empty box also represents the stuff in our lives, our luxuries, our treats, our treasures. Why is the box empty though? As we celebrate our Mass today, we hope that you will discover the reason for yourself.

Introduction to First Reading
Imagine the genie of the lamp appeared right now and granted you three wishes. What would you wish for? What would you love to have? Or imagine you won the Lotto: how would you spend your fortune? Our First Reading talks about something that is priceless – that means it is worth more than all the wishes and Lotto winnings you could imagine. Let's listen to find out more.

First Reading
A reading from the book of Wisdom (7:7-11)

I prayed and was given understanding. The spirit of Wisdom came to me. I regarded her more highly than any throne or crown. Wealth was nothing compared to her. Precious jewels could not equal her worth; beside Wisdom all the gold in the world is a handful of sand, and silver is nothing more than clay. I valued her more than health and good looks. Hers is a brightness that never grows dim, and I preferred it to any other light.

When Wisdom came to me, all good things came with her.

The word of the Lord.

Introduction to Gospel
Our Gospel features a young man who is a good and kind person. He believes in God. He follows the Law. He also happens to be rich. That shouldn't matter, should it? When he meets Jesus and asks what he needs to do to have eternal life – to always be in the presence of God – he faces the greatest challenge. Let's listen.

Gospel
A reading from the holy Gospel according to Mark (10:17-30)

As Jesus was starting on his way again, a man ran up, knelt before him and asked him, 'Good Teacher, what must I do to receive eternal life?' 'Why do you call me good?' Jesus asked him. 'No one is good except God alone. You know the commandments: "Do not commit murder; do not commit adultery; do not steal; do not accuse anyone falsely; do not cheat; respect your father and mother."' 'Teacher,' the man said, 'ever since I was young, I have obeyed all these commandments.' Jesus looked straight at him with love and said, 'You need only one thing. Go and sell all you have and give the money to the poor, and you will have all the riches in heaven; then come and follow me.' When the man heard this, gloom spread over his face, and he went away sad, because he was very rich.

The Gospel of the Lord.

Dramatisation of Gospel
See Appendix III, p. 218.

Homily Suggestions

- Explain the term 'wisdom', personified as female in Scripture. Consider contrasting it with mere knowledge. Emphasise the depth of wisdom, the significance of experience and the role played by the Spirit in granting us wisdom in our everyday choices and decisions.

- Comment on the proclivity towards materialism and consumerism in the world today. For example, birthday and Christmas gifts are more and more extravagant. Highlight how in times of difficulty we can become more aware of the importance of thoughtful and inexpensive gifts, for example homemade cards and presents.

- Refer to the Gospel. Invite the congregation to reflect on Jesus. Was he materialistic? Was he more concerned with people and their welfare? Provide some time to reflect on what this means for how we should prioritise our lives (some may call it work–life balance, for example).

- Refer to the focal objects. Empathise with younger members of the congregation that the term 'wisdom' is difficult to understand because it is intangible. It may be easier for young people to see the value of something when it is physically obvious. Invite them to think of times they have spent with loved ones. Ask them to imagine 'bottling a memory' – it is intangible but real in some sense. Wisdom is similar – real but intangible.

- Set the congregation a challenge. Ask them to give up one luxury this week in light of this week's Gospel.

Prayer of the Faithful

We pray for our mammies and daddies. We thank them for all the food, clothing and gifts they give us, but also for their thoughtfulness, their trust in us and their unconditional love for us.

We pray for our Church. Bless all missionaries who help to bring the Good News to those in underdeveloped countries.

We pray for our leaders. Help them to make wise decisions for the good of all those in their care.

We pray for anyone who is blinded by illusion of wealth and materialism. Help them to see the beauty of God in the simple things of life.

We pray for our parish. Help us to share our time, wisdom and provisions in the spirit of true community.

Reflection/Thinking Prayer

Dear God,

Help us to see beauty in the simple things around us.

Help us to see the importance of just being there for each other.

Help us to judge what is really valuable in our lives.

We ask that we may be granted wisdom as we journey through difficult times.

We ask this through Christ our Lord.

Amen.

✠

Our Family Mass Resources for the Family Sunday Liturgy **Year B**

Twenty-Ninth Sunday in Ordinary Time

Colour Green

Suggested Décor Images from readings, children's artwork about being 'giving' or generosity

Theme The Suffering Servant

Entrance Procession Image of open hands, banner reading 'Thank you, Jesus'

Gospel Procession Candles, Lectionary

Welcome
Welcome to our Family Mass. We are happy to be in this sacred space to listen to the Word of God, to pray, to sing and to celebrate the Eucharist together.

Theme
We present an image of open hands. With our hands, we can either give or take. Jesus was a giving person. With his hands, he welcomed everyone, he broke bread with his disciples, he healed. In our readings today, we will hear how Jesus ultimately gave his life for us, so that we could enjoy the presence of God forever.

Our banner reads 'Thank you, Jesus'. Three simple words. But these are words we should say with our hearts every day. During our Mass, we hope to discover why we thank Jesus so much.

Introduction to First Reading
The word 'sacrifice' can mean to give up something: for example, during Lent we might give up sweets or chocolate. In our First Reading and our Gospel we will hear about the greatest sacrifice of all. We will also learn more about the importance of giving. Listen carefully.

First Reading
A reading from the prophet Isaiah (53:10-11)

The Lord says, 'It was my will that he should suffer; his death was a sacrifice to bring forgiveness. And so he will see his descendants; he will live a long life, and through him my purpose will succeed. After a life of suffering, he will again have joy; he will know that he did not suffer in vain. My devoted servant, with whom I am pleased, will bear the punishment of many and for his sake I will forgive them.'

The word of the Lord.

Introduction to Gospel
Our First Reading may have been difficult to understand. That's okay. We heard about a servant of God who would suffer for the sake of others, who would give his life so that others could have life. Who do you think the First Reading referred to? Jesus. Jesus was a giving person, and in our Gospel he teaches his disciples that they need to be giving people too. Let's listen and allow Jesus to speak to us.

Gospel
A reading from the holy Gospel according to Mark (10:35-45)

Jesus called them all together and said to them, 'You know that the men who are considered rulers of the heathens have power over them, and the leaders have complete authority. This, however, is not the way it is among you. If one of you wants to be great, he must be the servant of the rest; and if one of you wants to be first, he must be the slave of all. For even the Son of Man did not come to be served; he came to serve and to give his life to redeem many people.'

The Gospel of the Lord.

Song
'Come Holy Spirit' (from *Alive-O*).[22]

Homily Suggestions
- Contrast selfishness to being a giving person. For example, compare a child who hoards toys or a child who shares, a person who is willing to give up watching their favourite programme to bring you to a match, and so on.

- Highlight that being giving and selfless is not the same as letting people take advantage of you.

- Refer to the Gospel: whilst Jesus used the word 'slave', concentrate or being of service to others, for example using your talent for singing to bring joy to those around you.

- Consider addressing some of the difficult terminology of the readings: 'suffering', 'redeem', 'heathen'. Highlight the main message of the importance of being of service to others and how Jesus was of service to us – his sacrifice brought us back into relationship with God.

---

[22] Bernard Sexton, *Alive-O 7 Teacher's Book* (Veritas, Dublin, 2003), p. 188.

- Mention how the image of the 'Suffering Servant' is a popular image of Jesus.
- Encourage the congregation to thank Jesus for such a gift, and challenge them to be giving in their daily interactions with others too.

Prayer of the Faithful

We pray for our mammies and daddies. We thank them for all they give us – our food, clothes and treats, and especially for their time and love.

We pray for our Church. Bless all in our Church who work for charity groups that give to those in need.

We pray for our leaders. Guide them as they work to give a good quality of life to all, especially the poor and marginalised.

We pray for those who are selfish. Grant them the wisdom to see the value of giving.

We pray for our parish. Bless all those who work for the needs of others, especially on a voluntary basis.

Reflection/Thinking Prayer
With these hands

A hand that held me when I took my first step,
A hand to feed me with food lovingly prepared,
A hand to help me cross the road,
A hand to hold me when I am scared.

Hands for high fives and rounds of applause,
Hands for inviting, playing games, having fun,
Hands for giving, reaching out to others,
Open hands offering friendship to everyone.

Thank you, Jesus, for giving so much.
You gave your whole life so that we may live
In the presence of God forever and ever.
With these hands, we promise to be generous and give.

To give of our time, our talents and gifts,
To offer a helping hand when needed.
To put others first and not just think of ourselves.
With these hands, we will show that you succeeded.

✠

Our Family Mass Resources for the Family Sunday Liturgy **Year B**

Thirtieth Sunday in Ordinary Time

Colour Green

Suggested Décor Images from readings

Theme God's Family

Entrance Procession Poster of a family tree, candle

Gospel Procession Candles, Lectionary

Welcome
Welcome to our Family Mass. Thank you for coming. Let us prepare to celebrate the sacred mysteries in this place.

Theme
We bring a poster of a family tree to the altar. Jesus was a Jew. The Jewish people cared a lot about their relatives, and had special regard for their ancestors – parents, grandparents, great-grandparents and so on. We record the names of our ancestors on family trees like these. In our Gospel we will hear Jesus called Son of David. We know that Mary and Joseph raised Jesus, not David. So what does this mean? Well, if we were to look at Joseph's family tree, we would find David. But also, 'Son of David' was a special name given to the person the Jews believed would be their Saviour and King, just as David was a great king.

But here is the best part: we all belong to God's family tree.

We bring a candle. A candle shows us the way. A candle helps us to see more clearly in the darkness. Our Gospel today tells us about a person who was blind but Jesus healed him and the man could see. Jesus is like our candle: he is our Light of the World.

Introduction to First Reading
In our First Reading, we will hear how God is described as a father to Israel, and that Ephraim, a leader, is described as his eldest son. Just as we explained in our Introduction, family trees were very important to the Jewish people. This was a good way for them to understand how everyone belongs to God's family. Let's listen.

First Reading
A reading from the prophet Jeremiah (31:7-9)

The Lord says this, 'Sing with joy for Israel, the greatest of the nations. Sing your song of praise, 'The Lord has saved his people; he has rescued all who are left.' I will bring them from the north and gather them from the ends of the earth. The blind and the lame will come with them, pregnant women and those about to give birth. They will come back a great nation. My people will return weeping, praying as I lead them back. I will guide them to streams of water, on a smooth road where they will not stumble. I am like a father to Israel, and Ephraim is my eldest son.'

The word of the Lord.

Introduction to Gospel
Our First Reading mentioned how God calls all people to him from everywhere, because we are all God's family. Jesus is the Light of our World who shows us this truth. In our Gospel, we will hear how Jesus brings sight to a blind man. Listen carefully: what does Jesus say made the blind man well?

Gospel
A reading from the holy Gospel according to Mark (10:46-52)

They came to Jericho, and as Jesus was leaving with his disciples and a large crowd, a blind beggar named Bartimaeus, son of Timaeus, was sitting by the road. When he heard that it was Jesus of Nazareth, he began to shout, 'Jesus! Son of David! Take pity on me!'

Many of the people scolded him and told him to be quiet. But he shouted even more loudly, 'Son of David, take pity on me!'

Jesus stopped and said, 'Call him.'

So they called the blind man. 'Cheer up!' they said. 'Get up, he is calling you.'

He threw off his cloak, jumped up, and came to Jesus.

'What do you want me to do for you?' Jesus asked him.

'Teacher,' the blind man answered, 'I want to see again.'

'Go,' Jesus told him, 'your faith has made you well.' At once he was able to see and followed Jesus on the road.

The Gospel of the Lord.

Song
'Every Valley' (from *Alive-O*).[23]

Homily Suggestions
- Refer to the family tree. Emphasise that God calls everyone to be in his family. Infer the significance of this openness and welcome for our interactions with others. We ought to be tolerant and inclusive in our daily interactions too.
- Refer to the candle and the Gospel in which the blind man sees. Highlight how Tradition refers to Jesus as the Light of the World. Like a candle, Jesus sheds light, shows the truth and guides us.
- Mention how Jesus said in the Gospel that the blind man's faith made him well. Talk about the importance of our faith too. When we are faced with difficult decisions or problems and cannot see a solution, we can pray for guidance from our friend, Jesus – like a candle to show us the right path.
- Talk about families. Stress the importance of family to the Jewish people, to God, to all of us. Suggest that, this week, members of the congregation should make a special effort to spend time with their families. Perhaps members of the family that we have not seen for a while could be invited for a family get-together and so on.

Prayer of the Faithful
We pray for our families. Be with us as we try to spend more quality time together.

We pray for our Church. Bless the faithful all over the world.

We pray for our leaders. Help them to work towards a world of justice and equality where everyone is treated with respect.

We pray for those who are away from their families at this time. Comfort them in the knowledge that you are always with them.

We pray for our parish community. Help us to be kind and fair to each other, treating others with love and respect because all of us belong to the one family – God's family.

Reflection/Thinking Prayer
As we prepare to go back to our daily lives
help us to bring with us some wisdom from today's Family Mass.

Help us to treasure our own families –
our mammies, daddies, brothers, sisters, grandparents, cousins, aunts and uncles.

We pray that we will treat each other with love as fellow children in God's family.

As Jesus is the Light of the World,
we pray that he will help us to see more clearly.

To see the truth
to see the way forward
to see how we can make a difference to others and the world around us.

We ask this through Christ our Lord.

Amen.

✠

---

[23] Bob Dufford SJ, *Alive-O 8 Teacher's Book* (Veritas, Dublin, 2004), p. 284.

Our Family Mass Resources for the Family Sunday Liturgy **Year B**

Thirty-First Sunday in Ordinary Time

Colour Green

Suggested Décor Images from readings, hearts

Theme Love – the Greatest Commandment

Entrance Procession Large image of a heart, banner reading 'Love one another'

Gospel Procession Candles, Lectionary

Welcome
Welcome to our Family Mass. It is an important and special time for us to be together in the presence of God. Let us try our best to take part in this important celebration of God's love for us, and our love for God.

Theme
We bring an image of a heart to the altar. We can feel our hearts beating. It shows us how alive we are. A heart also makes us think of love. We love our families, our friends and our pets. When we love someone, we try our best to bring happiness to that person. We might make them laugh, listen to their stories or play with them.

Our Mass today reminds us how important love is in our lives. Jesus said that to 'love one another' is the greatest commandment. It is the best thing that we can do. Our banner reads 'Love one another'. When we love each other as God loves us, then we are already trying our best to be the good people that God wishes us to be.

Introduction to First Reading
Our First Reading comes from the time of Moses, who led the Israelites out of slavery and who told them about God's Law – how God wanted his people to live. In particular Moses emphasised how we should love God. Let's listen.

First Reading
A reading from the book of Deuteronomy (6:2-6)

Moses said to the people, 'As long as you live, you and your descendants are to honour the Lord your God and obey his laws that I am giving you, so that you may live in that land a long time. Listen to them, people of Israel, and obey them! Then all will go well with you, and you will become a mighty nation and live in that rich and fertile land, just as the Lord, the God of our ancestors, has promised.

Israel, remember this! The Lord – and the Lord alone – is our God. Love the Lord your God with all your heart, with all your soul, and with all your strength. Never forget these commands that I am giving you today.'

The word of the Lord.

Introduction to Gospel
Remember the Ten Commandments – the Law that Moses received from God on Mount Sinai? The Pharisees and Sadducees followed these guidelines and thought that they would trick Jesus by asking him to choose which of the commandments was most important. Let's listen to how Jesus responded.

Gospel
A reading from the holy Gospel according to Mark (12:28-34)

A teacher of the Law came to Jesus with a question: 'What commandment is the most important of all?'

Jesus replied, 'The most important one is this: "Listen, Israel! The Lord our God is the only Lord. Love the Lord your God with all your heart, with all your soul, with all your mind, and with all your strength." The second most important commandment is this: "Love your neighbour as you love yourself." There is no other commandment more important than these two.'

The Gospel of the Lord.

Song
'Listen' (from *Alive-O*).[24]

Homily Suggestions
- Emphasise how both readings have a simple message for us – that we must love God with all our heart, soul and strength, and we must love our neighbour as ourselves. Allow some time for meaningful reflection on this simple yet profound message.

- Show how Jesus exemplifies how to live by this simple message. Everything about Jesus –

---

[24] Mary MacDonnell, *Alive-O 4 Teacher's Book* (Veritas, Dublin, 1999), p. 339.

his kindness and thoughtfulness, his teaching, healing and actions – shows his love for God and how he loved others just the same.

- Refer to the Gospel – 'love God, and love one another'. Highlight the image of the heart. Talk about how we can use the word 'love' so easily; for example, I love chocolate! Emphasise love as is meant in the Gospel reading – respect, treatment, relationship. Caution against thinking of it as only 'lovey-dovey' love, i.e. hugs and kisses. Rather, love as the joining force between us all – our families, our friends, our planet.
- Ask the congregation to think about how they can:
  - Love God – for example, keeping God part of their daily lives
  - Love your neighbour – for example, thinking about how you would feel if you were 'in their shoes', giving your time and using your talents for the good of others.

Prayer of the Faithful

We pray for our families. May the love we have for each other fill our homes with happiness.

We pray for our Church. May she be a shining example to all of loving God and loving our neighbour.

We pray for our leaders. Help them to work towards peace in our world – bringing love where there is hatred, and justice where there is inequality.

We pray for those who feel unloved. Help them to know that God loves them, and guide the people around them to be more understanding and caring towards them.

We pray for our parish family. May we build a real, living community with the love of God always at its heart.

Reflection/Thinking Prayer
Choose Love![25]

Choose Love!
Love God!
Love one another!
God of love, you love each one of us with an everlasting love.
You want us to live with you forever in love in heaven.
Teach us, as we live, to choose love each day.

Response Choose love!

In all we say … (R)

In all we do … (R)

In all we think … (R)

In all we pray for … (R)

In all we work for … (R)

In all we hope for … (R)

In our homes … (R)

In our school … (R)

In our play … (R)

In the fun … (R)

In the good times … (R)

In the hard times … (R)

As we try to live the Kingdom lives … (R)

God our Father, fill our hearts with your love so that we may truly know how to love you and each other on earth and in heaven.
Amen.

⊕

---

25 From *Alive-O 8 Teacher's Book* (Veritas, Dublin, 2004), p. 241.

Our Family Mass Resources for the Family Sunday Liturgy **Year B**

Thirty-Second Sunday in Ordinary Time

Colour Green

Suggested Décor Images from readings

Theme 'Good goods in small parcels'

Entrance Procession Empty bowl

Gospel Procession Candles, Lectionary

Welcome
Welcome to our Family Mass. Each and every one of us is welcome here today and every day. Don't worry if you don't know all the words to the songs, or all the prayers yet. Your presence here shows that you love God. Sometimes that is simply enough. Let's celebrate being here together.

Theme
We bring only one object in our entrance procession today. It is an empty bowl. Why bother, you may ask? In both our readings today we will hear about the problem of not having enough for basic needs such as food for the next meal. Sometimes our bowl of life can feel empty, as if we have very little left to offer. We feel as if we are not good enough.

But there is something else we bring to our Mass every single time – ourselves. It might not seem like much, but we all made the effort to come here today. Isn't that something?

Our Mass today encourages us to have hope and recognise the value of whatever talents, gifts and possessions we have. The real value. There is a saying, 'There are good goods in small parcels.' As we celebrate our Mass today, allow God to explain this to you.

Introduction to First Reading
Do you remember when Jesus fed the thousands with just five loaves and two fish? Our First Reading is very similar. It tells us about the prophet Elijah who meets a widow, that is a woman whose husband has died. The widow doubts she has enough food to spare to feed Elijah. Let's listen to what happened.

First Reading
A reading from the first book of Kings (17:10-16)

Elijah went to Zarephath, and as he came to the gate of the town, he saw a widow gathering firewood. 'Please bring me a drink of water,' he said to her. And as she was going to get it, he called out, 'And please bring me some bread too.'

She answered, 'By the living Lord your God I swear that I haven't got any bread. All I have is a handful of flour in a bowl and a drop of olive-oil in a jar. I came here to gather some firewood to take back home and prepare what little I have for my son and me. That will be our last meal, and then we will starve to death.'

'Don't worry,' Elijah said to her. 'Go ahead and prepare your meal. But first make a small loaf from what you have and bring it to me, and then prepare the rest for you and your son. For this is what the Lord, the God of Israel, says: "The bowl will not run out of flour or the jar run out of oil before the day that I, the Lord, send rain."'

The widow went and did as Elijah had told her, and all of them had enough food for many days. As the Lord had promised through Elijah, the bowl did not run out of flour nor did the jar run out of oil.

The word of the Lord.

Introduction to Gospel
Here we meet another widow. She put a few coins into a collection box. Jesus notices her doing this, as well as many others who did the same. But Jesus explains to his disciples how incredible a deed this woman has just done.

Gospel
A reading from the holy Gospel according to Mark (12:41-44)

As Jesus sat near the Temple treasury, he watched the people as they dropped in their money. Many rich men dropped in a lot of money; then a poor widow came along and dropped in two little copper coins, worth about a penny. He called his disciples together and said to them, 'I tell you that this poor widow put more in the offering box than all the others. For the others put in what they had to spare of their riches; but she, poor as she is, put in all she had – she gave all she had to live on.'

The Gospel of the Lord.

Dramatisation of Gospel
See Appendix III, p. 219.

Homily Suggestions
- Refer to the appearance of widows in both readings. Explain the social standing of widows at the time.
- Highlight how the women in both readings did not realise the significance of their 'small' efforts. Similarly, we may not realise the impact of our actions, however trivial, on those around us.
- Refer to the empty bowl. Highlight that it is not in fact empty – it is full of air. Draw a parallel that something we might not see as special, God sees its worth; a gesture we might consider trivial could in fact make someone's day, and so on.
- Invite the congregation to put themselves in the places of both widows in today's readings. Suggest that they may have felt fear, inadequacy, a sense of being insignificant. Reinforce that all of us can feel that way at times, but God sees each and every one of us as indispensable and irreplaceable.
- Challenge the congregation to see the value of the 'little things in life' this week. Offer the example of St Thérèse's 'Little Way' as a guide. Suggest that they become more aware of the value of 'small' gestures and kind words.

Prayer of the Faithful
We pray for our families. We thank them for all the 'little things' they do for us every day that make a big difference but might go unnoticed.

We pray for our Church. Bless all those who work tirelessly in your name who do not receive the thanks and recognition they deserve.

We pray for our leaders. Help them to look after those most in need in our society.

We pray for those who feel that they are not good enough. Help them to recognise their dignity and worth as children of God.

We pray for our parish. We thank the people who quietly contribute to our community in so many ways and yet are not recognised for their efforts.

Reflection/Thinking Prayer
Good goods in small parcels

There are good goods in small parcels,
Or so my Daddy told me.
You see I was the smallest in my class,
Everyone was picked for games before me.

But I had other talents not often seen:
I was gentle, kind and clever.
Some teachers saw this spark in me.
My parents saw it forever.

Did you know that a diamond –
That tiny white gem you see on rings –
Is the toughest element in the whole wide world
And one of the most valuable things?

You see there are good goods in small parcels,
Just as my Daddy said.
You might not think you have much to offer
But try to keep this thought in your head.

That smile you have, go on ... let's see it,
Tomorrow, just give it away.
It might not seem like much to you
But it might make someone else's day.

Give an extra hour or two
To sit with a relative or friend.
It might not seem like much to you
But to them, their joy will have no end.

There are good goods in small parcels,
My Daddy, he was right.
So do the best with whatever you have,
Give it all your strength and might.

✠

Our Family Mass Resources for the Family Sunday Liturgy **Year B**

Thirty-Third Sunday in Ordinary Time

Colour Green

Suggested Décor Images from readings

Theme Light and Eternal Life

Entrance Procession Different types of lights, lanterns and lamps

Gospel Procession Candles, Lectionary

Welcome
Welcome to our Family Mass. You are all welcome. In this sacred space, we will listen to the Word of God and celebrate the Eucharist in memory of Jesus. Let's do our best to listen well and take part as best as we can.

Theme
We bring many different lights to the altar. Just as there as many different lights, there are many different people who live and have lived in other places and at other times. Some people have passed away and are with God in heaven; others are yet to be born. Then here we are too. In today's Mass we will hear about people from many times and places. We will hear lots about light too.

Listen carefully and open your heart to the wisdom of God as we hear about light, life and the end of all time.

Introduction to First Reading
Our faith regards the angel Michael as a great defender. He is mentioned in our reading which tells of a vision of the end of time by the prophet Daniel. Listen carefully. You will also hear about lights.

First Reading
A reading from the prophet Daniel (12:1-3)

At that time the great angel Michael, who guards your people, will appear. Then there will be a time of troubles, the worst since nations first came into existence. When that time comes, all the people of your nation whose names are written in God's book will be saved. Many of those who have already died will live again: some will enjoy eternal life, and some will suffer eternal disgrace. The wise leaders will shine with all the brightness of the sky. And those who have taught many people to do what is right will shine like the stars forever.

The word of the Lord.

Introduction to Gospel
Our Gospel today also describes the end of time. When we think of the end, like the end of a film or a game, we might think that it is over, finished and most of all, sad. But listen to our Gospel. Feel the sense of hope it describes. Imagine the wonderful gathering and unity that awaits us.

Gospel
A reading from the holy Gospel according to Mark (13:24-32)

In the days after the time of trouble the sun will grow dark, the moon will no longer shine, the stars will fall from heaven, and the powers in space will be driven from their courses. Then the Son of Man will appear, coming in the clouds with great power and glory. He will send the angels out to the four corners of the earth to gather God's chosen people from one end of the world to the other.

The Gospel of the Lord.

Song
'Christ be our Light' (from *Alive-O*).[26]

Homily Suggestions
- Refer to the different types of light. Although different, they share the element of light. Similarly, the world is full of different people who speak many languages, live in different cultures and do various jobs. Some people are alive now, others yet to be born, still others already passed away. All share the one light within them, as children of God, made in the image of God – the light of Christ.

- Reiterate that our faith's understanding of the end of time is that we will all be together again as the family of God. It is not a sad time, like the sadness we might experience at the end of holidays, for example.

- Stress that we must do our very best to be good people while here on earth because of the great gift of eternal life that Jesus won for us.

---

26 Bernadette Farrell, *Alive-O 8 Teacher's Book* (Veritas, Dublin, 2004), pp. 273–274.

- Refer to eternal life. Explain that Jesus defeated death and was raised to new life so that we could enjoy the presence of God for all time. Death is not the end. There is the eternal life with God. Some younger children may benefit from the use of the term 'heaven'.

- Refer to the stars in the readings. When the sun sets, we see the stars. The stars are always there, only the brightness of the sun prevents us from seeing them. The darkness allows us to see them. When the sun sets for all time, at the end of time, we can imagine our eternal life as the stars. Always there, together, only visible now because of the darkness.

- Emphasise the togetherness and gathering in both readings. This may be of particular benefit to anyone in mourning. Stress that God and all God's family will be together.

Prayer of the Faithful
We pray for our families, especially those who have passed away and already enjoy eternal life with you in heaven.

We pray for our Church. Bless all the faithful, those here on earth, those preparing to share in the glory of God's presence and those already with God in heaven.

We pray for our leaders. May they be guided by your light in providing a quality standard of life for all people.

We pray for those who are sick or afraid. Grant them strength and bring the light of healing and hope to their lives.

We pray for our parish. Help us to be shining examples of what it means to belong to God's family.

Reflection/Thinking Prayer
Dear God,

We thank you for all the many different ways you show us your love.

We thank you for the various gifts and blessings you give us.

We thank you for the wondrous gift of life.

We thank you for the gift of eternal life, to be forever in your loving presence.

The light that will never go out.

We pray that we will recognise this light – you – within each one of us.

We pray that we will use our talents and gifts to help this light shine.

Shine brightly for all to see.

We ask this through Christ our Lord.

Amen.

⊕

Our Family Mass Resources for the Family Sunday Liturgy **Year B**

Our Lord Jesus Christ, Universal King

Colour White

Suggested Décor Images from readings, children's artwork of Jesus

Theme Christ the King

Entrance Procession Candles, crown, shepherd's staff, report card

Gospel Procession Candles, Lectionary

Welcome
Welcome to the final Family Mass of this liturgical year. Next week, we begin a new year in the Church. Let's make the most of our celebration today. Pray with our hearts, sing with our souls and join together in the presence of God's love.

Theme
We bring a crown. Christ is our King. When we call Christ 'King', we might picture him on a throne, but Jesus is not like the kings in our stories and films. Christ leads his people by example – he teaches us how to love God and to love one another. We honour Jesus by trying our best to follow his teachings. We try to be good and faithful people to God.

We bring a shepherd's staff. It reminds us that Jesus is the Good Shepherd. He looks after all his people with tenderness and love. He provides for our needs and guides us when we are lost.

We bring a report card. At the end of this Church year, we will examine how we have fared in following the message of Jesus to love God and love one another.

Introduction to First Reading
Sometimes the prophets had special dreams called visions, shown to them by God. Our reading today describes a vision of the prophet Daniel about someone. Who do you think it might be?

First Reading
A reading from the prophet Daniel (7:13-14)

During this vision in the night, I saw what looked like a human being. He was approaching me, surrounded by clouds, and he went to the one who had been living for ever and was presented to him. He was given authority, honour and royal power, so that the peoples of all nations, races and languages would serve him. His authority would last forever, and his kingdom would never end.

The word of the Lord.

Introduction to Gospel
When Jesus was arrested, the Governor who was in charge, Pilate, asked him about the claim he had heard that Jesus was being called a king. After all, the Jews were meant to answer only to the Emperor and within their own towns, to the Governors – a king would be a threat to the Governor. In our Gospel, we will hear how Jesus and Pilate talk about the meaning of the word 'king'.

Gospel
A reading from the holy Gospel according to John (18:33-37)

Pilate went back into the palace and called Jesus. 'Are you the King of the Jews?' he asked him. Jesus answered, 'Does this question come from you or have others told you about me?' Pilate replied, 'Do you think I am a Jew? It was your own people and the chief priests who handed you over to me. What have you done?' Jesus said, 'My kingdom does not belong to this world; if my kingdom belonged to this world, my followers would fight to keep me from being handed over to the Jewish authorities. No, my kingdom does not belong here!'

So Pilate asked him, 'Are you a king then?'

Jesus answered, 'You say that I am a king. I was born and came into the world for this one purpose, to speak about the truth. Whoever belongs to the truth listens to me.'

The Gospel of the Lord.

Song
'Kingdom Come!' (from *Alive-O*).[27]

---

[27] Fr Peter O'Reilly, *Alive-O 8 Teacher's Book* (Veritas, Dublin, 2004), p. 298.

Homily Suggestions

- Refer to focal object of the crown – compare images of kings in films, e.g. *The Chronicles of Narnia*. Sometimes kings can be portrayed as unkind, giving orders and doing nothing themselves. Highlight how God deserves our respect and commitment, but that God is more like the Good Shepherd (refer to the focal object of the shepherd's staff) – leading by example. That example is the life of Jesus.

- Refer to the focal object of the report card. Rather than thinking about grades and percentages, ask the congregation to imagine how this report card would look if it showed how well we fared in this past year loving God and loving one another. Leave some moment for silent contemplation and encourage the congregation to identify areas in which they 'can do better'.

Prayer of the Faithful

We pray for our mammies, daddies, brothers and sisters. We thank you for their love throughout this year.

We pray for our Church. Thank you for your blessings on the Church in this past year. We ask you to guide the Church in her mission in the new year to come.

We pray for our leaders. May they follow the example of the Good Shepherd, leading with kindness, respect and providing for those most in need.

We pray for those in our parish who have died in the past year and for their loved ones who mourn their passing. May those who have died enjoy your loving presence in heaven, and we ask you to comfort the bereaved.

We pray for our parish family. Thank you for being with us in all our ups and downs this year. We ask you to bless our homes as we enter the new Church year.

Reflection/Thinking Prayer

Using the focal object of the report card:

Imagine you are reading your report card from Jesus for this year.

What might it say?

Take a few moments to think about how you have loved God and loved one another.

Allow a pause after each of the following

When have you shown kindness to others?

When have you put the needs of others before your own?

When have you thanked others for all they do for you?

How have you shown that God is an important part of your life?

How have you put special time aside just to be with God?

For all the times that we have tried our best and have done God's will, we thank you God for your help and guidance.

For all the times that we have not done so well, we are sorry and ask for your forgiveness.

We pray that God will show us the way to try even more in the coming year to love God and love one another as Jesus taught us.

Together we pray:

Our Father,
Who art in heaven
Hallowed be thy name
Thy Kingdom come
Thy will be done
On earth as it is in heaven.
Give us this day our daily bread
And forgive us our trespasses
As we forgive those who trespass against us
And lead us not into temptation
But deliver us from evil.
Amen.

✠

Our Family Mass Resources for the Family Sunday Liturgy **Year B**

VI. Some Major Feast
Feast of Saint Patrick

Colour Green

Suggested Décor Images from readings, children's artwork of theme of St Patrick*

Theme St Patrick, Answering God's call

Entrance Procession Candles, shamrock, crosier, image of child's hand in parent's hand

Gospel Procession Candles, Lectionary

Welcome
Welcome to our Family Mass. Amidst all the parties and parades let's take this special time together in our sacred space to celebrate St Patrick. He answered God's call and we remember him for bringing the Good News to Ireland. Let's try to listen to God's Word and welcome God into our lives too.

Theme
We bring some shamrock to the altar. It is an image that people associate with Patrick and our country.

We bring a crosier. This is like a shepherd's staff – a long stick that shepherds use in their work looking after sheep. It is used by our Church leaders to show how they follow in the footsteps of Jesus, the Good Shepherd. We often see images of St Patrick with a crosier. He was like a shepherd to the people of Ireland – guiding them to the love of God and teaching them the Good News.

We present an image of a child's hand within a parent's hand. In our First Reading, we will hear how God knows and calls to us even from before we are born. He is always there to hold our hand and guide us. St Patrick's life changed when he was just a boy. He answered God's call. We can too.

Introduction to First Reading
Jeremiah was a prophet many years before Jesus. He taught people about God, but he was often made fun of, laughed at and felt miserable. Jeremiah had no confidence in himself, giving excuses to God, such as that he was too young for such a task. Let's listen to how God encouraged Jeremiah and helped him to answer God's call to be a prophet.

First Reading
A reading from the prophet Jeremiah (1:4-9)

The Lord said to me, 'I chose you before I gave you life, and before you were born I selected you to be a prophet to the nations.' I answered, 'Sovereign Lord, I don't know how to speak; I am too young.' But the Lord said to me, 'Do not say that you are too young, but go to the people I send you to, and tell them everything I command you to say. Do not be afraid of them, for I will be with you to protect you. I, the Lord, have spoken!'

Then the Lord stretched out his hand, touched my lips, and said to me, 'Listen, I am giving you the words you must speak. Today I give you authority over nations and kingdoms to uproot and to pull down, to destroy and to overthrow, to build and to plant.'

The word of the Lord.

Introduction to Gospel
The friends of Jesus travelled far and wide to talk to different people about him, about the Good News that God loves us. In our Gospel today, we listen to the instructions given to Jesus' friends on how to spread the Good News – what to do and what to say. Let's listen.

Gospel
A reading from the holy Gospel according to Luke (10:1-12, 17-20)

The Lord said to them, 'Go! I am sending you like lambs among the wolves. Don't take a purse or a beggar's bag or shoes; don't stop to greet anyone on the road. Whenever you go into a house, first say, 'Peace be with this house.' If a peace-loving man lives there, let your greeting of peace remain on him; if not, take back your greeting of peace. Stay in that same house, eating and drinking whatever they offer you, for a worker should be given his pay. Don't move around from one house to another. Whenever you go into a town and are made welcome, eat what is set before you, heal the sick in that town, and say to the people there, "The Kingdom of God has come near you."'

The Gospel of the Lord.

Song
'St Patrick's Song' (from *Alive-O 2*).

Homily Suggestions
- Refer to the First Reading. Compare the reluctance and lack of confidence of Jeremiah to the young Patrick from our stories. Ask the congregation to imagine how Patrick must have felt on returning to Ireland – afraid of rejection, afraid of failure … imagine how Patrick may have felt during his eventful youth.

- Reiterate how Patrick had an eventful childhood, grew in knowledge and love of God, to the point that we remember him for bringing Christianity to Ireland. Emphasise that Patrick's example shows us how, from humble beginnings, even one person has the potential to make such a big difference.

- Refer to the Gospel – God urges his messengers to be determined and focused. Ask the congregation to think about the difference that Patrick made! Mention that he most likely gained followers along the way who helped him in his work, but still … it is with Patrick that we associate Christianity coming to Ireland. Present Patrick as a follower of Jesus, spreading the news, just like the friends of Jesus that we hear about in our Gospel. Emphasise the mandate that Jesus gave to his disciples. We are called to carry out this mission also.

- Refer to shamrock (focal object). Give the example of how Patrick is reputed to have used it as a teaching aid (the Trinity or Sign of the Cross)

- Invite the congregation to thank God for sending Patrick to teach us about Christianity, and to pray that we continue to nourish our faith too, i.e. remind how our faith is a life-long endeavour.

- Refer to the focal object of the crosier – the sign of shepherd: remind the congregation how Jesus is seen as the Good Shepherd. Mention how Patrick is often depicted with a crosier and that bishops still have crosiers as signs of office in the Church today.

- Present the image of the child's hand in the parent's hand. In reference to the First Reading ('I chose you before I gave you life … Do not be afraid of them, for I will be with you to protect you …'), speak about how encouraging it is to know how much God loves us, guides us and looks after us. Jeremiah used his youth as an excuse not to answer God's call; Patrick's eventful youth must have been difficult too; and yet both saw that God was there for them, and they answered God's call.

- Emphasise how our young people can be capable of so much, given the support and guidance we owe them. Encourage the youth of the congregation to be brave like Jeremiah and Patrick, to listen to God's guidance and to have the confidence to answer God's call.

- Refer to how priests, religious, teachers and parents in the local community make a difference. Extend this to include how Irish missionaries across the world have contributed greatly to the spread of Christianity, just like St Patrick. Affirm that in this way, it is certainly a day to be proud to be Irish!

Prayer of the Faithful
We pray for our families. May our homes be places of prayer.

We pray for our Church. Bless all those who travel to spread your Good News.

We pray for our leaders. Guide them in providing what is best for our country's people.

We pray for young people. May they be inspired by Jeremiah and Patrick to do your will.

We pray for our parish. May everyone in our community enjoy the celebrations of this feast day and remember the important influence Patrick had on our faith.

Reflection/Thinking Prayer
Today we will thank God for sending Patrick to Ireland:[1]

Response Thank you, God, for Patrick

For Patrick's courage (R)
For Patrick's love of God (R)
For Patrick's care of others (R)
For all the work Patrick did to help others to know about God's love (R)

---

[1] Taken from *Connecting School and Parish: An Alive-O 1–4 Handbook for Classrooms Visitations* (Veritas, Dublin, 2001), p. 157.

Together we pray Patrick's favourite prayer:

Christ be with me
Christ be beside me
Christ be before me
Christ be at my right hand
Christ be at my left hand
Christ be with me everywhere I go
Christ be my friend forever and ever. Amen.

* Most children will encounter a number of lessons in school on the life of St Patrick. The media also presents different images and stories at this time. Consider arranging to use some artwork from a range of classes/youth groups to decorate the Church for this feast day.

✢

Our Family Mass Resources for the Family Sunday Liturgy **Year B**

Feast of the Assumption

Colour White

Suggested Décor Images from readings, children's artwork of Mary*

Theme The Assumption

Entrance Procession Candles, flowers, image of Mary and infant Jesus, crown

Gospel Procession Candles, Lectionary

Welcome
Welcome to our Family Mass. Let's remember that we are in a special place. Together we will listen to the Word of God and celebrate the Eucharist. Let's try to keep a prayerful atmosphere in which we can welcome God's presence into our lives.

Theme
The Gospels do not mention Mary's death. From very early in the Church's history, we believe that Jesus took his beloved mother Mary, body and soul, into heaven, to share in God's glory. We call this the Assumption. Today we celebrate how special Mary is. She is a 'one of a kind' whose 'yes' to God's call brought Jesus into our world. We honour Mary as our Mother too.

As a token of our love for Mary, we bring some flowers.

To show that we honour Mary as Queen of Heaven, we bring a crown.

Introduction to First Reading
The First Reading comes from the book of the Apocalypse which is full of visions and images. It describes a terrifying moment when a woman, about to give birth, is apparently trapped by a dragon who wants to eat the child as soon as he is born. It reminds us of the importance of Jesus, who was Mary's son. It must have been very difficult for Mary to see her son go through everything, including death on the cross. In the reading, God protects both the mother and the baby. Let's listen to find out how.

First Reading
A reading from the book of the Apocalypse (12:4-6, 10)

The red dragon stood in front of the woman, in order to eat her child as soon as it was born. Then she gave birth to a son, who will rule over all nations with an iron rod. But the child was snatched away and taken to God and his throne. The woman fled to the desert, to a place God had prepared for her, where she will be taken care of for twelve hundred and sixty days. Then I heard a loud voice in heaven saying, 'Now God's salvation has come! Now God has shown his power as King! Now his Messiah has shown his authority!'

The word of the Lord.

Introduction to Gospel
Do you remember when the Angel Gabriel appeared to Mary and asked her to be the Mother of God's Son? What an amazing event that was! We can only imagine how Mary must have felt. Scared? Excited? Nervous? Our Gospel is about her visit to her cousin Elizabeth, who was also pregnant by the power of the Holy Spirit. When Elizabeth saw Mary, they talked about how happy Mary was to do God's work – to be the Mother of his Son. Let's listen.

Gospel
This reading requires three participants.
A reading from the holy Gospel according to Luke (1:39-56)

Narrator Soon afterwards, Mary got ready and hurried off to a town in the hill-country of Judea. She went into Zechariah's house and greeted Elizabeth. When Elizabeth heard Mary's greeting, the baby moved within her. Elizabeth was filled with the Holy Spirit and said in a loud voice:

Elizabeth You are the most blessed of all women, and blessed is the child you will bear! Why should this great thing happen to me, that my Lord's mother comes to visit me? For as soon as I heard your greeting, the baby within me jumped with gladness. How happy you are to believe that the Lord's message to you will come true!

Narrator Mary said:

Mary My heart praises the Lord; my soul is glad because of God my Saviour, for he has remembered me, his lowly servant! From now on, all people will call me happy, because of the great things the mighty God has done for me. His name is holy; from one generation to another he shows mercy to those who honour him. He has stretched out his mighty arm and scattered the proud with all their plans. He has brought down mighty kings from their throne, and lifted up the lowly. He has filled the hungry with good things, and sent the rich away with empty hands. He has kept the promise he made to our ancestors, and has come to the help of his servant Israel. He has remembered to show mercy to Abraham and to all his descendants forever!

Narrator Mary stayed about three months with Elizabeth and then went back home.

The Gospel of the Lord.

Homily Suggestions
- Refer to the First Reading: reassure the congregation that it is not literal, but a symbolic vision. Focus on the importance of Mary in God's plan.
- Refer to the Gospel: explain how Mary's response to Elizabeth became an important prayer called the Magnificat. Ask the congregation to think of other prayers about Mary. Suggest some as examples.
- Mention how we see Mary as the Queen of Heaven (referring to crown) but emphasise that we venerate her but do not worship her, i.e. we only pray to God, and we ask Mary to pray to God for us too.
- Suggest how amazing Mary was – a young woman who went through so much, who saw her only Son suffer, etc. Confirm that Mary is a role model for us. She is known as the First Disciple.
- Clarify that we can think of Mary as our mother too. Relate how special Mary is to how special all our mothers are. Remind the congregation that it is important to treasure our mothers.

Prayer of the Faithful
We pray for all our mothers. Bless them with health and happiness.

We pray for our Church. May she look to Mary as an example of strong and true faith in God.

We pray for our leaders. May they follow the example of Mary by making good decisions and protecting those in need.

We pray for women everywhere who suffer in any way, through sickness, violence or the loss of a child. Be with them in their hour of need.

We pray for our parish. Help us to be inspired by Mary to do God's work and build a faithful community.

Reflection/Thinking Prayer[2]
Mary did what God asked of her.

We now ask Mary to help us to do what God wants us to do. We ask her to help us to grow in God's love as Jesus grew in God's love. We pray:

Response Hail Mary, full of grace

Help us, Mary, to be kind and gentle (R)

Help us, Mary, to be caring at home (R)

Help us, Mary, to be caring when we play together (R)

Help us, Mary, to remember to take special care of children who are younger than ourselves (R)

Help us, Mary, to remember to care for the trees and plants and all of the world of nature (R)

Let us pray together:
Hail Mary, full of grace,
The Lord is with thee
Blessed art thou among women
And blessed is the fruit of thy womb, Jesus.
Holy Mary, Mother of God,
Pray for us sinners,
Now, and at the hour of our death.
Amen.

*As this Feast Day occurs during the summer holidays, it may be easier to collect children's artwork of Mary during the rest of year. This would facilitate a wider collection of artwork to cover various aspects of Mary's life as depicted in the Gospels.

⊕

---

[2] From *Prayer Services for 4–12 Year Olds* (Veritas, Dublin, 2005), p. 481

Our Family Mass Resources for the Family Sunday Liturgy **Year B**

Feast of All Saints

Colour White

Suggested Décor Images from readings, *see overleaf

Theme All Saints Day

Entrance Procession Candles, flowers, one of the items from the list of Suggested Décor

Gospel Procession Candles, Lectionary

Welcome
Welcome to our Family Mass. Today we especially remember those of our family who have died. All those who loved God during their lifetime now enjoy the true happiness of being with God in heaven. We remember that it can be hard to think about those who have died but we will try our best to take part in our celebration today with the love and respect that they would like us to show.

Theme
We bring (*chosen item from procession ideas*) to the altar. We remember that those who have died are still part of God's family. During their lives, they loved God and now they enjoy the fullness of heaven. We can look to them as an example of how we can improve our lives, and we can continue to pray for them and ask them to pray for us.

We bring some flowers to the altar. We look to the colour and beauty of these flowers. We often bring flowers to the graves of our loved ones to show that we are still thinking about them. We keep the saints alive in our memories through prayer, through talking about the members of our families who have died, and by allowing ourselves to be inspired by their lives.

Introduction to First Reading
Our First Reading comes from the last book of the Bible. It is full of visions or images. This particular reading is a vision of the saints in heaven. It mentions the Lamb, another name for Jesus. Listen for the description of all the people dressed in white robes – these are the Saints, who have gone through all the ups and downs of life on earth and are now enjoying the happiness of being fully with God.

First Reading
A reading from the book of the Apocalypse (7:9-10, 13-14)

After this I looked, and there was an enormous crowd – no one could count all the people! They were from every race, tribe, nation, and language, and they stood in front of the throne and of the Lamb, dressed in white robes and holding palm branches in their hands. They called out in a loud voice: 'Salvation comes from our God, who sits on the throne, and from the Lamb!'

One of the elders asked me, 'Who are these people dressed in white robes, and where do they come from?'

'I don't know, sir. You do.' I answered. He said to me, 'These are the people who have come safely through the terrible persecution.'

The word of the Lord.

Introduction to Gospel
Our Gospel is taken from a speech by Jesus about happiness. We know that God wants us to be happy. Today we think about those who have died and enjoy the true happiness of being with God in heaven. Let's listen.

Gospel
A reading from the holy Gospel according to Matthew (5:1-10)

Jesus saw the crowds and went up a hill, where he sat down. His disciples gathered around him, and he began to teach them:

Happy are those who know they are spiritually poor; the Kingdom of heaven belongs to them.

Happy are those who mourn; God will comfort them!

Happy are those who are humble; they will receive what God has promised!

Happy are those whose greatest desire is to do what God requires; God will satisfy them fully!

Happy are those who are merciful to others; God will be merciful to them!

Happy are the pure in heart; they will see God!

Happy are those who work for peace; God will call them his children!

Happy are those who are persecuted because they do what God requires; the Kingdom of heaven belongs to them!

The Gospel of the Lord.

Litany of the Saints and Prayer of Remembrance[3]
We think of all the saints in heaven with Jesus and we ask them to pray for us as we say:

Response Pray for us

Mary, the Mother of Jesus (R)

St Joseph (R)

St Patrick (R)

St Brigid (R)

St Columba (R)

(Other saints, especially local or patron saints could be included here.)

We remember all those who have died and we ask God to bless them, as we say:

Response May they live forever with the saints

God loves all the granddads and grannies who have died (R)

God loves all the dads and mums who have died (R)

God loves all the friends and neighbours who have died (R)

Amen.

Homily Suggestions
- Refer to the Beatitudes: describe how the saints are those who have done their best throughout their lives – coping with various events – and now enjoy the true happiness of being completely with God.

- Clarify who saints are – all those who loved God, members of our families, ordinary good people, as well as those who are now well known.

- Mention the local/patron saint in particular; give a brief description of how their lives reflected their love for God.

- Clarify how the saints are part of God's family, too. We remember them, pray for them and ask them for their intercessions. Mention how we sometimes name children after certain saints or how children choose their confirmation names, etc.

- Suggest that the congregation choose a saint to research and look at ways in which we can imitate them, for example being more prayerful, doing more for charity, etc.

Prayer of the Faithful
We pray for our families. We especially remember the members of our family who have died. We ask you to bless them. May they rest in peace.

We pray for our Church. May she treasure her saints as members of God's family who have put God first in their earthly lives, and now enjoy happiness in heaven.

We pray for our leaders. May they be inspired by the saints to work for the good of others.

We pray for those who mourn the loss of loved ones. Comfort them in their hour of need.

We pray for our parish family. We remember those who have lived in our community and who are now saints in heaven with God. We thank them for their good example. May they rest in peace.

---

3 From *Prayer Services for 4–12 Year Olds* (Veritas, Dublin, 2005), p. 17–18.

Reflection/Thinking Prayer
Today we celebrate the lives of those we love who are now saints in heaven with God.

We celebrate the lives of the saints from long ago, and from other places whose goodness on earth has given them the reward of happiness with God in heaven.

We pray that we will be inspired by their example of how to be true followers of Jesus.

The following is a blessing by Blessed John Henry Newman:

Lord, may you support us all day long
till the shadows lengthen and evening falls,
and the busy world is hushed,
and the fever of life is over and our work is done;
then in your mercy, Lord, grant us a safe lodging,
a holy rest and peace at last.[4]

* Suggested Décor – a few options to consider, depending on the size of parish:

- A display of the names of those in the parish who have died in the last year.

- An appropriately decorated hardcover book called 'Book of the Living' including names of loved ones who have died.[5]

- Children's artwork of the lives of some saints, or lives of loved ones who have died.

---

[4] From Brendan Quinlivan, *Liturgies for Post-Primary Schools* (Veritas, Dublin, 2002), p. 16.

[5] Ibid.

E. Appendices

Appendix I
Mass Responses and Everyday Prayers
Signing

Mass Responses and Everyday Prayers[1]

As primary school children work through religious education programmes such as *Alive-O*, they will encounter the main Mass responses and everyday prayers. Perhaps a particular set of responses or prayers could be given special attention across a number of Family Masses to encourage children to join in.

This section presents the main Mass responses and everyday prayers.

The Lord be with you
And with your spirit.

A reading from the holy Gospel according to ... /*Sliocht as an Soiscéal naofa de réir ...*
Glory to you, O Lord/*Glóir duit, a Thiarna.*

The Body of Christ/*Corp Chríost*
Amen/Áiméan.

Kyrie, eleison
Lord have mercy/*A Thiarna, déan trócaire*

Lord have mercy/*A Thiarna, déan trócaire*

Christ have mercy/*A Chríost, déan trócaire*

Christ have mercy/*A Chríost, déan trócaire.*

Lord have mercy/*A Thiarna, déan trócaire*

Lord have mercy/*A Thiarna, déan trócaire*

---

1 Taken from *Roman Missal* (Veritas, Dublin, 2011).

Our Family Mass Resources for the Family Sunday Liturgy **Year B**

Confiteor

I confess to almighty God,
and to you, my brothers and sisters,
that I have greatly sinned,
in my thoughts and in my words,
in what I have done,
and in what I have failed to do,
through my fault, through my fault,
through my most grievous fault;
therefore I ask blessed Mary, ever virgin,
all the Angels and Saints,
and you, my brothers and sisters,
to pray for me to the Lord our God.
Amen.

Gloria

Glory to God in the highest
and on earth peace to people of good will.
We praise you,
we bless you,
we adore you,
we glorify you,
we give you thanks for your great glory,
Lord God, heavenly King,
O God, almighty Father.
Lord Jesus Christ, only Begotten Son,
Lord God, Lamb of God, Son of the Father,
you take away the sins of the world,
have mercy on us;
you take away the sins of the world,
receive our prayer;
you are seated at the right hand of the Father,
have mercy on us.
You alone are the Holy One,
you alone are the Lord,
you alone are the Most High,
Jesus Christ,
with the Holy Spirit,
in the glory of God the Father.
Amen.

Confiteor

A phobal Dé, tugaimis ár bpeacaí chun cuimhne
chun gurbh fhiú sinn na rúndiamhra naofa a
cheiliúradh.
Admhaím do Dhia uilechumhachtach,
agus daoibhse a bhráithre,
gur pheacaigh mé go trom,
le smaoineamh agus le briathar, le gníomh agus le
faillí,
trí mo choir féin, trí mo choir féin, trí mo mhórchoir
féin.
Ar an ábhar sin, impím ar Naomh-Mhuire Síor-
Ógh,
ar na hAingil agus ar na Naoimh,
agus oraibhse, a bhráithre, guí ar mo shon
chun ár dTiarna Dia.
Go ndéana Dia uilechumhachtach trócaire orainn,
go maithe sé ár bpeacaí dúinn,
agus go dtreoraí sé chun na beatha síoraí sinn.
Amen.

An Ghlóir

Glóir do Dhia sna harda,
agus ar talamh síocháin do lucht dea-thola.
Molaimid thú;
móraimid thú;
adhraimid thú;
tugaimid glóir duit;
gabhaimid buíochas leat as ucht do mhórghlóire;
a Thiarna Dia, a Rí na bhflaitheas;
a Dhia, a Athair uilechumhachtaigh.
A Thiarna, a Aonmhic, a Íosa Críost.
A Thiarna Dia, a Uain Dé, Mac an Athar,
tusa a thógann peacaí an domhain, déan trócaire
orainn;
tusa a thógann peacaí an domhain, glac lenár
nguí.
Tusa atá i do shuí ar dheis an Athar, déan trócaire
orainn.
Óir is tú amháin is Naofa; is tú amháin is Tiarna;
is tú amháin is Ró-Ard,
a Íosa Críost,
mar aon leis an Spiorad Naomh: i nglóir Dé an
tAthair.
Amen.

Apostles' Creed
I believe in God,
the Father almighty,
Creator of heaven and earth.
and in Jesus Christ, his only Son, our Lord,
who was conceived by the Holy Spirit
born of the Virgin Mary.
suffered under Pontius Pilate,
was crucified, died, and was buried;
he descended into hell;
on the third day he rose again from the dead;
he ascended into heaven,
and is seated at the right hand of God the Father almighty;
from there he will come to judge the living and the dead.
I believe in the Holy Spirit,
the holy catholic Church,
the communion of saints,
the forgiveness of sins,
the resurrection of the body,
and life everlasting. Amen.

Cré na nAspal
Creidim i nDia,
an tAthair uilechumhachtach, Cruthaitheoir neimhe agus talún,
agus in Íosa Críost, a Aon-Mhacsan,
ár dTiarna,
a gabhadh ón Spiorad Naomh,
a rugadh ó Mhuire Ógh,
a d'fhulaing páis faoi Phointias Píoláit,
a céasadh ar an gcros, a fuair bás agus a adhlacadh,
a chuaigh síos go hifreann,
a d'éirigh an treas lá ó mhairbh,
a chuaigh suas ar neamh,
atá ina shuí ar dheis Dé an tAthair uilechumhachtach;
as sin tiocfaidh sé chun breithiúnas a thabhairt ar bheo agus ar mhairbh.
Creidim sa Spiorad Naomh,
sa Naomh-Eaglais Chaitliceach,
i gcomaoin na naomh,
i maithiúnas na bpeacaí,
in aiséirí na colainne,
agus sa bheatha shíoraí. Amen.

Nicene Creed

I believe in one God,
the Father almighty,
maker of heaven and earth,
of all that is, visible and invisible.
I believe in one Lord Jesus Christ,
the only Begotten Son of God,
born of the Father before all ages.
God from God, Light from Light,
true God from true God,
begotten, not made, consubstantial with the Father;
through him all things were made.
For us men and for our salvation
he came down from heaven,
and by the Holy Spirit was incarnate of the Virgin Mary,
and became man.
For our sake he was crucified under Pontius Pilate,
he suffered death and was buried,
And rose again on the third day
in accordance with the Scriptures.
He ascended into heaven
and is seated at the right hand of the Father.
He will come again in glory
to judge the living and the dead
and his kingdom will have no end.
I believe in the Holy Spirit, the Lord, the giver of life,
who proceeds from the Father and the Son.
Who with the Father and the Son is adored and glorified,
who has spoken through the Prophets.
I believe in one, holy, catholic and apostolic Church.
I confess one baptism for the forgiveness of sins
and I look forward to the resurrection of the dead
and the life of the world to come. Amen.

Nicene Creed

Creidim in aon Dia amháin,
an tAthair uilechumhachtach,
a rinne neamh agus talamh,
agus an uile ní sofheicthe agus dofheicthe.
Agus in aon Tiarna amháin Íosa Críost, Mac Aonghine Dé,
an té a rugadh ón Athair
sula raibh aon saol ann,
Dia ó Dhia, solas ó sholas,
Fíor-Dhia ó Fhíor-Dhia;
an té a gineadh agus nach ndearnadh,
agus atá de chomhshubstaint leis an Athair:
is tríd a rinneadh an uile ní.
Ar ár son-na, an cine daonna, agus ar son ár slánaithe,
thuirling sé ó neamh.
Ionchollaíodh le cumhacht an Spioraid Naoimh é
i mbroinn na Maighdine Muire
agus ghlac sé nádúr daonna.
Céasadh ar an gcros é freisin ar ár son faoi Phointias Píoláit;
d'fhulaing sé páis, agus adhlacadh é.
D'aiséirigh an treas lá de réir mar a d'fhógair na Scrioptúir;
chuaigh suas ar neamh; tá ina shuí ar dheis an Athar.
Tiocfaidh sé an athuair faoi ghlóir,
le breithiúnas a thabhairt ar bheo agus ar mhairbh,
agus ní bheidh deireadh lena ríocht.
Creidim sa Spiorad Naomh,
Tiarna agus bronntóir na beatha,
an té a ghluaiseann ón Athair agus ón Mac.
Tugtar dó adhradh agus glóir,
mar aon leis an Athair agus leis an Mac:
is é a labhair trí na fáithe.
Creidim san aon Eaglais, naofa, chaitliceach, aspalda.
Admhaím an t-aon bhaisteadh amháin
chun maithiúnas na bpeacaí.
Agus táim ag súil le haiséirí na marbh,
agus le beatha an tsaoil atá le teacht. Amen.

Sanctus

Holy, holy, holy Lord God of hosts.
Heaven and earth are full of your glory.
Hosanna in the highest.
Blessed is he who comes in the name of the Lord.
Hosanna in the highest.

Sanctus

Is naofa, naofa, naofa thú,
a Thiarna, Dia na slua.
Tá neamh agus talamh lán de do ghlóir.
Hósanna sna harda.
Is beannaithe an té atá ag teacht in ainm an Tiarna.
Hósanna sna harda.

Our Father

Our Father who art in heaven
hallowed be thy name.
Thy kingdom come,
thy will be done
on earth as it is in heaven.
Give us this day our daily bread
and forgive us our trespasses
as we forgive those who trespass against us.
And lead us not into temptation
but deliver us from evil. Amen.

An Phaidir

Ár nAthair atá ar neamh,
go naofar d'ainm.
Go dtaga do ríocht,
go ndéantar do thoil ar an talamh
mar a dhéantar ar neamh.
Ár n-arán laethúil tabhair dúinn inniú,
agus maith dúinn ár bhfiacha,
mar a mhaithimidne dár bhféichiúna féin.
Agus ná lig sinn i gcathú,
ach soar sinn ó olc. Áiméan.

Agnus Dei

Lamb of God, you take away the sins of the world:
have mercy on us.
Lamb of God, you take away the sins of the world:
have mercy on us.
Lamb of God, you take away the sins of the world:
grant us peace.

Agnus Dei

A Uain Dé, a thógann peacaí an domhain,
déan trócaire orainn.
A Uain Dé, a thógann peacaí an domhain,
déan trócaire orainn.
A Uain Dé, a thógann peacaí an domhain,
Tabhair dúinn síocháin.

Prayer before Communion

Lord Jesus, come to me.
Lord Jesus, give me your love.
Lord Jesus, come to me and give me yourself.
Lord Jesus, friend of children, come to me.
Lord Jesus, you are my Lord and my God.
Praise to you, Lord Jesus Christ.

Paidir roimh Chomaoineach

A Thiarna Íosa, tar chugam.
A Thiarna Íosa, tabhair dom do ghrá.
A Thiarna Íosa, tar chugam agus tabhair tú féin dom.
A Thiarna Íosa, a chara na bpáistí, tar chugam.
A Thiarna Íosa, is tú mo Thiarna agus mo Dhia.
Moladh leat, a Thiarna Íosa Críost. Áiméan.

Our Family Mass Resources for the Family Sunday Liturgy **Year B**

Prayer after Communion
Lord Jesus, I love and adore you.
You're a special friend to me.
Welcome, Lord Jesus, O welcome.
Thank you for coming to me.
Thank you, Lord Jesus, O thank you
for giving yourself to me.
Make me strong to show your love
wherever I may be.
Be near me, Lord Jesus, I ask you to stay
close by me forever and love me, I pray.
Bless all of us children in your loving care
and bring us to heaven to live with you there.
I'm ready now, Lord Jesus,
to show how much I care.
I'm ready now to give your love
at home and everywhere. Amen.

Paidir tar éis Comaoineach
A Thiarna Íosa, gráim agus adhraim thú.
Is tú mo chara dílis.
Fáilte romhat, a Thiarna Íosa.
Go raibh maith agat as teacht chugam.
Go raibh maith agat, a Thiarna Íosa,
as ucht tú féin a thabhairt dom.
Cabhraigh liom do ghrá a léiriú
cibé áit a mbím.
Bí taobh liom, a Thiarna Íosa,
fan in aice liom go deo.
Beannaigh sinn, na páistí, atá faoi do chúram
agus tabhair ar Neamh sinn chun cónaithe leat
féin.
Táim réidh anois, a Thiarna Íosa,
Tá grá agam go leor.
Táim réidh anois le do ghrá a thabhairt
sa bhaile is don saol mór. Áiméan.

Hail Mary
Hail Mary, full of grace,
the Lord is with thee.
Blessed art thou among women
and blessed is the fruit of thy womb, Jesus.
Holy Mary, mother of God,
pray for us sinners,
now, and at the hour of our death.
Amen.

'S É do Bheatha, a Mhuire
'S é do bheatha, a Mhuire,
atá lán de ghrásta,
tá an Tiarna leat.
Is beannaithe thú idir mhná,
agus is beannaithe toradh do bhroinne, Íosa.
A Naomh Mhuire, a mháthair Dé,
guigh orainn, na peacaigh,
anois agus ar uair ár mbáis.
Áiméan.

Glory be to the Father
Glory be to the Father
and to the Son,
and to the Holy Spirit;
as it was in the beginning,
is now and ever shall be,
world without end. Amen

Glóir don Athair
Glóir don Athair,
agus don Mhac,
agus don Spiorad Naomh;
mar a bhí ó thus,
mar atá anois,
mar a bheas go brách,
le saol na saol. Áiméan.

E. Appendices

Prayer to Jesus
Christ be with me.
Christ be beside me.
Christ be before me.
Christ be behind me.
Christ at my right hand.
Christ at my left hand.
Christ be with me everywhere I go.
Christ be my friend, for ever and ever.
Amen.

Paidir D'Íosa
Críost liom.
Críost romham.
Críost i mo dhiaidh.
Críost ionam.
Críost ar mo dheis.
Críost ar mo chlé.
Críost i mo chuideachta is Cuma cá dtéim.
Críost mar chara agam, anois is go buan.
Áiméan.

Prayers to Mary
Mary, mother of Jesus,
I want to live and love like you.
I want to love the Father,
I want to love like Jesus. Amen.

Mother of Jesus, blessed are you.
Mother of Jesus, my mother too.
Help me to live like Jesus
and help me to live like you.
Amen.

Paidir do Mhuire
A Mhuire, a Mháthair Íosa,
Teastaíonn uaim maireachtáil
agus grá a thabhairt cosúil leatsa.
Teastaíonn uaim grá a thabhairt don Athair.
Teastaíonn uaim grá a thabhairt mar a dhéanann Íosa.

A Mháthair Íosa, is beannaithe thú.
A Mháthair Íosa, is tú mo mháthairse freisin.
Cabhraigh liom maireachtáil cosúil le hÍosa,
agus cabhraigh liom maireachtáil cosúil leatsa.

Prayers to the Holy Spirit
Holy Spirit, I want to do what is right.
Help me.
Holy Spirit, I want to live like Jesus.
Guide me.
Holy Spirit, I want to pray like Jesus.
Teach me. Amen.

Spirit of God in the heavens.
Spirit of God in the seas.
Spirit of God in the mountain-tops.
Spirit of God in me.
Spirit of God in the sunlight.
Spirit of God in the air.
Spirit of God all around me.
Spirit of God everywhere.
Holy Spirit, Spirit of God,
Help me. Amen.

Paidreacha don Spiorad Naomh
A Spiorad Naoimh, ba mhaith liom an rud ceart a dhéanamh.
Cabhraigh liom.
ASpioraid Naoimh, ba mhaith liom maireachtáil mar a mhair Íosa.
Treoraigh mé.
A Spioraid Naoimh, ba mhaith liom guí mar a ghuigh Íosa.
Múin dom é. Áiméan.

Spiorad Dé sna spéartha.
Spiorad Dé sna farraigí.
Spiorad Dé ar na sléibhte.
Spiorad Dé ionam.
Spiorad Dé i solas na gréine.
Spiorad Dé san aer.
Spiorad Dé thart timpeall orainn.
Spiorad Dé i ngach áit.
A Spiorad Naoimh, Spiorad Dé, cabhraigh liom.
Áiméan.

Signing

The *Alive-O* programme teaches some of our everyday prayers accompanied by actions and gestures. This extra visual dimension can enhance our experience of prayer by increasing our comprehension and being more inclusive to those of our congregation who have difficulty with spoken language. Of course, younger people have great fun with the movements too! Here is a sample of the action-prayers from the Alive-O programme.

Hail Mary

Hail Mary, full of grace
(Arms outstretched at the side, palms facing upwards)
The Lord is with thee.
(Arms lifted high above the head)
Blessed art thou among women.
(Arms outstretched in front, palms facing upwards)
And blessed is the fruit of thy womb, Jesus.
(Cradle and gently rock the 'baby' in arms)
Holy Mary, Mother of God,
Pray for us sinners
Now and at the hour of our death. Amen.

Praise the Lord

All the nations of the earth,
(Stretch first one hand, then the other, out in a circular motion)
Praise the Lord
(Raise both hands up to the heavens)
Who brings to birth
(Lower both hands, palms facing down)
The greatest star,
(Sweep one hand in an arc and hold in that position)
The smallest flower,
(Hold out a cupped hand)
Alleluia.
(Bring both hands side by side over head and down.)

Our Father

Our Father, who art in heaven
(Arms crossed over chest)
Hallowed be thy name
(Arms extended, level with shoulders)
Thy Kingdom come
(Arms extended high above head)
Thy will be done on earth as it is in heaven
(Head bowed, hands together in front)
Give us this day our daily bread
(Beckoning actions towards body)
And forgive us our trespasses
(Head bowed, hand on heart)
As we forgive those who trespass against us
(Handshake of friendship towards child beside them)
And lead us not into temptation
(Arms extended in front, hands making a 'pushing away' gesture)
But deliver us from evil
(Hands together in front, head bowed)
Amen.
(Hands outstretched, level with shoulders.)

In God's Space

In you
(Open hands with palms up)
we live
(Raise right hand – or 'starting hand' – high)
and move
(Raise other hand high)
and have our being.
(Raised hands arc across and fold on chest.)

Worth a look!

The **National Chaplaincy for Deaf People** released a DVD in 2005 called *Liturgical Signs and Prayers* to enable interpreters to understand liturgies for deaf people. It is also an aid to educators and parents to teach deaf children and those interested in learning the liturgical signs and prayers of the Church. The Dublin Deaf Choir is also affiliated with this organisation. For more information and contact details, please refer to the *Recommended Resources* section.

Appendix II
Additional Prayers and Services

This appendix contains a collection of prayers, poems and stories for the most common themes and occasions. They can be incorporated into any Mass or service. You might even find that some of the material is more appropriate for the homily. Some items are suitable for children to read aloud, others would be best read by adults as they address the younger members of the congregation. This provides for a welcome variety in material and broader participation in the Family Mass.

For more details of the *Alive-O* products, as well as other materials that are of benefit when sourcing prayers or services for special occasions, please refer to the *Recommended Resources* section.

The *Alive-O* programme contains a treasury of prayers, services and rituals that can be used or adapted for a Family Mass. Special occasions and important family events are addressed by way of story, poem, drama, plays, reflections and activities. In addition, many members of the congregation will already be familiar with them, reinforcing a home–school–parish link.

***

Advent
Patient People (from *Alive-O 7*)
Advent is like a waiting room
for those who take time to make
an appointment with the Spirit of Christmas,
the real one, that is, not the fake
that's everywhere available, twenty-four seven
and in jingling tills rejoice;
the one you plug-in and it squawks 'Merry Christmas'
in battery-operated voices;
the one whose lights get brighter and brasher
with every year that goes by,
as they try to outdo each other: they'll never
outshine that star in the sky.
Those who have made an appointment
with the true Spirit of Christmas know
that waiting rooms are unpopular places
in today's world of get-up-and-go.
What can you do in a waiting room but wait
and wait … till the time is right
and the door to Christmas swings open
and patient people gain insight
to the Christian meaning of Christmas
which sings out in true festive voice,
'Come! Your waiting is over!
Emmanuel! God with us! Rejoice!'

Celebrating Children and Childhood

For celebrating the innocence, humility and closeness of children to God

Why is it, Lord[1]
Why is it, Lord,
That parents see puddles and think wellies
And our children see magic mirrors
Waiting for a pebble-plop
To ripple into smiles?

Why is it, Lord,
That parents see snow and think gloves
And our children see sleds and slides
And the tingle of a snowflake's farewell kiss
Upon the palm?

Why is it, Lord,
That parents see toys and think tidy
And our children see the endless possibilities
For fantasy and play?

Why is it that when we were growing up
We somehow grew away?
Away from all the joy and wonder
In the everyday?
From carefree to careful,
From outgoing to anxious,
From confident to concerned?
And unless we regain our vision of God
In the here and now
How shall we ever know Him then?

Help us to be humble.
To be led by our children
Into the small joys and special moments
Where miracles abound,
So that hand in hand
We may enter with them
The Kingdom of Heaven. Amen.

By Christy Kenneally

Prayer before playing[2]
Praise God for the fun of it.
Glory to God for the friends in it.
Fair play to God for it.

Prayer after playing[3]
Thank God for the fun of it.
Thank God for the friends in it.

For Holiday Times/Times of Travel

Journey Prayer[4]
Arise with me in the morning,
Travel with me through each day,
Welcome me on my arrival.
God, be with me all the way. Amen.

Prayers to Bless the Arrival of Each Month[5]

January
God of New Beginnings, bless us in the month of January – it is the time of new beginnings, the time of promises, the time of hope. We place our hopes and dreams in the care of our loving God that we may become better people when our hopes and dreams come true.

February
God of new life, we bless you in the month of February – it is the time of spring, the time of growth, the time of life. We place our lives in the care of our loving God that we may grow in strength and maturity.

March
God of faith, we bless you in the month of March – it is the time of St Patrick, the time of St Joseph and the time when God became a human in the womb of Mary. We place our faith in the care of our loving God that we may have a source of strength in our time of need.

April
God of the resurrection, we bless you in the month of April – it is the time of Easter, the time of resurrection, the time of eternal life. We place our eternal souls in the care of our loving God that we may live lives worthy of the promises made to us.

---

1 From *Prayer Services for 4–12 Year Olds*, p. 29.
2 From *Children's Everyday Prayerbook for 8–12 Year Olds* (Veritas, Dublin, 2011), p. 7.
3 Ibid.
4 From *Children's Everyday Prayerbook for 7–10 Year Olds*, (Veritas, Dublin, 2007), p. 18.
5 Adapted from *Liturgies for Post-Primary Schools*, pp. 25–28.

May
God of work, we bless you in the month of May – it is the time of study, the time of preparation, the time of perseverance. We place our work and study in the care of our loving God that we may grow in knowledge.

June
God of wisdom, we bless you in the month of June – it is the time of exams, the time of testing, the time of remembering what we have learned. We place our examinations in the care of our loving God that we may receive the reward of our efforts.

July
God of friendship, we bless you in the month of July – it is the time of holidays, the time of sport and games. We place our friendships in the care of our loving God that we may grow closer to one another.

August
God of nature, we bless you in the month of August – it is the time of reaping, the time of harvest, the time of thanksgiving. We place the rewards of our work in the care of our loving God that we may grow in respect for the created world.

September
God of change, we bless you in the month of September – it is the time of return to school, the time of autumn, the time of transition. We place the new opportunities in the care of our loving God that we may grow with every passing year.

October
God of joy, we bless you in the month of October – it is the time of Mary, the time of motherhood, the time of parenthood. We place our parents in the care of our loving God that we may mature in love and respect for all they do for us.

November
God of all who ever lived, we bless you in the month of November – it is the time of all saints, the time of all souls, the time of remembering. We place all who have died in the care of our loving God that we may share eternal life with all those we love.

December
God who became man, we bless you in the month of December – it is the time of families, the time of charity, the time of Christ's birth. We place our families in the care of our loving God that we may be people of charity and love.

For World Day of Peace, 1 January

The Prayer of St Francis[6]
Lord, make me an instrument of your peace.
Where there is hatred, let me sow love.
Where there is injury, pardon,
Where there is doubt, faith,
Where there is despair, hope,
Where there is darkness, light,
Where there is sadness, joy.

O Divine Master,
Grant that I may not so much seek
To be consoled as to console,
To be understood as to understand,
To be loved as to love.
For it is in giving that we receive,
It is in pardoning that we are pardoned,
It is in dying that we are born to eternal life.

Prayer of Praise (to celebrate Spring/Creation)
All the nations of the earth,
Praise the Lord,
Who brings to birth,
The greatest star,
The smallest flower.
Alleluia.

---

6 From *More Liturgies for Post-Primary Schools*, p. 37.

St Brigid (1 February)

Prayer to St Brigid (from *Alive-O*)
Saint Brigid of Ireland,
Help us, we pray,
To be kind and loving
In our work and our play.

Prayer to St Brigid[7]
Brigid, you were a woman of peace,
You brought harmony where there was conflict.
You brought light into the darkness.
You brought hope to the downcast.
May the mantle of your peace
Cover those who are troubled and anxious,
And may peace be firmly rooted
In our hearts and in our world.
Inspire us to act justly and revere all God has made.
Brigid, you were a voice for the wounded and the weary.
Strengthen what is weak within us.
Clam us into a quietness that heals and listens.
May we grow each day into greater wholeness –
In mind, body and spirit.
Amen.

Prayer for the Sick[8]
(World Day of the Sick, 11 February)

God of compassion, we are always under your care and you know the needs of our bodies, hearts and minds. Give us the healing that you desire for us and help us to follow and embrace your plans. Inspire our trust, nourish our faith, be our hope.

St Valentine[9]
God of love, you give us St Valentine as an example of love. His love for you was great. As we celebrate the feast of this loving and caring saint we ask you to bless our relationships. May the love and affection we share for each other always be respectful and honest. May we always follow the example of your Son Jesus Christ who is Lord forever and ever. Amen.

Focusing on the Cross at Easter

Cross in My Pocket[10]
I carry a cross in my pocket
A simple reminder to me
Of the fact that I am a Christian
No matter where I may be.

This little cross is not magic
Nor is it a good luck charm.
It isn't meant to protect me.
From every physical harm.

It's not for identification
For all the world to see.
It's simply an understanding
Between my Saviour and me.

When I put my hand in my pocket
To bring out a coin or key.
The cross is there to remind me
Of the price he paid for me.

It reminds me, too, to be thankful
For my blessings day by day
And strive to serve him better
In all that I do and say.

It's also a daily reminder
Of the peace and comfort I share
With all who know my master
And give themselves to his care.

So, I carry a cross in my pocket
Reminding no one but me
That Jesus Christ is Lord of my life
If only I'll let him be.
By Verna Thomas

---

7 Taken from local parish bulletin, Skerries Parish.
8 Taken from http://www.sacredspace.ie [accessed 13 June 2010].
9 Adapted from *Liturgies for Post-Primary Schools*, p. 30.
10 From *Liturgies for Post-Primary Schools*, pp. 45–46.

A Prayer for Mothering Sunday
Ideally, this would be read out by a daughter, mother and grandmother. If not, a child and two women of appropriate age would suffice, or simply use whichever section is applicable.

Child
Thank you, Mammy, for everything you do for me.
For the cuddles, the hugs, for tucking me in nice and cosy.
For bringing me to places to have fun and to learn.
For playing games with me, even when you have so much to do yourself.
Thank you for all the lunches, dinners and special treats.
For looking after me when I'm sick.
For the little things you do that mean so very much.
I thank God for you and ask God to bless you.

Mammy
Thank you, Mam, for being there for me through my childhood and as I grew up.
Thank you for your advice, even though I didn't always welcome it.
Thank you for supporting me as I started my adult life.
Thank you for teaching me how to be a mother myself.
I thank God for you and ask God to bless you.

Grandmother
Thank you, Mother, for being there for me.
I still talk to you and think of you often.
I miss you but, in this way, I keep your memory alive.
I thank God for having you in my life and I pray that you are happy in heaven with God.

Together
We ask for our Mother Mary's blessing on us all.
Amen.

Prayers for Father's Day

Happy Father's Day – *An Acrostic*
Holding my hand when we're on an adventure
Answering my endless questions of 'Why?, Why? Why?'
Pushing my bicycle home when I get too tired.
Picking me up from school as a surprise.
You are loved for all this and much more!

For reading me bedtime stories,
And giving in when I say 'just one more time!'
Together we have such great fun and laughs
Here's to lots more to come!
Every day I should tell you out loud that I love you,
Remembering that you love me so much too.
So today I say a special prayer for you.

Day of peace and quiet – I hope you enjoy it.
And some special time together to show you how much I care.
You are in my prayers always, not just today.

***

Dear God,
Bless all our daddies.
They have lots of responsibilities.
Be with them, and comfort them when they find things difficult.
Our daddies like to be strong and protective.
Thank you for their determination and their good health.
We ask you to look after our daddies who are sick or in need of help.
We thank you for our daddies and all that they teach us, and do for us.
We pray that you will be with them in a special way today,
Because we love our daddies so very much.
We ask this through Christ our Lord.
Amen.

This is the World that God Made[11]
(A prayer for farmers, millers, bakers)

This is the world that God made.
This is the field
that is part of the world that God made.

This is the wheat
that was planted by the farmer
that grows in the field
that is part of the world that God made.

This is the flour
that was ground by the miller
that comes from the wheat
that was planted by the farmer
that grows in the field
that is part of the world that God made.

This is the bread
that was made by the baker
that contains the flour
that was ground by the miller
that comes from the wheat
that was planted by the farmer
that grows in the field
that is part of the world that God made.

This is our tea when we eat the bread
that was made by the baker
that contains the flour
that was ground by the miller
that comes from the wheat
that was planted by the farmer
that grows in the field
that is part of the world that God made.

This is the day when we say 'THANK YOU'
to the baker,
the miller,
the farmer,
and to God
for giving us bread by which we live
in the wonderful world which God made.
© 2005 T.W.Brighton

Child's Thanksgiving Prayer[12]
(for harvest-time)

Thank you God for all that grows,
Thank you for the sky's rainbows,
Thank you for the stars that shine,
Thank you for these friends of mine,
Thank you for the moon and sun,
Thank you God for all you've done!

Charity
(For example, St Vincent de Paul, 27 September)

Sharing our Time, our Talent and our Treasure[13]
Charity is about giving of ourselves to others. We are asked by God to make sacrifices so that we can help our brothers and sisters who are in need. A clock reminds us of the time we have. We ask God to help us use our time wisely so that we can all play a part in making the world a better place to live in.

We all need a helping hand in life. We are loved by the hugs of our family. We are supported by the handshakes of our friends. We are encouraged by the pat on the back that spurs us to do more. We ask God to help us to be more helpful to those in need.

True riches do not always come from money. We can sometimes be rich in what we have or own, but be poor in what we share. At the collection, we offer a contribution to those who need it. May the sharing of our treasure make us rich in friendship and rich in the sight of God.

---

[11] From http://www.farmingmatters.org.uk/seasons/harvest.html [accessed 13 June 2010].

[12] From http://www.prayer-and-prayers.info/thanksgiving-prayers/childs-thanksgiving-prayer.htm [accessed 13 June 2010].

[13] Adapted from *Liturgies from Post-Primary Schools*, p. 7.

A Child's Prayer for Grandparents[14]
(National Grandparents' Day, 28 September)

Dear God, please bless my grandparents.
Thank you for the life they gave my parents
   and for the life they give to me.

For the ways they helped me and made me
   strong, I give thanks.

For the ways they love me no matter what,
   I rejoice.

For the ways they have paved the road
   that leads me here, I am grateful.

Let them grow in wisdom and joy in life.
Let them find peace and rest from their work.
Let them be healed of every sickness and pain.
And let them see with their own eyes
   the glory of your Son, Jesus,
     in the love of their children and grandchildren.

Bless them always until they come to rest in you.
We ask this through Christ our Lord.
Amen.

For the Feast of Guardian Angels, 2 October

Prayer to the Guardian Angel[15]
Angels sent by God to guide me,
be my light and walk beside me;
be my guardian and protect me;
on the paths of life direct me.

The Guardian[16]
An angel was assigned to you,
On the day you were born;
It watched you as a slumbering babe,
And kept you safe from harm.
It followed every childhood step,
Then guarded you as you grew;
The dangers that you never saw,
God and your angel knew.
For the Father gave an angel,
A mission to fulfil;
To keep and guard your every step,
Was the Heavenly Father's will.
To gently guide you on your path,
To stand and so battle for you;
A constant, holy companion,
Until life's journey is through.
An angel was assigned to you,
On the day that you were born;
A Guardian sent to walk with you,
To keep you safe from harm
   By Allison Chamber Coxsey

---

[14] From http://www.dsjliturgy.blogspot.com/2006/08/prayer-for-grandparents.html. Copyright © 2005, Diana Macalintal [accessed 13 June 2010].

[15] From *Children's Everyday Prayerbook for 8–12 Year Olds* (Veritas, Dublin, 2011), p. 9.

[16] From Brendan Quinlivan, *More Liturgies for Post-Primary Schools* (Veritas, Dublin, 2003), pp. 5–6.

Blessing for Animals[17]
(in relation to St Francis, 4 October)

Blessed are you, Lord, God of all creation.
We praise you for every living creature in our world:
You made the birds that fly and sing;
You made the fish that swim in the sea;
You made all the animals that live on the land;
You made us in your own image.
Bless our animals:
They bring us comfort and joy,
They give us company and peace.
Help us to be like St Francis in the care we give to our pets.
We ask this through Christ our Lord.
Amen.

Prayer of St Teresa of Avila
(Feast day 15 October, also Doctor of Prayer)[18]

Christ has no body now, but yours,
No hands, no feet on earth but yours.
Yours are the eyes through which
he looks compassion on this world,
Yours are the feet with which he walks to do good,
Yours are the hands with which he blesses all the world.
Yours are the hands.
Yours are the feet.
Yours are the eyes.
You are his body.

For the month of November/Remembering the Dead

Prayer for those who mourn (from *Alive-O*)
Gentle God,
You love all of us.
Wipe away the tears of those who are sad
And help all of us to remember Jesus
Who died and rose from the dead.
May we live forever with Jesus
And be happy forever.
Amen.

A Letter to Grandad
Have you met Grandma in heaven?
You always believed that you would:
Though you were happy, you missed her.
(I know she'd meet you if she could.)

What's it like there in heaven?
There's only so much we can say,
Only so much we imagine,
A place where each tear's wiped away.

I hope you're happy in heaven
Where God will make everything new –
That's what it says in the Bible,
But, Grandad, I so, so miss you.
I know what it says in the Bible,
But, Grandad, I so, so miss you.
John.
   By Gabriel Fitzmaurice (from Alive-O 6)

---

[17] From *Prayer Services for 4–12 Year Olds*, p. 52.
[18] Taken from *Alive-O 8 Teacher's Book* (Veritas, Dublin, 2004), p. 108.

A Prayer Service/Litany of the Saints[19]

Symbols needed

Mary	a rosary
St Joseph	a carpenter's tool
Apostles	a bishop's/shepherd's staff
Martyrs	a red rose
Founders	a cross
Teachers	a catechism
Holy men and women	a Bible
Saints of Ireland	a Bridget's Cross

We turn to the examples of our heroes of faith. We try to learn from their lives and examples so that we may receive the same reward – the fullness of life with our loving God.

> Mary said yes to God when he called on her. She trust in God's promise and risked everything for love of him.
> Holy Mary Mother of God
> Pray for us.

God put his son into the loving and protective care of an honest and decent man.

> St Joseph, protector of the Christ-child.
> Pray for us.

The mission of Jesus was continued by those he gathered around him and to whom he gave the gift of the Holy Spirit.

> Saints Peter and Paul, St John and all the Holy Apostles
> Pray for us.

In the history of the Church many paid with their lives for believing in Jesus. Their faith was so strong that their love of God was stronger than their love of life itself.

> St Stephen, St Agnes, St Maximillian Kolbe and all the Holy Martyrs
> Pray for us.

In every generation people responded to the call to build up God's kingdom. In their ministry they gathered people around them to help.

> St Francis, St Dominic, St Ignatius and all the Holy Founders
> Pray for us.

Many dedicated their lives to the service of young people. They strove to help all to mature in faith and knowledge of God.

> St John Bosco, Blessed Edmund Rice and all Holy Teachers
> Pray for us.

People of prayer always draw us closer to God by their acts of worship and devotion.

> St Clare, St Thérèse of Lisieux and all Holy Men and Women of Prayer
> Pray for us.

The faith we have received has been preserved and handed on to us by people down through the generations, often at great cost to themselves.

> St Patrick, St Bridget, St Oliver and all Holy Men and Women of Ireland
> Pray for us.

God of our ancestors, your holy saints are present to us as we gather today. Give us the courage to follow their example. Guide us in the ways of faith that we might lead others to you through Christ our Lord. Amen.

---

19 From Brendan Quinlivan, *More Liturgies for Post-Primary Schools* (Veritas, Dublin, 2003), pp. 17–20.

For times of transition such as Graduation, Beginning/End of School Year

A Parent's Blessing[20]
When you were born
Our hearts were so full of happiness
That there was no room in us
For words.

When you were growing
Our hearts were so full of care for you
That we spoke soothingly
And sometimes sharply,
Fearful for your safety,
But always
In the deepest places of our hearts
We spoke lovingly.

Today,
As we watch you moving forward with your friends
We marvel at all you have done
And become.
Our spirits sing praise to God
For the gift that is you.
And, though our hearts
Have stretched to love others,
Yet, there is a place within us
That is yours, and only yours
Always.

For the light you have shone on us,
For the life you have called us to,
For the special gift of God
You are now, and will ever be,
Thank you.
   By Christy Kenneally

Blessing for New School Year[21]
God, our Loving Father, you care greatly for all your children. We want to grow in every way this year closer to you and each other. We stand before you ready to travel further along the road of life and the journey of faith. Help us, and open our hearts to your truth. Bless all our activities in this year ahead so that we may see your plan for us in all we do.

Bless the work that we do, help us to grow in knowledge and understanding.

Bless the games that we play, help us to grow in strength and fairness.

Bless the things we create, help us to grow in imagination and joy.

Bless the time we will spend together, help us to grow in harmony and peace.

Bless the time we spend in prayer, help us to grow in faith, hope and love.

Help us ever loving Father to meet the challenges that this new year will bring.

Amen.

Test Prayer for Suffering Students![22]
Now that I lay me down to study
I pray the Lord I won't go nutty.
If I should fail to learn this junk,
I pray the Lord I will not flunk.

But if I do, don't pity me at all;
Just lay my bones down in the study hall.
Tell my teachers I did my best.
Then pile the books upon my chest.

Now I lay me down to rest,
And pray I'll pass tomorrow's test.
If I should die before I wake,
That's one less test I'll have to take.
Amen.

---

20 From *Prayer Services for 4–12 Year Olds*, p. 32.
21 From *Liturgies for Post-Primary Schools*, p. 2.
22 Ibid., p. 56.

For Teachers

Why God Created Teachers[23]

When God created teachers,
He gave us special friends
To help us understand his world
And truly comprehend
The beauty and the wonder
Of everything we see,
And become a better person
With each discovery.
When God created teachers,
He gave us special guides
To show us ways in which to grow
So we can all decide
How to live and how to do
What's right instead of wrong,
To lead us so that we can lead
And learn how to be strong.
Why God created teachers,
In his wisdom and his grace,
Was to help us learn to make our world
A better, wiser place.

The Ten Commandments in Modern Format[24]

- **First** Love the Lord your God alone, with all your heart.
- **Second** Respect the Lord's name.
- **Third** Keep the Lord's Day holy.
- **Fourth** Honour your parents.
- **Fifth** All life is in God's hands; do not destroy life.
- **Sixth** Be faithful in marriage.
- **Seventh** Do not steal.
- **Eighth** Do not speak falsely of others.
- **Ninth** Do not desire a person who already belongs with another.
- **Tenth** Do not be greedy for things that already belong to others.

Prayer for Changing the Clock at Spring/Summer

As we put our clocks forward one hour,
We spring into longer days and shorter nights.
We thank God for all the new life we see around us at this time of year
We pray that God will provide good weather for our farmers so that their crops will have all they need to grow well.
We pray that we enjoy the longer evenings, playing and going for walks together.
We ask God to keep us safe when we travel to visit family or go on holiday.
We ask this through Christ our Lord. Amen.

Prayer for Changing the Clock at Autumn/Winter

As we put our clocks back one hour,
We prepare for longer nights and shorter days.
We thank God for the warmth and cosiness of our homes in this colder, darker time of year.
We ask God to be with us on our outdoor adventures in the cold, bright sunshine.
We especially pray that God will be with the elderly and those who live alone.
We ask God to keep them safe and warm.
We thank God for our hot dinners on cold nights.
We pray that we will be safe as we travel on darker roads.
We ask this through Christ our Lord. Amen.

---

[23] From *More Liturgies for Post-Primary Schools*, pp. 81–82.
[24] From *Children's Everyday Prayerbook for 8–12 Year Olds* (Veritas, Dublin, 2011), p. 19.

Prayers about the Environment[25]
We praise you Lord.
You have given us many lovely colours.
Green is one of those special colours –
You have painted many shades of green.

You have made our countryside
Colourful and beautiful –
With green fields and green meadows,
With green hills and green valleys.

You know Lord, that green
is soft and soothing.
It is relaxing and refreshing.
Green does not tire our eyes.

Green gives us life.
Green gives us hope.
Thank you, God, for the colour green.

***

Litany[26]
Response Lord our God, we praise and thank you

We thank you for the rainbow that brightens the sky (R)

We thank you for the golden sun (R)

We thank you for the colours of the clouds in the vast blue sky (R)

We thank you for all the different shades of green (R)

We thank you for the silvery lakes and the shining sea (R)

We thank you for the brown bog and the purple heather (R)

We thank you for the bright flowers and the glossy leaves (R)

Amen.

***

---

[25] From Francesca Kelly, *Fifty Masses with Children* (Columba, Dublin, 1992), p. 80.

[26] Ibid, p. 82.

The 'Do It Anyway' Prayers
(The first version is attributed to Blessed Teresa of Calcutta, reputedly based on the second version by Kent Keith)[27]

People are often unreasonable, irrational, and self-centred. Forgive them anyway.

If you are kind, people may accuse you of selfish, ulterior motives. Be kind anyway.

If you are successful, you will win some unfaithful friends and some genuine enemies. Succeed anyway.

If you are honest and sincere, people may deceive you. Be honest and sincere anyway.

What you spend years creating, others could destroy overnight. Create anyway.

If you find serenity and happiness, some may be jealous. Be happy anyway.

The good you do today will often be forgotten. Do good anyway.

Give the best you have, and it will never be enough. Give your best anyway.

In the final analysis, it is between you and God. It was never between you and them anyway.

***

People are illogical, unreasonable, and self-centered. Love them anyway.

If you do good, people will accuse you of selfish ulterior motives. Do good anyway.

If you are successful, you win false friends and true enemies. Succeed anyway.

The good you do today will be forgotten tomorrow. Do good anyway.

Honesty and frankness make you vulnerable. Be honest and frank anyway.

The biggest men and women with the biggest ideas can be shot down by the smallest men and women with the smallest minds. Think big anyway.

People favor underdogs but follow only top dogs. Fight for a few underdogs anyway.

What you spend years building may be destroyed overnight. Build anyway.

People really need help but may attack you if you do help them. Help people anyway.

Give the world the best you have and you'll get kicked in the teeth. Give the world the best you have anyway.

---

[27] From http://www.prayerfoundation.org/mother_teresa_do_it_anyway.htm [accessed 1 May 2011].

Appendix III
Dramatisations of Gospel Readings

These are optional, but can add to the liturgical experience when used appropriately. Depending on the suitability of local conditions, a dramatisation can help illustrate the message of Sacred Scripture. It also provides a facility for inviting greater participation from children and adults alike.

It will involve additional input in terms of practise. In some examples, the participants may have to learn lines.

The dramas provided here can be used, adapted or omitted in accordance with what makes *your* Family Mass the best liturgical experience for all involved.

First Sunday of Advent

Needs Narrator(s), servants of the house, master, doorkeeper, mask.

Scene 1 Mime. Master and servants are happy together (miming everyday tasks of cleaning, gardening, waving at passers-by. All characters are happy).

Narrator Once upon a time, long before phones, television and cars, there lived a man with his servants in a cosy little cottage. It was the only house along a road between two distant towns. Passer-bys would stop there to rest and would always be welcome. The master made sure to keep his garden neat and tidy. His servants left out food for the birds and kept the cottage clean, warm and cosy. They lived a happy life together – the master looked after them like they were all one, big, caring family.

Scene 2 Mime. Master leaves. Once he is gone, the servants just sit down and put up their feet. Some sleep.

Narrator One day, the master explained that he had to go away on an important journey. He would be gone for one month. He asked his servants to keep the cottage just like it would be when he was there – welcoming, warm, clean and cosy. Of course, they agreed, so off he went. But no sooner had he left, than the servants talked and agreed that they would take it easy until a few days before the master was due back. Then they would do a big clean-up and make it look as if they had been doing as he asked all along. Sure, he would never know the truth, would he?

Scene 3 Mime. Master arrives. Looks in a 'window' and scratches his head to show he is confused and thinking. He puts on a mask and knocks at the 'door'. He is ignored. Then he takes off the mask, walks in and the servants stand up looking shocked.

Narrator Only two weeks later, the master was on his way back. He was back early because he missed his home and his friends. He was looking forward to getting back to his cosy cottage. As he came closer, he noticed something strange. The grass was not cut. The garden was messy. There were no birds because no food had been left out for them. He crept up to a window and looked in. There were his servants just relaxing, surrounded by dirty dishes and dirty clothes. It seemed as if they had done nothing for the whole time he was away. He was confused. He hoped that they had at least welcomed any passers-by who had needed rest. The master decided to put on a disguise and test them. He knocked on the door, changed his voice and asked for shelter. At first he was ignored, then yelled at to go away. Heartbroken, the master took off his disguise, opened his door and walked in. The servants were shocked. They hadn't expected their master for at least another week. What now?!

Second Sunday of Advent
Interview with John the Baptist.

Needs John the Baptist, interviewer.

Interviewer Ladies and Gentlemen, here is the man in the desert we have heard people talking about, John the Baptist.

John, you're wearing a sackcloth and we hear you eat locusts and wild honey. First question – why?

John I just make do with whatever I find. It's not important what I wear or what I eat. What's important is that people listen to what I have to say.

Interviewer Which is what?

John We mustn't delay any longer. It's time to give up bad habits and old ways. We all need to make a fresh start, to be ready to welcome the one who comes after me.

Interviewer Why are you called John the Baptist?

John I baptise people with water. They confess

their sins, give up their bad ways and by baptising them with water, I suppose you could say they are cleansed – a much better state in which to welcome someone special, wouldn't you say?

Interviewer And who is this someone special. People say you're pretty special yourself!

John Me! I'm nothing compared to the one who is coming. I can say only this: I baptise with water, but the one who comes after me will baptise with the Holy Spirit.

Nativity Play (from *Alive-O*)

The Moment We've Been Waiting For[1]

Characters
Mary
Joseph
Melchior
Balthasaar
Caspar
Naomi – a young shepherdess
Benjamin – a young shepherd
Isaac – a solo singer
A group of shepherds
Centurion
Simeon
Anna
A group of soldiers
A choir of angels
A group of innkeepers
A child carrying a star

For all the songs in this play, a choir, assembled nearby or on stage, may assist the singing. They should stand when they sing, and sit and watch when not singing.

During the singing of the opening song, the three wise men make their way through the audience and on to the stage. Melchior carries a 'telescope' (perhaps a tin-foil tube). Caspar carries a rolled-up map and various instruments such as a large blackboard-size protractor, a set-square, etc. Balthasaar carries a compass (a home-made one, large enough to be clearly visible). As the song continues, they peer at the sky; study the map;

---
1 From *Biblical Dramas for 4–12 Year Olds* (Veritas, Dublin, 2005), pp. 11–15.

examine the compass and swap instruments. They adopt many different poses and gestures for the duration of the song (such as scratching the head, as if puzzled; each king, in turn, pointing towards a different direction while the other two shake their heads in disagreement; sitting down and waiting, drumming fingers impatiently, and so on). They may also join in the singing.

Act 1, Scene 1
The three wise men sing this song, assisted by the choir.

'Following A Star'[2]

Verse 1
Why are we waiting here, why?
Why are we waiting here, why?
Waiting for the joy and hope the baby brings
To us and to the world.

Chorus
We are the wise men,
Caspar, Melchior and Balthasaar.
We are the wise men,
Following a star.

Verse 2
Why are we watching here, why?
Why are we watching here, why?
Watching for a new star in the sky above
To guide us on our way.

Verse 3
Why are we wondering here, why?
Why are we wondering here, why?
Wondering if the road we're on will ever end,
If the new King will be there.

Melchior (*pointing in the direction of the ceiling at the back of the room/hall*) Look at all those stars!
Balthasaar and Caspar (*each with one hand 'shading' their eyes as they very obviously peer at the audience*) Never mind all those stars, look at all these stars!
Melchior They're not stars, not real stars…
Balthasaar How do you know they're not real stars … they might be able to sing and dance and …

---
2 Ibid., p. 59.

Our Family Mass Resources for the Family Sunday Liturgy **Year B**

Caspar This play could do with some good singers and actors. Let's ask them and see.
Melchior Don't be silly! I mean, they're not the kind of stars in the story.
Balthasaar and Caspar What story?
Melchior This story…
The kings, assisted by the choir, sing these words to the tune of 'Once Upon A Time'.[3]

Verse 1
Gather round, and a story you will hear.
It's a story that's retold every year
About a baby, a manger and a star
And wise men from afar.
You can hear it in once upon a time.

Verse 2
Gather round and a story you will hear.
It's a story that's retold every year
About a mother, some shepherds, angels too.
Sing glory Allelu.
You can hear it in once upon a time.
All three stare silently for a moment.
Melchior There is a new star in the sky tonight? I wonder why!
Balthasaar That's what I'm wondering too.
Caspar I wonder if it's a sign – a star-sign?
All three stare silently for another moment.
Balthasaar and Caspar Why are we watching?
Melchior Because we are waiting.
Balthasaar and Caspar Why are we waiting?
They begin to sing together, 'Why are we waiting, why are we waiting' etc.
Melchior (*impatiently*) Because we are wise. All wise people watch and wait.
Balthasaar I wonder why!
Caspar Me too. (*Turning to Melchior*) Why do all wise people watch and wait, Melchior?
Melchior (*crossly*) You two are only half-wise, otherwise you would know why. Wise people watch and wait because they don't want to miss anything. (*Melchior becomes excited.*) Watch out! The star is moving! (*He rushes around, gathering up the equipment, before heading off in the direction of the star.*)
Balthasaar (*in a laid-back voice*) I see that.
Caspar (*equally laid back*) I wonder why it's moving!
Balthasaar (*making no moves to follow the star*) If something is moving, you can follow it.

Caspar (*making no moves either*) True. You cannot follow a thing that does not move.
Balthasaar You are a very wise man, Caspar.
Melchior (*rushes back on stage, agitated*) Come along, come along, we must follow the star, hurry!
Balthasaar Hurry, Caspar.
Caspar Hurry Balthasaar.
The three hurry off stage.

Act 1, Scene 2
Centurion accompanied by soldiers and carrying a roll-book enters the stage. He/she addresses the audience directly.
Centurion You there (*pointing at someone who may or may not have been planted there*) in the front row – where are you from?
(*The person answers and, as they do so, the centurion pretends to write the details in the book.*) You must go to Bethlehem. Caesar's orders. (*The centurion repeats this process twice more.*)
Melchior enters the stage and says with agitation:
Melchior It'll take till Christmas to count all these at the rate you're going.
Centurion Everyone must be counted. Caesar's orders.
He points as if to call out another person, but Melchior interrupts him.
Melchior But we must move on, the story must be told tonight.
Centurion (*repeating*) Everyone must be counted. Caesar's orders.
Melchior I'll tell you what I'll do. (*He whispers in the centurion's ear and then turns, addressing the audience directly.*) Do you want to hear the rest of the story? Are you sure? Well then, you must all promise this centurion that as soon as this story is told tonight, you will all go to Bethlehem to sign Caesar's book. Do you promise? Louder …
Centurion (*to audience*) Repeat after me – We promise.
Audience repeats We promise.
To go to Bethlehem.
Audience repeats To go to Bethlehem.
To be counted.
Audience repeats To be counted.
Very well then. (*He leaves the stage, but just before he exits he turns to Melchior one last time and points a warning finger.*) Remember – you promised!
Melchior Now, let's get on with the story. (*He exits.*)

---
[3] Ibid., p. 71.

Act 1, Scene 3

A long queue of people wind across the stage like a snake. Those at the front of the queue are the main speaking characters, Mary, Joseph, Naomi, Benjamin, Simeon and Anna.
They sing the following to the tune of 'The Passover Song'.[4]

Chorus
Watching and waiting and waiting and watching.
Watching, waiting, wondering too.
Watching and waiting and waiting and watching
For a Saviour – a Saviour who (last chorus 'A Saviour true').

Verse 1
Will lead us to the freedom of God's kingdom,
Will tell us the story of God's love,
Will share the bread and wine of life with humankind,
And send us the Spirit from above.

Verse 2
Will teach us to call God 'Our Father',
Will heal the sick and comfort those who cry,
Will right the wrongs to those who've been ill-treated,
Bring new life to all those who've died.

Two soldiers enter the stage.
Soldier 1 That's enough of that noise.
Soldier 2 We could arrest you for singing such rebel songs. Be quiet and stand to attention for our centurion.
The centurion enters the stage, still carrying the large roll-book from earlier. He pretends to do a rough head-count. As he is doing so, the cross young woman says:
Naomi Some day, we will have a true leader, someone to put these Roman soldiers in their place. *(The others in the queue nod and mumble assent.)* A leader from among our own people who will show everyone how to treat people fairly and justly.
Benjamin We have been waiting for a leader like that for a long, long time. How much longer do we have to wait?
Simeon My name is Simeon. I have spent my whole life watching and waiting for him. God will send us a leader, I am sure of it.

Anna My name is Anna. I too have spent a lifetime watching and waiting for the one whom God promised to send. I have prayed. I know it will not be long now.
Naomi Well, whenever he comes, it will not be a moment too soon.
Benjamin Speaking of sooner – the sooner we get back to our flocks on the hillside, the better. They will be scattered far and wide by now. It'll take all night to gather them together.
Centurion That's enough talking! Be quiet! *(Turning to his soldiers)* Who are all these people and where are they from? *(pointing to the queue on stage)*
Soldier 1 These are David's people and they have come from Nazareth.
Centurion And who are all these? *(pointing to the audience)*
Soldier 2 These are all *(mentioning the name of the school)* and they come from *(mentioning the name of the locality)*.
Centurion *(repeating the names just mentioned)* Never heard of them! Take the whole lot of them to the Scriptorium to sign up.
Handing the book to soldier 1, he says (obviously referring to the audience)
They don't look too intelligent.
(Turning from the soldier he addresses the audience)
Can you lot all write your own name? Well… speak up.
Allow a moment for an audience response.
Shaking his head as he leaves the stage, the centurion says in a loud voice:
Definitely a rather 'stupid' lot! *(He turns to soldier 2)* Now, we need to sort out our accommodation for the night. Are there any innkeepers in the queue?
Soldier 1 Anyone who has an inn, step forward.
A group of innkeepers step forward. They can be as numerous or as few as you wish. They sing to the tune of 'My Body Clock'.[5]

Verse 1
Today is just the busiest we've been for quite some time,
With crowds of people queuing up and waiting just to sign.
They come from near, they come from far, all looking for a place.

---

[4] Ibid., p. 81.

[5] Ibid., p. 70.

We've never been so busy; we just cannot keep pace.

Chorus
I haven't got a room, no room for anyone.
I haven't got a room; no room, no room.

Verse 2 (The soldiers)
We are Caesar's soldiers, we're the rulers of this land
And what we soldiers want – we get! So, take heed! Understand!
Turn your guests out of their rooms; make way for Caesar's men
Or it'll be the worse for you, your families and your friends!

Chorus
We soldiers want a room; all rooms, every room.
We soldiers want a room; all rooms, all rooms.

Verse 3 (Joseph stepping forward with Mary)
We two have travelled far this day and Mary is with child.
We need a room where we can stay; the night is wet and wild.
The moment we've been waiting for is very soon to come.
Shepherds, kings and angels wait the birth of Mary's son.

Chorus (Mary and Joseph, while innkeepers and soldiers shake their heads)
Please let us have a room; one room, any room.
Please let us have a room; one room, one room.

Verse 4 (Melchior entering, and trying to hurry things along)
Not a room of any kind, or so the story goes,
Except for one kind woman, who's had children and she knows
That every newborn baby and its mother need a bed.
'I've a stable in the hills, you can go there,' she said.
'You can go there,' she said, 'go there and make a bed.
You can go there,' she said, 'go there, go there.' (*Melchior points off stage.*)
Melchior That's that sorted out. Now, take all these people away to sign the book.
He ushers the soldiers, the centurion and the queue off stage and then he leaves himself. Mary and Joseph struggle along at the back of the queue.
Joseph Sit down Mary. Take a moment to rest yourself. You must be tired out.
Mary (*sits down, Joseph sits beside her*) Yes Joseph, let's take a moment to rest.
Mary and Joseph sing 'Mary, Our Mother'.

'Mary, Our Mother'[6]
Chorus
Mary, our mother, the Lord is with you.
Guide us, protect us in all that we do.

Verse 1
Angel Gabriel said to you,
'You will be mother of Jesus.'
Verse 2
With Elizabeth you rejoiced,
'I will be mother of Jesus.'

Verse 3
In a manger in Bethlehem
You became mother of Jesus.

Mary We have had many precious moments, Joseph, but right at this moment, we need to move on and find the stable where we can stay. I have a feeling this baby will be here soon.
Mary and Joseph walk a few 'laps' of the stage. As they do so, the choir sing two verses of 'Carol Of The Journey'.[7]

Act 1, Scene 4
A group of shepherds sit around in a semi-circle. Naomi and Benjamin are standing, one on either side of the semi-circle, recounting their experience of earlier on in the day.
Naomi Some day a leader will come from among our own people, who will put an end to the soldiers' rule. Then we will never again have to sign our names in Caesar's book.
Benjamin I have never seen such a long queue. It took ages to sign.
Third Shepherd We have gathered all your sheep, as well as our own, for the night, so there is nothing for you to do. You look worn out. Sit down and take a rest. Isaac was just about to sing 'The Lost Sheep' song for us.

---
6 Ibid., p. 69.
7 Ibid., p. 56.

They sit down. Isaac stands up and sings. The others join in the chorus.

'The Lost Sheep'[8]
Verse 1
The poor little sheep, he started to weep
All lost and alone in the wood.
He didn't cry 'Mummy', he didn't cry 'Mum',
He just started bleating as loud as he could:
'Baa, baa, baa, I've lost my Ma-ma, maa, maa,
Baa, baa, baa, I've lost my Ma-ma.'

Verse 2
Back home in the shed, the mother sheep said,
'My baby is not by my side.'
She didn't cry 'Sonny', she didn't cry 'Son',
She just started bleating and here's what she cried:
'Maa, maa, maa, I've lost my baba, baa, baa.
Maa, maa, maa, I've lost my baba.'
Verse 3
The shepherd came in and said with a grin,
'See mother I've brought home your boy!'
He didn't cry 'Mummy'; she didn't cry 'Son',
They just started bleating aloud in their joy:
'Maa, maa, maa, I've found my baba, baa, baa.'
'Baa, baa, baa, I've found my mama!'
During the last chorus a choir of angels enter the stage and join in the singing. If there are a lot of angels to be 'got on stage', they could begin to enter during the last verse, singing along with Isaac. The shepherds are so 'shocked' that their mouths drop open, they stare and forget to finish the song.
Melchior (*rushing on stage*) Wait, wait! This is wrong. This is not part of the story. The angels are supposed to sing *Glo-o-o-o-o-o ria in excelsis deo*, not maa, maa, maa and baa, baa, baa!
Angel 1 Who are you?
Melchior I'm Melchior, one of the three wise men.
Angel 2 Then it's you who are wrong – in the wrong place at the wrong time.
Angel 3 The wise men don't come into the story until the end.
Melchior Yes I know, but for now I'm just supervising, to see that the story is told properly.
Angel 1 Well for now we're just joining in the song because it's a good song.
Angel 2 We sing the same Gloria song every year, it's nice to have a change.

Melchior Very well, but can you get on with the proper story now please, otherwise we may run out of time and we wise men might not get to see the baby at all! (*He exits*)
Angels sing the shepherds' verse of 'Carol of The Journey'. As they finish, Naomi becomes very excited.
Naomi This is it! This is it! (*she shouts to the other shepherds*). This is the sign we have been waiting and watching for, wondering who would be our leader!
Benjamin She's right. All the watching and waiting and wondering is finally over! We must go and see this new baby who will be our Saviour!
The Other Shepherds (*together*)
But what about our sheep, our lambs? We can't just run off and leave them, they might wander away and get lost …
Angel 1 Don't worry about your sheep; we will look after them for you.
Melchior (*hurrying on stage again*) Go on, go on, go on will you, or the story will never get to the end and we'll be wandering about from East to West for another year!
He ushers the shepherds off stage.
Angel 3 (*to the other angels*) Do any of you know anything about minding sheep?
Angels shake their heads, shrug their shoulders and generally murmur 'No'.
Angel 2 I know, let's sing to them.
Angel 1 I say, I say, I say, what kind of songs do sheep like?
Angels (*together*) We don't know; what kind of songs do sheep like?
Angel 1 Why lullabaa-aas of course!
All the angels exit the stage singing choruses of 'The Lost Sheep' song as they go.

Act 2, Scene 1

Mary, carrying the baby, and Joseph, carrying a little lamb, enter stage and place the baby in a manger and the lamb beside it. They look at it for a moment, smiling.
Mary This is the moment we've been waiting for, Joseph. It seems such a long time ago since the day the angel came and told me the good news … Do you remember, Joseph?
Joseph Indeed I do. (*Leaving Mary's side and coming forward to address the audience.*)
The moment the angel appeared
Mary grew worried, and yet …

---
8 Ibid., p. 79.

Mary (*coming forward to join him*) The moment I first heard the news.
Is a moment I'll never forget.
Joseph The moment she left on her journey
Mary grew worried, and yet …
Mary The moment Elizabeth hugged me
Is a moment I'll never forget.
Joseph The moment I mentioned 'Bethlehem'
Mary grew worried, and yet …
Mary (*looking at Joseph*) The moment you said 'I'll be with you'
Is a moment I'll never forget.
Joseph The moment the keeper said 'No room'
We both grew worried, and yet …
Mary The moment yon little lamb bleated
Is a moment I'll never forget.
Joseph (*picking up the baby*) The moment the baby first cried
We both grew worried, and yet …
Mary The moment our baby first smiled
We thought, this is the best moment yet!

All cast except the wise men and soldiers assemble on stage, grouped around the manger. All together, they say the following poem.

'The Crib Community'
Amidst all the tinsel and glitter
And fuss and bother and din,
To our house every Christmas
A whole community moves in.
Several men, one woman, one baby,
Where on earth will they fit?
Sheep, lambs, a cow and a donkey,
With a manger and straw – and that's it!
After settling their babe in the manger
They arrange themselves out before him,
Then spend Christmas Days, feasting their gaze;
It's obvious they simply adore him!
Amidst all the hustle and hassle
There's something so graceful about them,
Although they don't say or do anything
It wouldn't be Christmas without them!

Led by a child carrying a star, Caspar and Balthasaar enter. They present their gifts as the choir sings the kings' verse of 'Carol Of The Journey'.

Naomi Only two wise men! Shouldn't there be three?

Caspar and Balthasaar There were three of us. We've watched and waited like the story says, now we are wondering …
Benjamin Wondering … what are you wondering about at this late stage? The story is almost over, the baby is born.
Caspar and Balthasaar We're wondering where Melchior has got to.
A great marching of feet is heard. Melchior, protesting loudly and being roughly escorted by soldiers, enters from the back of the hall/performance area and makes his way on stage.
Melchior You cannot arrest me. I am an Eastern king. You have no authority over me.
Centurion You may be an Eastern king, but here in this country, Rome rules. OK! You are under arrest. You made a bargain and you did not keep it.
Naomi (*stepping forward*) The moment has finally come: the beginning of the end of Roman rule in our country.
She takes the baby in her arms and shows it to the centurion.
This baby, born tonight in this stable, is our king. He will lead us to freedom from Rome's rule. You will see.
Centurion (*laughing mockingly*) Hah! This is a king! A baby born in a stable … Show me his army, show me his might and his power! Hah! Go back to your sheep, girl, for sheep will be all this baby will ever lead.
Soldiers all laugh.
Anna (*Taking the baby from Naomi*) You are right, soldier. This baby will grow up to be a shepherd, but he will be a good shepherd like King David, his ancestor.
Simeon (*stepping forward*) Yes, you are right soldier, he will never have a powerful army like Caesar's. For he will always be on the side of those who have no power, no might.
Mary You are only partly right, Naomi, for yes, this baby will be a great leader. But his kingdom will not be a particular place – it will be anywhere and everywhere that people live together in the spirit of Christmas, in the spirit of peace on earth and goodwill to all.
Angel choir sing their chorus of 'Carol of the Journey'.
When they finish, Melchior, who is still being held by the soldiers, attempts to go and give his gift to the baby. He struggles to break free.
Centurion Where do you think you're going?

Melchior Let me go, I must give my gift to the baby.
Centurion If you were really a wise man, you would keep your gift for Caesar, to try and make up for breaking your bargain.
Melchior It's not my fault that all those other people didn't turn up to sign your book. They promised me they would. It is they and not I who have broken the promise.
Caspar and Balthasaar But they have turned up! Look, there they are (*pointing to the audience*). They are just waiting for the story to be over. Then they will sign the book. (*Turning to address the audience*) Won't you? … won't you? …
Melchior (*still 'under arrest', speaks to the audience*) I'll tell you what, if you agree to sign the book, then clap your hands now.
(*Caspar, Balthasaar and the others on stage begin to clap their hands. Hopefully, the audience will join in.*) Thank goodness for that! (*The soldiers let go of him and he presents his gift.*) At last, the story is all told (*with a great flourish*). THIS is the moment we have all been waiting for!
Total cast shout
Hurray for Baby Jesus; Hurray for Christmas; Hurray, Hurray, Hurray!

Finale
Everyone sings:
'This Is The Moment'[9]

Verse 1
Mary and Joseph tried to find a place to stay in Bethlehem,
But they were turned away at every door.
They settled in a stable where baby Jesus soon was born.
'This is the moment we've waited for.'

Chorus
As the star rose in the sky on that first Christmas night,
Mary took him in her arms and held him oh so tight.
The moment had arrived and he gave a little smile to the world,
A smile to the world.

Verse 2
The sound of angels filled the sky.

---
9 Ibid., p. 86.

Shepherds heard each word they sang:
'Go see the baby and wait no more.'
Three wise men in the morning light
Found that star, it was so bright.
'This is the moment we've waited for.'

The Baptism of the Lord
Needs John, Jesus, voice representing God, white blanket/cloak.

John I baptise you with water. But one comes after me who baptises with the Holy Spirit.

John places the blanket/cloak around Jesus.

Voice You are my own dear Son. I am pleased with you.

Second Sunday of Easter
Needs Narrator, Jesus, Disciples.

Three tableaus are presented as three scenes, each with a brief narration.

Scene 1 Frightened-looking disciples huddled together.

Narrator Their friend Jesus had been killed. Crucified. The disciples were afraid. Their leader was gone. Would they be next?

Scene 2 The disciples look toward Jesus with a mixture of disbelief and shock.

Narrator Jesus appeared, saying, 'Peace be with you'.

Scene 3 Jesus with arms open, smiling at the disciples. The disciples look happy and spread out holding hands, no longer huddling together in fear.

Narrator The disciples recognise their friend. Jesus is risen. Again, he says, 'Peace be with you'. He gives them his Spirit uniting them. Together they will witness the Risen Jesus and will continue his work of spreading the Good News of God's love for all.

Fourth Sunday of Easter
Needs Narrator, two shepherds, another person who is not a shepherd.

Scene Two shepherds and another character are sitting together, chatting.

Shepherd 1 I'm just passing through here. I'm taking my flock to the other side of the valley in the morning.

Shepherd 2 It's a great life, isn't it?

Third Person I think you're both crazy! They're only sheep – and you let yourself be stuck up in those mountains for weeks. It's been really cold lately too. If it was me, I'd leave them there and go home.

Shepherd 1 Oh no. I couldn't do that do them!

Third Person But they're sheep. It's not like they're people!

Shepherd 2 You don't understand. I know every single one of them. I know when one is upset or afraid or getting sick.

Shepherd 1 It's the same with me. They're my family.

Third Person But it's just a job. There are better jobs. Safer ones. Warmer ones!

Shepherd 2 No. It's not a job. This is what I'm meant to do. My flock need me.

Shepherd 1 I feel the same. They come first.

Third Person So you both choose to do this?

Shepherd 1 Yes!

Shepherd 2 Absolutely!

Narrator Jesus is the Good Shepherd. We are his flock. He chooses to be our shepherd, to put our needs first, to love us no matter what.

Fifth Sunday of Easter
Needs Three figures. Central figure in white to represent Jesus, black cloak/blanket.

Tableau 1 All figures holding hands, standing and smiling.

Tableau 2 Central figure holding onto just one other figure. Both are standing and smiling. Other figure is crouched and covered in black cloak/blanket.

The Ascension of the Lord
Needs: Narrator, group of Apostles, Jesus.

Scene depicts Apostles huddled together, looking uncertain and frightened.

Apostle 1 I'm staying here. It's too dangerous out there.

Apostle 2 But what about what Jesus told us?

Apostle 3 I just don't know. We'd be taking a risk. Who knows what could happen to us?

Apostle 4 Maybe we were mistaken?

Jesus enters, shaking his head, looking disappointed and a little angry.

Jesus What are you doing? Why are you not out there doing what I asked of you?

Apostle 4 But ... but ... but ...

Jesus Be not afraid! I am with you. And when I go back to my Father in heaven, the Holy Spirit will be with you.

Narrator After the Lord Jesus had talked with them, he was taken up to heaven and sat at the right side of God. The disciples went and preached everywhere, and the Lord worked with them and proved that their preaching was true by the miracles that were performed.

Third Sunday in Ordinary Time
Needs: Narrator, Simon, Andrew, James, John, Jesus.

Scene Simon and Andrew, James and John form two groups miming hauling nets and fishing. Jesus approaches and beckons to them. They leave their work and follow him.

Narrator An ordinary day.
  An ordinary place.
  A lakeside.
  Some fishermen.
  Nets. Boats.
  But then … a face.

  No ordinary face.
  No ordinary person.
  'Come with me.'
  'Follow me.'
  'Simon, Andrew.'
  'James and John.'

Fifth Sunday in Ordinary Time
Needs Narrator, Jesus, Simon, Simon's mother-in-law, other figures.

Tableau 1 Simon's mother-in-law is lying down. Simon points to her while looking at and beckoning Jesus to approach.

Narrator Simon's mother-in-law was very sick. He brought Jesus to her at his house.

Tableau 2 Simon's mother-in-law is standing with Jesus and Simon. All are happy.

Narrator Jesus held her hand and she was cured. She got up and invited Jesus to stay for a meal.

Tableau 3 A queue of other figures form in front of Jesus.

Narrator Many other people with all kinds of sicknesses arrived throughout the night to be cured by Jesus. Before dawn, Jesus left and went to a quiet place to be alone.

Sixth Sunday in Ordinary Time
Needs Narrator, Jesus, sick man (wearing mask).

Tableau 1 A sick man wearing a mask is alone and dejected.

Narrator A man with a skin disease was shunned by everyone around him. No one dared to come near to me. They were afraid. He was alone and in pain.

Tableau 2 Jesus holds the hand of the sick man who kneels before him.

Narrator Jesus did what no one else did. He allowed the sick man to be near him. In fact, he reached out to the man and held his hand. He agrees to heal the man.

Tableau 3 The cured man no longer wears a mask. He stands away from Jesus.

Narrator The cured man told everyone what had happened, even though Jesus had asked him not to. Many people heard about Jesus and came to him for healing. Sometimes Jesus went off on his own to a quiet place for some time just to himself.

Seventh Sunday in Ordinary Time
Needs First aid kit, the paralysed man, Teacher of the Law.

Scene 1 The paralysed man, seated, holds the first aid kit.

Paralysed Man I've been to healers before. Nothing worked. I knew God would never give up on me though. I always held onto hope. My body may have failed me, but I could still speak, still think, still feel. When I heard about this Jesus, something inside me told me this was it, I just had to get to see him. I felt called. I asked my neighbours to carry me. And all credit to them, they carried me the whole way there. When we couldn't get through the door they still found a way. Imagine, they lifted me through the roof! God bless them. And then I saw him. Jesus. I was mesmerised. To be honest, I can't even remember what he said to me. But whatever it was, I could feel it running through my body from my heart outwards. This body, which for years has been like a stone cage to me. And I felt as light as a feather. I knew God would never give up on me. I don't need this anymore [*throws first aid kit aside and stands*] but I will try to do my best with this hands and legs of mine that work again. Thanks be to God!

Teacher of the Law I know that man was paralysed. I've seen him before. Bless his faith, he never gave up on God. He still prayed sincerely despite his hardship, but what happened that day … I just don't know what to think. Only God can forgive our sins. I know the Law. I live it with all my heart. But how can this Jesus say those words, 'Your sins are forgiven'? And yet, I saw that man get up and walk … I just don't know …

Eleventh Sunday in Ordinary Time
Needs Three children, narrator.

Tableau 1 One child crouching as small as possible.

Narrator There once was a seed small and tiny.

Tableau 2 Second child kneeling, hands beginning to stretch out.

Narrator And this seed began to grow.

Tableau 3 Third child standing tall, arms outstretched.

Narrator It grew tall, strong and mighty.

Tableau 4 All three children standing tall, arms outstretched and holding hands.

Narrator And from it, all life, joy and love did flow.

Fourteenth Sunday in Ordinary Time
Needs Narrator, three characters sitting down, Jesus.

Scene 1 Jesus stands facing the characters who are seated listening to him.

Narrator Jesus travelled far and wide teaching, preaching and healing. News of his miracles and sermons reached his hometown of Nazareth. Jesus returned there and spoke with a group. Just as he had done elsewhere, he taught them about God.

First Person Wow! That was something else! I've never felt like that after a preacher before.

Second Person But that's just Jesus from over there. Mary and Joseph couldn't have taught him all that. How does he know it all?

Third Person What do you think about all this healing; and I even heard he can perform miracles?

Scene 2
The three characters stand up and face away from Jesus. Jesus looks dejected.

Narrator More and more, they talked about how Jesus could not possibly be for real. They talked about when he was a child – just like them. Finally they agreed that he must be pretending or acting. No one from their locality could be what people said Jesus was.

Jesus (*to congregation*) All they need is to believe. Have faith.

Sixteenth Sunday in Ordinary Time
Needs Narrator, Jesus, some disciples, some additional characters as 'crowd'.

Tableau 1 Jesus and his disciples sit down looking very tired and rubbing their tummies with hunger.

Narrator Jesus and his disciples spent all day teaching. They were so busy they didn't even have anything to eat. By evening time, they were hungry and exhausted. All they wanted was to rest, have something to eat and have some time to themselves.

Tableau 2 Jesus and his disciples are faced by a crowd with outstretched arms.

Narrator More people approached Jesus and his disciples. They were hungry to learn more, to be healed, to listen to the Good News. What would Jesus and the disciples do? Tell them to go away and leave them be; after all, it had been a long hard day. Or would Jesus and the disciples put the needs of the crowd first?

(*long pause*)

Tableau 3 Jesus and his disciples join with the crowd. Some kneeling, some standing, some sitting – representing an active preaching session with attentive listeners.

Narrator What do you think?

Twenty-Second Sunday in Ordinary Time
Needs Jesus, three characters, cup, sheet.

Scene 1 Jesus approaches a person who is miming washing his/her hands.

Jesus Excuse me? I have something very important to say to you.

First Person Not now! Can't you see I have to wash my hands. It's the Law! (*frustrated*)

Scene 2 Jesus approaches a second person who is miming cleaning a cup.

Jesus Excuse me? I have something very important to say to you.

Second Person Go away! It's not a good time! I'm busy washing this cup the way the Law says I have to.

Scene 3 Jesus approaches a third person who is making a bed (using sheet).

Jesus Excuse me? I have something very important to say to you.

Third Person Leave me alone please. I have to follow the Law and make this bed in a certain way.

Scene 4 An exasperated Jesus addresses all three.

Jesus You hypocrites! You say you follow the Law but yet you ignore me! What you are doing is just a habit. Don't you realise that? A habit human beings made for themselves. What's the point of following a rule when you don't follow it with your heart? God's Law is to love one another as I have loved you. Are you doing that? Or not?

Twenty-Sixth Sunday in Ordinary Time
Needs Narrator, Jesus and some disciples wearing white, another figure wearing green.

Tableau 1 Jesus and some disciples wearing white are huddling together in a group. The figure in green stands to one side.

Narrator Jesus and his disciples worked together as a group, spreading the Good News and healing people.

Tableau 2 Jesus stands alone. His disciples put the hands palms outwards to shut out the figure in green, now facing Jesus and the disciples.

Narrator Another person also healed. But Jesus' disciples thought that this was wrong. He wasn't part of their group. They told Jesus their concerns.

Tableau 3 Jesus, disciples and the figure in green all join hands together.

Narrator Jesus told his disciples that whoever does God's work belongs with God just as Jesus and his disciples do. God's love is offered to everyone.

Twenty-Eighth Sunday in Ordinary Time
Needs Narrator, Jesus, Rich young man.

Scene 1 A rich young man approaches Jesus. He is pleading with him, asking him something of great importance.

Narrator Jesus looked at him and loved him.

The man, young and rich, stood at his feet.

Rich Young Man I have done all the Law has asked.

> I do not misbehave or cheat.
> Am I worthy of you now Lord?
> What else need I do?
> All I want is the Reign of God.
> How can I be more like you?

Scene 2 Jesus takes the hand of the rich young man and begins to instruct him.

Narrator Jesus looked at him and loved him.

Jesus You have done very well, my child,
> You have read and learned your Scripture.
> And its dictums you have applied.
> I have come to teach a new Law,
> To build on what has gone.
> Live out what I now teach you.
> Then you can come along.

Rich Young Man Thank you, Jesus! I will do anything.
> Nothing can be too much.

Jesus Then sell all you have.
> Give your wealth to the poor

Scene 3 *The rich young man turns away from Jesus.*

Narrator But to do this, the young man did not rush.
> Jesus looked at him and loved him.

The young man was close to tears.
He turned his back, and walked away.
The loving face haunted him for all his years.

Thirty-Second Sunday in Ordinary Time
Needs Interviewer, widow, rich man, Jesus.

Interviewer Good morning everyone. Here we are at the Temple treasury. As you know, people put in some money and that money goes to help others in need. We thought you might like to hear from those who contribute. Excuse me, may we have a quick word?

Rich man Yes?

Interviewer Tell us, why do you give money to the treasury?

Rich man Well, I have plenty to spare so a few coins that I won't miss might put a loaf of bread on someone else's dinner table.

Interviewer That's very kind of you.

Rich man Like I said, I won't miss it. I have plenty more.

Interviewer Here's a woman. Excuse me, may we ask you a few questions?

Widow Alright. What would you like to know?

Interviewer Why do you give money to the treasury?

Widow My late husband always did, so since he died I've kept up the tradition. It's not much though. I'm embarrassed that I only had a few coppers to put in.

Jesus Excuse me.

Interviewer What? We're in the middle of an interview here.

Jesus I want everyone to know about the good deed this lady just did.

Interviewer She paid into the treasury like everyone else – what makes her so special?

Jesus Don't you see? She gave all she had. She has nothing left for herself. The first person you spoke to has plenty to spare. But she gave all she had.

Interviewer I see. Thank you. That is important. She gave all she had.

Appendix IV
Penitential Rite

Introduction

The Penitential Rite prepares us to hear the Word of God and to receive the Eucharist by reminding us that only God's mercy and grace make us worthy to participate. Following 'a brief pause for silence' (GIRM, 51), it provides an opportunity in a public setting for the general confession of minor transgressions that do not need to be confessed in the sacrament of Penance. The 'Kyrie eleison' (Greek for 'Lord, have mercy'), i.e. the 'Lord, have mercy … Christ, have mercy … Lord, have mercy', asks the Risen Lord to have mercy on our sins. Based on an ancient litany, it is Jesus who is addressed in each case (rather than Father, Son and Spirit).[1]

For the Season of Advent
Coming together as God's family, with confidence let us ask the Father's forgiveness, for he is gentle and full of compassion.

Lord, you come to gather us into the peace of your Kingdom. Lord have mercy.

Jesus, you come in word and actions to make us better people. Christ have mercy.

Lord, you come in glory to save all your people. Lord have mercy.

For the Season of Christmas
Coming together as God's family, with confidence let us ask the Father's forgiveness, for he is gentle and full of compassion.

Dear Jesus, you are the prince of peace. Lord have mercy.

Dear Jesus, you are the Son of God and Son of Mary. Christ have mercy.

Dear Jesus, you are the Word made flesh. Lord have mercy.

For the Season of Lent
Coming together as God's family, with confidence let us ask the Father's forgiveness, for he is gentle and full of compassion.

I confess to almighty God,
and to you, my brothers and sisters,
that I have greatly sinned,
in my thoughts and in my words,
in what I have done,
and in what I have failed to do,
through my fault, through my fault,
through my most grievous fault;
therefore I ask blessed Mary, ever virgin,
all the Angels and Saints,
and you, my brothers and sisters,
to pray for me to the Lord our God.
Amen.

For the Season of Easter and the Feast of the Baptism of the Lord
Rite of Blessing and Sprinkling Holy Water

Dear friends,

This water will be used to remind us of our baptism. Let us ask God to bless it and to keep us faithful to the Spirit he has given us.

Dear God, your gift of water brings life to the earth and nourishes our bodies. It washes away our sins and brings us to eternal life.

We ask you now to bless this water.

Renew the living spring of your life within us and help us to be the best people we can be.

We ask this through Christ our Lord.

For the Most Holy Trinity
Coming together as God's family, with confidence let us ask the Father's forgiveness, for he is gentle and full of compassion.

Lord, you came to heal our relationships, with each other and with God. Lord, have mercy.

Jesus, you heal the wounds caused by our wrongdoings. Christ have mercy.

Lord, you came to help us. Lord, have mercy.

---

1 This introductory paragraph is taken from Pat Mullins, *The Mass* (Veritas, Dublin, 2009), pp. 29–30.

For the Body and Blood of Christ

Coming together as God's family, with confidence let us ask the Father's forgiveness, for he is gentle and full of compassion.

Lord Jesus, you healed the sick. Lord, have mercy.

Christ, you forgave sinners. Christ have mercy.

Lord Jesus, you give us yourself to heal us and bring us your strength. Lord, have mercy.

For Christ, the Universal King

Coming together as God's family, with confidence let us ask the Father's forgiveness, for he is gentle and full of compassion.

Lord, you welcome everyone. Lord, have mercy.

Christ, you invite us into your Kingdom. Christ, have mercy.

Lord, you are the Son of God and friend to us all. Lord, have mercy.

For the Feast of St Patrick

Coming together as God's family, with confidence let us ask the Father's forgiveness, for he is gentle and full of compassion.

Dear Jesus, you have shown us the way to the Father. Lord have mercy.

Dear Jesus, you are the Way, the Truth and the Life. Christ have mercy.

Dear Jesus, you are the Good Shepherd. Lord, have mercy.

For the Feast of the Assumption

Coming together as God's family, with confidence let us ask the Father's forgiveness, for he is gentle and full of compassion.

Jesus, you raise us to new life. Lord have mercy.

Jesus, you forgive our sins. Christ have mercy.

Jesus, you feed us with your body and blood. Lord have mercy.

For the Feast of All Saints

Coming together as God's family, with confidence let us ask the Father's forgiveness, for he is gentle and full of compassion.

Dear Lord, you raise us to new life in the Spirit. Lord have mercy.

Dear Lord, you bring us peace. Christ have mercy.

Dear Lord, you bring light to those in darkness. Lord have mercy.

Our Family Mass Resources for the Family Sunday Liturgy **Year B**

For Sundays 2, 3, 5, 9, 10, 13–15, 23–26 and 28 in Ordinary Time
Coming together as God's family, with confidence let us ask the Father's forgiveness, for he is gentle and full of compassion.

Jesus, our friend, you are with us always. Lord have mercy.

Jesus, our friend, you show us how to be faithful. Christ have mercy.

Jesus, our friend, you came to save us. Lord have mercy.

For Sundays 4, 16, 17, 21, 22, 27, 29, 31 and 33 in Ordinary Time
Coming together as God's family, with confidence let us ask the Father's forgiveness, for he is gentle and full of compassion.

Jesus, you are the Word of God. Lord, have mercy.

Lord, you show us how to love God and one another. Christ, have mercy.

Jesus, you welcome us into your Kingdom. Lord, have mercy.

For Sundays 6–8 and 30 in Ordinary Time
Coming together as God's family, with confidence let us ask the Father's forgiveness, for he is gentle and full of compassion.

Dear Jesus, you came to heal the sick. Lord, have mercy.

Dear Jesus, you came to call sinners. Christ, have mercy.

Dear Jesus, you are our Saviour. Lord, have mercy.

For Sundays 18–20 and 32 in Ordinary Time
Coming together as God's family, with confidence let us ask the Father's forgiveness, for he is gentle and full of compassion.

Lord, you are the light of the world. Lord have mercy.

Jesus, you are the Way, the Truth and the Life. Christ, have mercy.

Lord, you are the Bread of Life. Lord, have mercy.

F. Recommended Resources

Books and Materials

Family Liturgies; The Mass; Readings

Bernadette Sweetman, *Our Family Mass: Resources for the Family Sunday Liturgy, Year A* (Veritas, Dublin, 2010)

Celebrating the Mystery of Faith, Revised Edition: A Guide to the Mass (National Centre for Liturgy, 2011)

The Columba Lectionary for Masses with Children (Years A,B, C), (Columba Press, Dublin)

Directory for Masses with Children (Congregation for Divine Worship, 1973)

Clann Dé ag an Aifreann : Leabhar Aifrinn agus Urnaithe Céad Chomaoineach (Veritas, Dublin, 2009)

With the Risen Jesus at Mass: A First Communion Mass and Prayer Book (Veritas, Dublin, 2009)

The New Missal: Explaining the Changes (National Centre for Liturgy, 2011)

Sr Francesca Kelly, Fifty Masses with Children (Columba Press, Dublin, 1992)

Maeve Mahon & Martin Delaney, *THUMB (That's His/Her Useful Mass Book)* (Veritas, Dublin, 2010)

Megan McKenna, *Lent: Sunday Readings* (Veritas, Dublin, 2008)

Megan McKenna, *Lent: Daily Readings* (Veritas, Dublin, 2008)

Share the Good News, National Directory for Catechesis in Ireland (Irish Episcopal Conference, 2010)

Sing the Mass: Anthology of Music for the Irish Church (National Centre for Liturgy in association with the Advisory Committee on Church Music, 2011)

Katie Thompson, *The Liturgy of the Word with Children: A Complete Programme that follows the guidelines of the Bishops' Conference* (Kevin Mayhew, Suffolk, 2004)

Liturgical Signs and Prayers: A DVD (National Chaplaincy for Deaf People, Dublin, 2005)

Pat Mullins, *The Mass: Understanding What's What* (Veritas, Dublin, 2009)

Primary and Post-Primary Resources

The Alive-O/Beo go Deo programme (Books, Audio CDs, DVDs) – available from Veritas

Eleanor Gormally, *Connecting School and Parish: An Alive-O 1–4 Handbook for Classroom Visitations* (Veritas, Dublin, 2001)

Brendan O'Reilly, *Connecting School and Parish: An Alive-O 5–8 Handbook for Classroom Visitations* (Veritas, Dublin, 2007)

Brendan O'Reilly et al, *Prayer Services for 4–12 year olds adapted from Alive-O Religious Education Programme* (Veritas, Dublin, 2005)

Clare Maloney, *Biblical Dramas for 4–12 year olds adapted from Alive-O Religious Education Programme* (Veritas, Dublin, 2005)

Clare Maloney, *More Alive-O stories and poems* (Veritas, Dublin, 1997)

Brendan Quinlivan, *Liturgies for Post-Primary Schools* (Veritas, Dublin, 2002)

Brendan Quinlivan, *More Liturgies for Post-Primary Schools* (Veritas, Dublin, 2003)

Gerry Campbell, Kathleen Byrne, *God and Time Embrace: Prayer Services for School and Parish* (Veritas, 2010)

Books on Prayer

Children's Everyday Prayerbook for 4–7 Year Olds (Veritas, Dublin, 2011)
Children's Everyday Prayerbook for 8–12 Year Olds (Veritas, Dublin, 2011)
Leabhar Urnaithe Laethúil do Pháistí idir a ceathair agus a seacht mbliana d'aois (Veritas, Dublin, 2008)
Leabhar Urnaithe Laethúil do Pháistí idir a seach agus a deich mbliana d'aois (Veritas, Dublin, 2007)
Rosemary and Peter Atkins, *Prayer-Bytes: Everyday Prayers for Young People* (Veritas, Dublin, 2006)
Rosemary and Peter Atkins, *Prayer Kids: Modern Prayers for children today* (Veritas, Dublin, 2008)
Ed Hone and Roisín Coll, *All Together: Creative Prayer with Children* (Veritas, Dublin, 2009)
Clare Maloney, *Will Our Children Have Family Prayer?* (Veritas, Dublin, 1999)
Gwen Costello, *Praying with Children* (Twenty-Third Publications, Connecticut, 2007)
Kelley Renz, *God Listens to Our Children: Kids' Prayers for Every Day of the Liturgical Year* (Our Sunday Visitor, Indiana, 2006)
Catherine Wiley (ed.), *Prayers for Grandparents* (Veritas, Dublin, 2010)

Other recommended books
Leo Buscaglia, *The Fall of Freddy the Leaf: A Story of Life for All Ages* (Slack, New Jersey, 1982)
William J. Bausch, *A World of Stories for Preachers and Teachers* (Twenty-Third Publications, Connecticut, 2007)

Suppliers of Catechetical and Religious Materials
Veritas Ltd. 7–8 Lower Abbey Street, Dublin 1, Ireland.
www.veritas.ie

Dominican Publications, 42 Parnell Square, Dublin 1, Ireland
www.dominicanpublications.com

Columba, 55A Spruce Avenue, Stillorgan Industrial Park, Blackrock, Co. Dublin
www.columba.ie

Websites

General Liturgy
http://www.liturgy-ireland.ie
National Centre for Liturgy, Maynooth

http://www.litmus.dublindiocese.ie
The Dublin Diocesan Liturgical Resource Centre

http://www.cumannnasagart.ie
Liturgical Planning as Gaeilge

http://www.osb.org/liturgy/
Site of the Benedictines of St John's Abbey, Minnesota, providing links to liturgy websites and online resources

http://www.usccb.org/liturgy/
The Liturgy section of the United States Catholic Conference of Bishops

http://liturgy.nd.edu/
The Notre Dame Center for Liturgy

http://www.liturgyoffice.org.uk
The Liturgy Office of England and Wales

http://www.litcom.net.au
The Liturgical Commission of the Archdiocese of Brisbane, Australia

http://www.liturgyplanning.com
Comprehensive liturgical site by Emmaus Productions. Full access to resources requires an annual membership

Prayer Sites and Seasonal Resources
http://www.cilent.ie
Church Support and Catholic Ireland. A comprehensive day-by-day site on Lent, with specific reference to children

http://www.sacredspace.ie
Daily prayer and reflections

http://www.prayingeachday.org
Prayer site of the De La Salle brothers in England

http://www.universalis.com
US edition of the Divine Office and Daily Readings of the Mass online

http://www.cptryon.org/prayer/
Site run by the Passionist Order

http://www.cptryon.org/caritas/
'Virtual House of Prayer' run by the Sisters of Charity in Halifax, England

Our Family Mass Resources for the Family Sunday Liturgy **Year B**

Inclusive Liturgy
http://www.ncdp.ie
National Chaplaincy for Deaf People

http://www.cidp.ie
Catholic Institute for Deaf People, Dublin

http://www.trocaire.org
Overseas Development agency of the Catholic Church in Ireland

http://www.everybodyswelcome.org.uk
Information, articles support and activities from the Catholic Church of England and Wales. Offers a substantial list of links to similar websites about special needs

http://assembly/uca.org.au/worship/resources/10-guidelines/26-disabilitiesworshipguidelines.html
Guidelines from Australia on worship for those with special needs

http://www.cafod.org.uk
Catholic Aid Agency for England and Wales

Other sites of interest
http://www.veritas.ie
The website of Ireland's leading religious publisher and retailer

http://www.catholicbishops.ie
The website for the Irish Catholic Bishops' Conference. Comprehensive links to all dioceses, offices and agencies

http://www.catholicireland.net
An internet portal website for Irish Catholic activity and international links

http://www.nahc.ie/resources/
Liturgical resources from the National Association of Healthcare Chaplains, Ireland

http://www.thefurrow.ie
A journal for the contemporary Church, St. Patrick's College, Maynooth

http://www.mic.ul.ie/education/reled.htm
Children's Liturgy Project in Mary Immaculate College, Limerick

http://www.irishcatholic.ie
The website of the Irish Catholic newspaper

http://www.redcoms.org
The website of the Redemptorist Publications

http://www.domestic_church.com
US website offering activities and articles

http://www.faith-at-home.com
US website offering activities and articles

And remember ... the members of your congregation, your locality and the creativity of your own Family Mass team are all great, and often under-used, resources!

Postscript

Our Family Mass: Resources for the Family Sunday Liturgy
and *Share the Good News*, the National Directory for Catechesis in Ireland

As you use *Our Family Mass: Resources for the Family Sunday Liturgy*, it is appropriate to highlight how this resource relates and responds to our wonderful National Directory for Catechesis in Ireland, *Share the Good News*. The following is the relevant excerpt from the *Directory*:

98. Family Mass has become a popular form of ministry to families in a parish.[1] In Ireland today … children and young people need to know they belong to their faith community: 'Young members of the Church need to feel and believe that they have a valuable contribution to make to the local parish community.'[2] Family Mass, under the direction of the parish priest as the custodian of the sacred liturgy, has the added benefit of lifting the Sunday celebration for all those who attend. Very often, this type of celebration will become a form of ministry to the rest of the parish, as well as to young families. It is better celebrated as a Family Mass, not a Children's Mass. All members of the family and all age-groups have a role to play. Although a children's choir may be one focus of the celebration, everything should not be left to children, with adults becoming spectators rather than participants. In some parishes, parents/guardians of young children have also formed a choir with other adults, leading the congregational singing at the Family Mass once a month. A group of parents/guardians, trained over time in good liturgy, should act as leaders, stimulating others to organise lectors, procession, liturgical art, special events, after-Mass community gatherings etc. The Family Mass Team, working together with the parish's other faith development teams, can become a real focus for renewal in the parish. In the particular case where children are without religious support at home, have not been baptised or have not completed their journey of initiation, it is the responsibility of the Christian community to address the situation. It can do this, the General Directory for Catechesis suggest, 'by providing generous, competent and realistic support, seeking dialogue with the families, proposing adequate forms of education and providing catechesis which is proportionate to the concrete possibilities and needs of these children.'[3]

---

1 See Sacred Congregation for Divine Worship, *Directory on Children's Masses* (CTS, London, 1974)
2 Northern Ireland, Council for Catholic Maintained Schools, *Life to the Full: A Vision of Catholic Education*, p. 34
3 *GDC* 180